1997

The New Hollywood

For my mother,
Norma Bernardoni

The New Hollywood

What the Movies Did with the
New Freedoms of the Seventies

by

James Bernardoni

McFarland & Company, Inc., Publishers
Jefferson, North Carolina, and London

Also by James Bernardoni

George Cukor: A Critical Study and Filmography
(McFarland, 1985)

British Library Cataloguing-in-Publication data are available

Library of Congress Cataloguing-in-Publication Data

Bernardoni, James.
    The new Hollywood : what the movies did with the new freedoms of
the seventies / by James Bernardoni.
      p. cm.
    Includes bibliographical references (p.) and index.
    ISBN 0-89950-627-5 (lib. bind. : 50# alk. paper)∞
    1. Motion pictures—United States.   2. Motion picture industry—
United States. I. Title.
PN1993.5.U6B39   1991
791.43'0973—dc20   91-52742
                                                                 CIP

Manufactured in the United States of America

McFarland & Company, Inc., Publishers
  Box 611, Jefferson, North Carolina 28640

Contents

Foreword

James Bernardoni loved films, the film industry, and film criticism. Although his vast knowledge of film facts pleased and amazed his friends, Jim's chief pleasure came from viewing a film in which his and the director's expectations were realized. His hopes for the films of the newly independent directors of the seventies were as high as those of anyone who loved film. This book is Jim's answer to the questions: What benefits were achieved from the new freedom? How do the new films compare to the old?

Jim lived to complete his manuscript but died before the editorial and publication process had begun. Unfortunately, I do not know whom he would have acknowledged for their assistance in his research and the preparation of the text. I hope that whoever they are they will find gratification in the publication of the book.

Personally, I wish to thank Lee Amazonas for her help in preparing the captions for the stills included in the book.

Michael Williams
London, July 1990,
through Athens, Alabama,
September 1991

1

Introduction

At first, the New Hollywood seemed to be the real thing: a multi-faceted phenomenon with sufficient coherence, depth, and significance to persuade a number of observers that a genuine revolution had occurred in Hollywood, the primary source of what is arguably the most important art of the twentieth century.

The conditions for a revolution in Hollywood certainly seemed to be in place in the latter part of the sixties. There was the decaying regime: a studio system run by aging autocrats whose commitment to standardized technique and innocuous content seemed to make it impossible for genuine film artists to emerge in Hollywood. There was an external crisis: the initial challenge of television was followed by the consolidation of its position as *the* mass medium, a situation which by the end of the sixties had led to truly alarming declines in the box office receipts of American movies. There were the discontented masses: the educated young adults of the baby boom who were breaking free of outmoded social and attitudinal restrictions and who were looking for signs of the same breakthrough in American films. There was the indispensable elite, the energizing advanced guard: the so-called "movie generation," the visually literate men and women, many of them graduates of film schools, who were ready to make films that would at once express their unique visions and connect with the experiences and feelings of liberated young audiences. Finally, there was the timely appearance in France of a new critical stance that placed the films of the Old Hollywood — previously regarded (if they were considered at all) with critical disdain — in a new perspective, and suggested the possibility of a reconciliation between a studio system dedicated to the production of movies with mass appeal and a sensibility dedicated to the creation of cinematic art. The auteur theory implied that the restrictions and limitations on artistic freedom imposed by the big studio system created a potentially fruitful tension that could result in the ideal synthesis: films of artistic merit that are accessible to mass audiences. The auteur theory thus raised the possibility of a peaceful, bloodless revolution: Hollywood's decaying regime need not be overthrown but

1

only opened up to filmmakers prepared to exploit the possibilities it offered for making films that would serve both art and commerce.

For a time, as the sixties gave way to the seventies, it seemed that the revolution had indeed come, that a cadre of technically sophisticated filmmakers, frequently welcomed with open arms by a new generation of studio executives who were ready to try almost anything to reverse the decline in box office receipts, had set about the business of creating a New Hollywood. In the critical community optimism ran high. Joseph Gelmis, writing in 1970, expressed the euphoria of the era: "We are on the threshold of a technical and aesthetic revolution in movies which will inevitably restructure human consciousness and understanding. Accessibility of the means of production and changes in distribution and exhibition will democratize movies so there will be thousands made every year instead of just hundreds."[1] Richard Corliss, writing in 1980, offered this impressionistic snapshot of the New Hollywood when it was at its newest: "The decade [the seventies] began in a productive, promising turmoil, with young filmmakers leaping the barricades to take over the moguls' offices, foreign directors testing their skills against a new language (English) and, sometimes, a crazy new country (America), and the old men of the studios running for cover."[2]

The difference in tone — the movement from unguarded optimism to bemused irony — in the Gelmis and Corliss quotes suggests what happened as the seventies wore on: at about the same time (a hard to pinpoint historical moment) that the nation was waking up to what Joan Didion has called "the morning after the sixties," a new and decidedly pessimistic view of the New Hollywood began to emerge. As the seventies gave way to the eighties, the mood grew increasingly dark. In 1981 David Cook, after assuring us that "Hollywood is by no means dead," noted that "there are serious questions about the creative vitality of the American cinema."[3] Ernest Callenbach, in a 1984 *Film Quarterly* editorial entitled "Would Someone Care to Say What Is Going On Here?" wondered if we are witnessing the disintegration of the American film industry and the art form it has sustained.[4]

If Cook, Callenbach, and other observers who have deep misgivings about the current state of American films are right to be concerned — and I think they are — the question of what went wrong with the New Hollywood revolution and its promise of a renaissance in American films deserves serious attention.

One answer holds that the New Hollywood of the seventies, while it may have very briefly resembled a community of committed artists, very quickly reverted to being just a hit-making factory; the accountants and corporate dealmakers who took over the studios easily imposed their commercial values on the idealistic writers and directors fresh out of film school. In other words, the hoped-for creative tension between art and commerce never developed because the latter easily overpowered the former. This argument contends that what was significantly new about the New Hollywood was a new insecurity on the part of the men running the studios about the reliability of the hit-making process:

> Old Hollywood relied on a varied but conventional product to attract its mass audience. New Hollywood looks to lists of 'bankable' stars, trend-spotting, demographic studies — all of which adds up to a clear admission of failure, a loss of the intuitive certainty about its audience that old Hollywood had.... [T]he most striking aspect of the new Hollywood is its overwhelming conformism.[5]

A second answer maintains that the New Man of the New Hollywood, this person committed to the art of film, had a *Doppelgänger,* a calculating hustler more concerned with arranging deals to finance films than with following his or her artistic grail. Billy Wilder, a man who's been around long enough to take talk of revolution in Hollywood in stride, with considerably more than one grain of salt, has observed that "nowadays, 80 percent of a director's time is spent making deals and the remaining 20 percent making films. In the thirties and forties that ratio was the reverse."[6] The logic of this argument suggests that the serious artists of the New Hollywood were, in fact, careerists who were prepared to do anything necessary to assure that there would always be the next movie to direct or write; they thus lost sight of their goal of transforming Hollywood into a place where artistic considerations would consistently be given greater importance than they had previously been accorded.

A third answer points not to the internal contradictions of the New Hollywood but to changes in the external environment in which it functioned. One variation holds that the artistic ambitions of the New Hollywood were undermined by audiences' drift toward cultural conservatism; the New Hollywood, in effect, was deserted by audiences whose interest in innovative, personal films disappeared more or less simultaneously with their outer-directed mentality and dedication to social revolution. Andrew Sarris is a good spokesman for this view: "the American cinema has tended to become more vulgarly regressive through the Seventies. Even the most highly acclaimed directors have found that they cannot overcome the audiences' desire for such genre constants as fantasy, sentimentality, and violence."[7] A second variation holds that the New Hollywood revolution was simply overtaken and overwhelmed by a radically altered audiovisual environment that now features cable, discs, and, most important, video.

These perspectives on the New Hollywood share the assumption that a promising aesthetic phenomenon that might be called the New Hollywood cinema had begun to emerge in the late sixties–early seventies; they differ only in their explanations of the phenomenon's aborted development — whether it was subverted by corporate philistines, abandoned by filmmakers who under duress or by preference became dealmakers, ignored by audiences, or rendered irrelevant by the rise of competing visual media.

The sense of confusion and outrage about the premature death — or was it murder? — of an exciting evolution in the aesthetics of the American cinema strikes me as evidence of the failure to appreciate the real tragedy of the New Hollywood. The New Hollywood film, far from constituting an aesthetic advance, has marked a retreat in an art form that evolved during the Old Hollywood era, reaching a peak of aesthetic consolidation in the American cinema of the late forties and fifties. From this perspective, the New Hollywood cinema, considered as an aesthetic phenomenon, has not been thwarted in its development or driven to an early death but has merely passed into a maturity whose disappointing characteristics were already evident in its infancy.

Four fundamental aesthetic fallacies, evident in the films of the leading directors of the New Hollywood era as well as in those of the less talented and less clever directors who have formed the New Hollywood's second and third echelons, have made New Hollywood films inferior to the films of the Old Hollywood, or Big Studio, era.

The four fallacies are, first, the television fallacy, evident in its crudest form in Woody Allen's *Bananas* and on a higher level of sophistication in Robert Altman's *Nashville* and George Lucas's *American Graffiti;* second, the literary fallacy, which has been well represented in the New Hollywood, most notably in Allen's *Manhattan,* Terrence Malick's *Days of Heaven,* Bob Fosse's *All That Jazz,* and Francis Coppola's *Apocalypse Now;* third, the Hitchcockian fallacy, which can be seen in films as diverse as Brian DePalma's *Carrie* and Martin Scorsese's *Taxi Driver;* and, fourth, the Hawksian fallacy, one strain of which underlies Altman's *M*A*S*H,* while a second strain can be detected in Steven Spielberg's *Jaws* and *Raiders of the Lost Ark.*

The television fallacy is the belief that fictional television's combination of a restrictive, blatantly unrealistic narrative structure and an unrestrained, hyperactive visual style can form the basis of an aesthetics of film. Whether the New Hollywood directors whose films are marked by the television fallacy consciously transferred television aesthetics to film is, of course, a matter of speculation. Perhaps the *Doppelgänger* theory is relevant here: while the New Hollywood director was pursuing his or her art, a shameless twin was pursuing box office success at any cost; the latter, naturally enough, searched for the key to commercial success in television, whose vast audience just might be induced to pay to see films that duplicated the structural and stylistic features found in television. Perhaps the presence of the television fallacy in the New Hollywood can be explained by the sheer pervasiveness of television in postwar America: the New Hollywood directors were, inevitably, as influenced by television as they were by Old Hollywood auteurs, or foreign masters like Bergman and Fellini, or the theories and aesthetic principles they absorbed at film school.

The transference of television aesthetics to film has resulted in films that are

> overrun by a plague of zoom shots, telephoto lenses, and rack focus shots. Since all three of these devices rely on an artificial distortion of space for their effects, they can be regarded as completely reversing the wide-screen aesthetic of the Fifties that held spatial integrity as the key to film expression.... As the style of theatrical films increasingly imitated television technique ... the most important distinction between the two developed in the area of content, especially as all censorship in feature films virtually came to an end.[8]

The television fallacy's circuitous impact on the content of New Hollywood films may complete the explanation of the "vulgarly regressive" character of recent American films offered by Andrew Sarris: while it may be true that the reactionary audiences of the seventies were demanding films with reassuringly familiar content, there is also evidence that the New Hollywood, to differentiate stylistically indistinguishable films and television programs, offered audiences films of increasingly shocking and explicit content; thus it is the New Hollywood, not its audiences, that should be blamed for the "vulgar" part of the "vulgarly regressive" charge.

The literary fallacy — the belief that a film can be the equivalent of a novel, in terms of the kinds of experiences conveyed and the nature of the relationship the artist establishes with his or her audience — that is evident in the films of several New Hollywood directors can be partially accounted for if it is seen as a manifestation of the particular intellectual-aesthetic milieu in which the New Hollywood developed. All the talk about film as *the* art of our time that was common when the New Hollywood was in its formative stage resulted in a cultural atmosphere that

was, for ambitious new filmmakers, more than a little heady; it is not surprising that, in such an atmosphere, some New Hollywood directors
should come to think that film might subsume or even replace the novel.
They were encouraged to discount conventional strictures emphasizing
the distinctions between literary and cinematic communication by critical
heavyweights like Susan Sontag, a bellwether of intellectual trends in the
sixties:

> Like the novel, the cinema presents us with a view of an action which
> is absolutely under the control of the director (writer) at every moment.
> Our eye cannot wander about the screen, as it does about the stage. The
> camera is an absolute dictator.... In a similar way the novel presents
> a selection of the thoughts and descriptions which are relevant to the
> writer's conception, and we must follow these serially as the author leads
> us.[9]

Of course, there were persuasive arguments, particularly those derived
from the theoretical writings of Andre Bazin, that might have been made
in refutation of Sontag's assertions; but Bazin's humanistic ideas regarding film's obligation to convey reality and the film director's obligation to
respect the concept of freedom of audience response probably struck the
visionaries of the New Hollywood as severe restrictions on their art, and
the seemingly more challenging view of cinema and of the director's
power to determine response to his or her work propounded by Sontag
and others was undoubtedly more appealing to filmmakers setting out to
make a revolution. Even a usually cautious critic like Stanley Kauffmann
seemed to concur in the view that film can adequately convey states of being and modes of perception that are usually associated with literature
when he praised Bergman, Fellini, and Antonioni (who were among the
heroes of New Hollywood directors) for "extending the film into vast areas
of innermost privacy, even of the unconscious, that have been the prov-
ince of the novel and metaphysical poetry."[10]

If the intellectual-critical community's elevation of film to a preeminent position among the arts laid the groundwork for the literary
fallacy's appearance in the New Hollywood, a more specific cause of the
fallacy can be found in an apparent intersection of literary modernism
and the auteur theory.

Both literary modernism, which by the sixties had consolidated its
preeminent position in literature and literary criticism, and the auteur
theory accorded centrality to the concept of authorial vision. The concept
did not, however, have the same meaning in the two contexts. For modernist writers like Woolf and Proust, the concept of authorial vision

implied transforming the novel form into the verbal equivalent of their ineffable emotional states; the novel was to be an expression of the author's unique perceptions of people and events, rather than a vehicle for the mimetic rendering of them. As a concept of the auteur theory, authorial vision referred to a director's communication of a distinct point of view and a consistent body of thematic preoccupations through, within, and often in spite of the restrictions and conventions of mainstream narrative filmmaking; the Old Hollywood auteurs, unlike the masters of literary modernism, didn't claim exemption from the requirements of character delineation, narrative coherence, and spatial-temporal verisimilitude in the name of the higher requirement to make his medium an expression of his unique sensibility and perceptions.

The opposition between these two conceptions of authorial vision is at the heart of the apparent uncertainty experienced by New Hollywood directors as to what constitutes a "personal" film. On the one hand, there was the "personal" film of the auteur theory, which implied personal films within the framework of filmmaking for mass audiences, and which was in harmony with a modest, realism-oriented, Bazinian conception of film. On the other hand, there was the "personal" film extrapolated from literary modernism (whose initially avant-garde theories of the creative act have long since become orthodoxy and were surely absorbed at some point by New Hollywood directors), which makes authorial vision the preeminent determinant of the creative act, and which emphasizes the irrelevance of the conventions associated with realism and the necessity of appealing to mass audiences. The evidence of their films suggests that a number of New Hollywood directors were committed (again, it is impossible to say if this was a conscious and deliberate choice) to making films that were personal more in the modernist than in the auteurist sense. The result was the literary fallacy, which implicitly rejects a principle that was rarely, if ever, questioned in the Old Hollywood — namely, that "an art whose limits depend on a moving image, mass audience, and industrial production is bound to differ from an art whose limits depend on language, a limited audience, and individual creation."[11]

The combined effect of the literary and television fallacies left the New Hollywood film in a decidedly precarious state: the former resulted in films that futilely attempted to deny film's affinity for realism and that successfully denied audiences the pleasure of a relatively free response to the film experience, while the latter resulted in films whose adherence to a limiting, artificial structure and indulgence in inorganic stylistic displays made all but inevitable their failure to communicate significant meaning through appropriate style.

Since the remaining aesthetic fallacies that I have identified in the films of the New Hollywood are intimately connected with the auteur theory, a general word or two on that theory seems in order.

First, there is the question of just how important a role the auteur theory played in the New Hollywood. It seems accurate to say that the artistic vision that informed the New Hollywood directors' work was formed, in perhaps equal parts, of a commitment to the possibilities of film technology and an acceptance of at least the essential premise of the auteur theory. In numerous interviews and in their own occasional writings, New Hollywood directors have provided ample evidence of being aware of the auteur theory and, to a considerable extent, of regarding their careers in auteurist terms. The film school graduates among them — John Carpenter, Francis Coppola, Brian DePalma, Colin Higgins, David Lynch, George Lucas, Terrence Malick, John Milius, Paul Schrader, Martin Scorsese — certainly were directly exposed to auteurist ideas; the others — Woody Allen, Robert Altman, Bob Fosse, Steven Spielberg — were at least indirectly exposed to them, since auteurist premises informed much of the critical community's commentary on their work. It thus seems reasonable to assume that the auteur theory and auteurist criticism had significant influence on the work of New Hollywood directors.

Second, since what follows will focus on what I perceive to be negative consequences deriving from the auteur theory, it seems important to state my belief that the auteur theory represented an enormously fruitful advance in film criticism. The advance consisted, above all, in the theory's stress on formal questions of visual analysis. It is this aspect of the auteur theory that Andrew Sarris, its leading proponent in the United States, placed particular emphasis on:

> The art of the cinema is the art of an attitude, the style of a gesture. It is not so much *what* as *how*. The *what* is some aspect of reality rendered mechanically by the camera. The *how* is what the French critics designate somewhat mystically as *mise-en-scene*. *Auteur* criticism is a reaction against sociological criticism that enthroned the *what* against the *how*. [12]

The auteur theory, however, was not an unmixed blessing. As Peter Wollen put it, "[the theory] could be interpreted and applied on rather broad lines; different critics developed somewhat different methods within a loose framework of common attitudes. This . . . has allowed flagrant misunderstandings to take root."[13] Flagrant misunderstandings did indeed take root in the New Hollywood, and these misunderstandings are at the bottom of what I have designated the Hitchcockian and Hawksian fallacies.

The Hitchcockian fallacy can be traced to a misinterpretation of the auteur theory's correct emphasis on the totality of a director's stylistic choices — Sarris's *how* — as the locus of cinematic meaning, a principle that was most clearly, or at least most accessibly, illustrated in the films of Alfred Hitchcock. While a number of auteurist studies of Hitchcock, most notably Robin Wood's,[14] persuasively demonstrated that Hitchcock's style was not self-justifying but was always at the service of the organic development of significant and often profound themes, it would appear that some New Hollywood directors drew the wrong lessons from auteurist analyses of Hitchcock's mastery of cinematic technique. The point, so well exemplified in Hitchcock's films, that directorial style is the *source* of meaning in film was apparently misconstrued to mean that a demonstrable command of cinematic technique made "meaning," in the sense familiar from literary criticism, irrelevant. This view is reflected in Brian DePalma's remark regarding an upcoming film: "I'd like to try a change of pace and concentrate on a technical, stylistic exercise."[15] That remark captures the essence of the Hitchcockian fallacy, which is the belief that a film can properly be regarded as an exercise in style.

This misreading of auteurist assertions regarding the position directorial style occupies in the overall conception of film represents a variation on the old idea of "pure" cinema — the idea, that is, that the essence of film lies in directorial style, which is to be valued for its own sake and not judged in the context of style's obligation to serve some purpose beyond mere virtuosity. This view was rather persuasively refuted by Bazin and by auteurist critics, with the former insisting on directorial style's obligation to bring audiences into contact with unmediated reality and the latter valuing directorial style only to the extent that it approaches the ideal of the identification of style and meaning.

If the absolute centrality of the director links the literary and Hitchcockian fallacies, with the first regarding a film as a vehicle for the expression of its director's unique vision and the second as an autonomous construct whose purpose is fulfilled in its director's display of virtuosity, an emphasis on the technical aspects of filmmaking links the Hitchcockian and television fallacies. The Hitchcockian fallacy regards the full and imaginative exploitation of the technical elements of filmmaking as the most evident sign of directorial style, which in turn constitutes the "meaning" of, and sufficient justification for, a film; the television fallacy sanctions the use of the technical elements of filmmaking in an inorganic fashion, relying on them to generate a sense of visual variety and excitement without regard to what meaning, if any, their use generates. Both fallacies have thus contributed to the phenomenon, which has been increasingly remarked upon in recent years, of the New Hollywood film's seeming obsession with the technical-mechanical nature of film and its consequent indifference to film's communicative-intellectual nature.

It seems appropriate that Pauline Kael, the most outspoken anti-auterist among American film critics, should introduce the second of the New Hollywood aesthetic fallacies that can be traced to the auteur theory: "In fact it seems to be precisely this category that the *auteur* critics are most interested in — the routine material that a good craftsman can make into a fast and enjoyable movie. What, however, makes the *auteur* critics so incomprehensible is . . . their truly astonishing inability to exercise taste and judgment *within* their area of preference."[16] Kael notwithstanding, the best of the auteur critics did, in fact, make careful distinctions among the achievements of the directors of Old Hollywood genre films. The director in this category who was most admired among auteur critics was Howard Hawks. There would be, I think, little dispute that Hawks, along with Hitchcock, was the Old Hollywood director who received the most sustained and respectful scrutiny from auteur critics.

The elevation of Hawks, however, was problematic, at least insofar as he was perceived as an exemplary role model by auteur theory-conscious New Hollywood directors. The very considerable artistic achievements of Hawks are not as accessible to critical analysis as those of Hitchcock; understandably, the auteur critics were not totally successful in elucidating *why* so many of the seemingly routine entertainments directed by Hawks were in fact works of film art. The Hawksian fallacy was born in the gap between the exalted position accorded Hawks by the auteurists and the less than convincing critical studies that were offered in support of his elevation to the auteurist pantheon. The lack of solid, definitive criticism in support of Hawks's growing reputation resulted in a rather misleading interpretation of his achievements gaining currency in the New Hollywood, an interpretation that seemed to hold that the lesson to be learned from Hawks was that the most blatantly escapist entertainments would be transformed by the same mysterious alchemy at work in Hawks's films into works of genuine art. The result was that a number of New Hollywood directors who apparently admired what Hawks had achieved with Old Hollywood genre films set out to work within the same genres without fully understanding how Hawks had managed to transcend their inherent limitations.

Since, as Peter Wollen has noted,[17] one of the keys to understanding Hawks is the recognition that he reduced all the genres he worked in to two basic types, the adventure drama and the crazy comedy, the desire, whether conscious or not, of New Hollywood directors to emulate Hawks probably explains at least in part the abundance of adventure, comedy, and comedy-adventure films that have come out of the New Hollywood. And since, as Wollen went on to note, "having fun" is a very important value in the Hawksian canon, the number of throwaway, outlandishly silly New Hollywood adventure and comedy films can probably be explained as what results when directors who aspire to achieving a sense of profound, mysterious Hawksian "fun" fall short and achieve only a sense of rather elaborate and labored triviality.

There is an irony involved in the Hawksian fallacy. Pauline Kael, who, the above quote would seem to indicate, had had at least a vague premonition of the Hawksian fallacy and had warned against it, ended up promoting it. Kael, of course, did not refer to the Hawksian fallacy; what she promoted was something she called the "movie-movie," a film that pursued "fun" at all costs, that exhibited great quantities of "energy" (a key term in Kael's critical vocabulary), and that eschewed anything that might possibly be regarded as solemn or even serious. Kael's has been the most influential critical voice of the New Hollywood era; and her critical category, the "movie-movie," began turning up in the popular media under the label of the "pure entertainment" film. What was in essence the Hawksian fallacy thus came to be regarded as a *positive* phenomenon in much of the criticism and the mass media film reviews of the late seventies, although Kael herself has more recently shown signs of moving toward what seems to be the pessimistic consensus about the artistic achievements of the New Hollywood that has emerged in the eighties.

The pessimism seems warranted when one considers the combined effect on the films of the New Hollywood of the aesthetic fallacies I have described. V. F. Perkins, the brilliant auteurist critic, has provided an excellent framework in which to evaluate that effect:

> The movie is committed to finding a balance between equally insistent pulls, one towards credibility, the other towards shape and significance. And it is threatened by collapse on both sides. It may shatter illusion in straining after expression. It may subside into meaningless reproduction presenting a world which is credible but without significance.[18]

In the films of the New Hollywood we have seen the collapse Perkins speaks of. The literary and Hitchcockian fallacies, by giving absolute primacy to directorial expression, have violated film's obligation to convey a sense of credible reality; the television fallacy, by its frequent resort to devices that distort spatial and temporal reality, has also contributed to the shattering of the illusion of credibility. The television fallacy is also involved in the collapse of significance: both it and the Hawksian fallacy have resulted in films that reproduce a kind of media reality to which audiences may be willing to grant a certain degree of qualified credibility but which lacks significance because directors committed to those fallacies don't know how to use conventional narrative structures to express truths of enduring human significance.

In the pages that follow I will examine films of several of the most prominent directors of the New Hollywood era from a perspective that sees the films as clear examples of the aesthetic fallacies I have outlined above. Inevitably, the availability of films for repeated viewings somewhat distorted my selection; but I believe that the directors whose films receive detailed attention in these pages — Woody Allen, Robert Altman, Francis Coppola, Brian DePalma, Bob Fosse, George Lucas, Martin Scorsese, and Steven Spielberg — would be on nearly everyone's short list of the most important directors of the New Hollywood era.

I conclude with an examination of what in my view are the best films to come out of the New Hollywood thus far, films that do not suffer from the aesthetic fallacies that have undermined the majority of New Hollywood films. My purpose is not only to acknowledge the undeniable — that the New Hollywood has produced films of considerable artistic merit — but also to signal my hope that the admirable achievements of American film direction these films represent will, in the not-too-distant future, be a bit closer to the rule and a bit farther from the exception than they presently are.

Notes

1. Joseph Gelmis, *The Film Director as Superstar* (New York: Doubleday, 1970), p. ix.

2. Richard Corliss, "We Lost It at the Movies," *Film Comment,* January–February 1980, p. 34.

3. David Cook, *A History of Narrative Film* (New York: W. W. Norton, 1981), p. 638.

4. Ernest Callenbach, "Would Someone Care to Say What Is Going On Here?" *Film Quarterly,* Winter 1983-84, p. 1.

5. William Paul, "Hollywood Harakiri," *Film Comment,* March-April 1977, pp. 41, 59.

6. Quoted in Axel Madsen, *American Movies in the '70s* (New York: Thomas Y. Crowell, 1975), p. 89.

7. Andrew Sarris, "After *The Graduate*," *American Film*, July-August 1978, p. 36.

8. Paul, "Harakiri," p. 56.

9. Susan Sontag, *Against Interpretation* (New York: Delta, 1961), pp. 243–44.

10. Quoted in Robert Richardson, *Literature and Film* (Bloomington: Indiana University Press, 1969), p. 16.

11. George Bluestone, *Novels into Film* (Berkeley: University of California Press, 1957), p. 63.

12. Andrew Sarris, *The American Cinema* (New York: E. P. Dutton, 1968), p. 36.

13. Peter Wollen, "The *Auteur* Theory," in Bill Nichols, ed., *Movies and Methods* (Berkeley: University of California Press, 1976), p. 530.

14. Robin Wood, *Hitchcock's Films* (New York: Castle Books, 1965).

15. Quoted in Gelmis, *Superstar,* p. 32.

16. Pauline Kael, *I Lost It at the Movies* (Boston: Little, Brown, 1965), p. 297.

17. Wollen, "The *Auteur* Theory," pp. 532, 534.

18. V. F. Perkins, *Film as Film* (Harmondsworth, England: Penguin Books, 1972), p. 120.

2

The Television Fallacy

Bananas (1971)
American Graffiti (1973)

Critical detachment seems notably lacking in commentary on mainstream fictional television, which appears to be a subject that encourages the taking of extreme positions on a critical spectrum that runs from unyielding elitism to cynical populism. A critical consensus on the aesthetics of commercial television probably doesn't yet exist or has yet to emerge; but I have attempted to locate — or, more accurately, to fashion — one from the disparate views of critics who have reflected on the subject far more than I have. With a reasonably complete, if hardly exhaustive, statement of the aesthetic principles of commercial television in place, I can proceed to the main business at hand: an examination of what I have called the television fallacy — i.e., the transference to film of the aesthetic principles of commercial television.

In both film and television technology is, of course, inextricably connected with aesthetics. In the case of television, however, technology appears to have the kind of determining, defining relationship to aesthetics that, paradoxically, film technology lost as the result of technological advances.

The central fact of television technology is that the image is produced by way of a grid of dots located along five hundred lines, a method of transmission that generates chronic problems with the clarity of the televised image. That single technological fact, a given of television broadcasting, has far-reaching aesthetic implications. It gives rise to the "signal/noise" phenomenon that all television producers must deal with. The "signal" is the primary image to be conveyed; the "noise" is everything that threatens the clarity of that image, including any background visual information that competes with the primary image.[1] As a result, commercial television programming typically features simplified backgrounds that pose little threat to the clarity of the central image.

14

The constant preoccupation with the clarity of the televised image leads to an emphasis on close-ups and an accompanying deemphasis on details of background and decor that, while adding texture to the image, also tend to overload it. The same concern with clarity has given rise to a pronounced preference for those genres whose plots, themes, and emotions can be adequately communicated through bold movements, broad gestures, and straightforward, face-to-face dialogue exchanges.

If television technology has important aesthetic and substantive implications, the implications of the unique position television occupies among the mass media are equally important. Filmmakers, it seems safe to say, seek to create "interventions," visual constructs that alter audiences' thinking or, at a minimum, alter their routines; film audiences, in turn, expect films to be visual events that are intellectually or emotionally impressive enough to be remembered, however briefly, as distinct experiences. The producers of commercial television programs, in contrast, seek to create "artifacts," programs that can be assimilated into audiences' ongoing lives; television audiences expect television programs to be agreeable enough to become a welcome habit.

It follows that television producers are above all interested in achieving an unobtrusive "flow" of programming.[2] The smoothness of the flow depends, in the first place, on relatively bland, innocuous program content; and in the second place on breaking down total programming into discrete, relatively small quanta that don't require sustained attention from the viewer and don't encourage a high degree of viewer involvement (and that, not so incidentally, readily lend themselves to frequent commercial breaks). Commercial television's iron law of quanta flow has major aesthetic consequences: it explains in large part why both the long take featuring complicated camera movements and/or movement within the shot, and the prolonged stationary-camera shot are virtually unknown in commercial television programming.

The obvious risk inherent in seeking to make television an unobtrusive flow of programming is the loss of viewer attention: a program that is as familiar, comfortable, and unthreatening as your Uncle Fred runs the risk of becoming as boring as your Uncle Fred. Producers' ever-present fear of viewer boredom is what lies behind commercial television's marked proclivity for what Jerry Mander has called "technical events":

> Put on your television set and simply count the number of times there is a cut, a zoom, a superimposition, a voice-over, the appearance of words on the screen — a technical event of some kind. . . . Each technical event, each alteration of what would be natural imagery, is intended to

keep your attention from waning as it might otherwise.... The luring forward never ceases for very long. If it did, you might become aware of the vacuousness of the content that can get through the inherent limitations of the medium.[3]

One doesn't have to share Mander's adamantly negative view of television to acknowledge that he has made an important point about television aesthetics, a point made by William Paul[4] among others: far from being, as some have inexplicably claimed, a visually dull medium that offers little more than "talking heads," television is a visually hyperactive medium whose informing aesthetics are about as far removed from Bazinian unmediated realism as can be imagined.

Television aesthetics' affinity for a visually bold style at the service of thematically uncomplicated content has led to the relative neglect of character development in fictional programming. It is the static character's interaction with the situation that is the basis of most fictional programs, not the nuances of a character's evolution and change. Michael Malone has pointed out one semi-exception to this general bias against character development. What he calls the "tribal comedy," a variant of the situation comedy featuring a diverse assortment of characters connected by some external situation, initially features characters that constitute an ensemble of stock stereotypes; if, however, a series of this type is successful enough to continue beyond a season or two, the characters often begin to evolve into relatively interesting, reasonably credible individuals.[5] Malone's point is relevant here because it suggests the possibility that one reason films which adopt television's tribal comedy structure are frequently inferior to television programs with the same structure is that the former's characters remain locked into the stereotyped state that the latter's may have several seasons to break free of.

Films that adopt the tribal comedy structure are not the only ones that are inferior to the television programs that serve as their aesthetic models: not surprisingly, the transference of television aesthetics to film has resulted not only in films that are inferior *as films* but that also suffer in comparison to the best of entertainment programming offered on commercial television.

Woody Allen's *Bananas* is a case in point. The film is unmistakably (if unintentionally: I trust I shouldn't need to say I don't have special access to Woody Allen's thought processes) informed by television aesthetics. One of its most striking features is a fragmentation that strongly recalls television's quanta structure. One result of this fragmentation is that the film fails to convey the continuity and the sense of sustained involvement that I believe are indispensable characteristics of a good film.

But if *Bananas* attains television's goal of providing entertainment in minute particles, it doesn't (probably because Allen-the-performer's persona, at the time of *Bananas* still in flux, is too protean and disruptive, and the eruptions of black humor in the film too frequent) capture television's seductive, undisturbing flow — an indispensable quality of the best television programs.

Similarly, Allen's mise-en-scène is characterized by stylistic decisions that recall the "technical events" of television aesthetics. Allen rather frequently makes stylistic choices whose only apparent purpose is to hype sequences that he (apparently) thought would be visually dull if he had made choices more strictly related to the communication of coherent meaning. Yet Allen's stylistic flourishes are not quite frequent or blatant enough to achieve television's modest goal of staving off viewer boredom by treating the viewer to unceasing visual excitement. *Bananas,* to put it succinctly if harshly, is the worst of both worlds: neither a good film nor a particularly effective television program.

The first three segments of *Bananas* are each four minutes long, an indication of the metered uniformity of the film's quanta. First, there is a precredits segment showing Howard Cosell, the legendary television sportscaster, "covering" a political assassination in a fictional Latin American nation as if it were no different from the innumerable sports events he has covered for television audiences. The humor of most of the segment amounts to fairly timid television-baiting (Cosell is a notoriously vulnerable subject, hardly worth a self-respecting satirist's attention); toward the end, however, the humor takes on a darker hue as Cosell first "interviews" the assassinated president while he is literally in his death throes and then mindlessly wishes his successor good luck just after the latter has vowed to unleash a militaristic reign of terror in the country.

The next segment, immediately following the credits, introduces Fielding Melish (Woody Allen), who is seen performing his job of demonstrating and testing new products. The humor at this point shifts to the broadly physical as the elaborate "executive exerciser" Fielding is demonstrating becomes an uncontrollable, almost life-threatening menace during the course of the demonstration. The segment, amusing enough in itself, is nonetheless problematic because it establishes a character — a Keatonesque little man gamely confronting a mechanized world — who does not reappear in the film. The segment thus seems detachable, a four-minute gag bearing a strong resemblance to a television blackout sketch.

The third of the four-minute sketches begins well, with Allen's mise-en-scène establishing a persona and a milieu for Fielding that seem promising. The segment begins with a close-up of Fielding; as the camera tracks left with him, the initially blurred background comes into focus to reveal racks filled with pornographic magazines. The tracking camera eliminates Fielding from the frame, and the screen is filled with the magazine covers.

There is a cut to a medium shot of Fielding in the foreground-left of the frame; the magazines fill the right of the frame, and other customers can be seen in the background. Fielding is trying to select some pornographic magazines without the other customers becoming aware of his selection.

Next there is a cut to a medium shot of a rather forbidding, prudish-looking woman standing near the store's counter at the right of the frame; Fielding and the magazines fill the left of the frame. Allen's composition establishes an effective comic tension between Fielding, trying to accomplish his stealthy purchase, and the prude, who seems certain to notice what he's doing. A series of cuts between the two of them reiterates Fielding's paranoia and also partially justifies it by using the inquisitive prude to personify the intrusive New York milieu in which Fielding operates. This Fielding — the nervous but resourceful New Yorker — is the one we will most frequently see in the film, and in this vignette Allen's mise-en-scène economically and effectively establishes him.

Unfortunately, the segment concludes on a much less satisfying note. After making his pornographic purchases, Fielding finds himself in a confrontation with two young toughs (one of whom is a very young Sylvester Stallone) who are terrorizing the passengers in the subway car Fielding has boarded. Besides being a rather hackneyed, sitcom representation of the ubiquitous dangers of life in New York City, this subway segment-within-a-segment contains the first instance of a stylistic device that is a direct borrowing from television and that accentuates one of the major weaknesses of *Bananas*. This device might be called the "full-stop shot," a shot that, like a cinematic period, brings the segment in which it appears to an emphatic end. In this instance, the full-stop shot shows an elderly female passenger on the subway reading (and clearly enjoying) a pornographic magazine Fielding has abandoned in his flight from the punks. This device is Allen's favored solution to the problem of concluding the detachable quanta that constitute the major portion of *Bananas*. In aesthetic terms, it is a crude nonsolution, for the device soon becomes blatant and predictable and ends up underlining the fragmented, discontinuous nature of the film. Allen's full-stop shots are so reminiscent of the gags or "hooks" used to conclude television's quanta that one almost expects them to be followed by commercial breaks.

The sequence (it is one of the few instances in *Bananas* when that word, with its connotations of complexity and development, seems appropriate) that follows the subway incident is a high point of the film, the first demonstration of Allen's ability to embed meaning and create significance in and through his mise-en-scène.

The sequence, set in Fielding's apartment, begins with a shot of him answering a knock at the door. His caller is Nancy (Louise Lasser), who is circulating a petition in opposition to the new regime in San Marcos, the country whose coup was reported by Howard Cosell. There is a two-shot of Nancy and Fielding at the door that is sustained long enough to suggest the potential for intimacy between them. That suggestion, however, is quickly undermined by a symmetrical series of four shots. There is first a medium shot of Nancy speaking to Fielding off-camera. This is followed by a medium shot of Fielding in the living room, which is followed by a medium shot of Nancy entering the living room. Finally, there is a medium shot of Fielding speaking to Nancy off-camera. This series of shots effectively conveys the tentativeness of Nancy's entrance into Fielding's life and suggests that intimacy between them will not be instant and will probably be awkward.

There follows a series of three shots in which spatial tension stands in for psychological tension. The first and last of the shots are notable for being among the very few long takes in the film.

First, Fielding is seen in the midground-center of the frame, while Nancy, her back to the camera, occupies the foreground-center. The camera tracks back as Fielding enters the kitchen in the background-left of the frame; the resulting composition has Nancy and Fielding almost shouting their "casual" chatter from their respective positions at the extreme left and extreme right of the frame. The composition, besides suggesting the comic awkwardness of the encounter, also makes good use of the well-realized decor of Fielding's apartment, which seems to be a prime example of early tacky.

The second shot of the series is quietly brilliant. It is a medium shot of Nancy, who is talking to Fielding off-camera. The camera is placed behind what appears to be an empty shelf of a bookcase, so there is at least the suggestion of a frame around Nancy. The shot, moreover, is in soft-focus, so Nancy is presented in a very appealing, flattering manner. The choices Allen has made here — the isolation of one of the interlocutors in an ongoing dialogue, the placement of the camera, the use of soft-focus — suggest that the shot is meant to convey Nancy as seen from Fielding's highly subjective, rather romantic point of view.

The third shot in the series is a long shot of Nancy, in the living room at the left of the frame, and Fielding, who is in the kitchen at the right. At this point, Allen uses movement within the shot to reestablish the comic tension of the first shot of the series. Fielding walks left toward Nancy and the camera, stopping in the midground of the frame. The camera remains stationary as Fielding delivers a very nervous near-monologue which seems to both confuse and amuse Nancy, who remains in her position at the left. The camera remains stationary as Fielding, continuing his stream of words, first moves right toward the background of the frame and then left toward his previous position in the midground. In this shot Fielding has, in effect, put on an awkward but rather effective performance, with Nancy functioning as his audience. The direction of the shot — specifically, Allen's decision to sustain the shot for a con-siderable period without a cut, to keep both Fielding and Nancy in the frame for the duration of the shot, and to let Fielding dominate the shot by having a stationary camera record his movements — suggests that Fielding, besides seeing Nancy in a romantic-idealized light, also regards her as a complementary audience to his performer.

A series of medium shots of Nancy and Fielding ensues as she prepares to leave and he escorts her to the door. The last shot of the se-quence is excellent. There is a medium shot of Nancy and Fielding at the door; then she exits the apartment and the frame. Fielding, delighted that Nancy has given him her phone number, walks away from the door and toward the camera. As he moves, he indulges in an odd series of body movements (what he does cannot quite be described as dancing) that ex-presses his feeling of triumph. Nancy then reenters the frame from the background; she has recalled that Fielding never did sign her San Marcos petition. Fielding, caught in mid-performance, sheepishly signs the peti-tion and the sequence concludes. Allen, with admirable visual economy, has in this shot suggested that Nancy's practicality may intrude on, rather than complement, the ad hoc performances that Fielding is prone to give.

There is a danger of overrating this sequence, which gains con-siderably in comparison to most of what precedes and follows it. What is good about the sequence is that it reveals Woody Allen moving away from the undeveloped, uninvolving quanta of television aesthetics and toward a genuinely cinematic mise-en-scène. In this sequence, Allen assigns communicative roles to screen space, the duration of shots, and the details of decor, all of which is in accordance with film aesthetics but at variance with television aesthetics. He does not, to be sure, move as far as he might have: he fails, for example, fully to exploit the possibilities of spatial ten-sion, movement within (and out of) the frame, and stylized acting to achieve the exquisite male-female tension that Hawks created in *Bringing Up Baby*. But that is hardly a fair comparison. In the context of *Bananas*, the sequence seems masterful.

Allen does not long sustain the excellence he achieved in the initial Fielding-Nancy sequence. He follows it with two very brief segments, an easily detachable one showing Fielding at work, and a montage of shots showing Fielding and Nancy dating and demonstrating at the United Nations.

One of the longest and (probably not coincidentally) best shots of the film follows. Fielding and Nancy are in his bedroom, about to make love for the first time. She is stretched out on the bed, filling the center of the frame. A stationary camera observes Fielding moving to the right, left, and background of the shot as he frantically tries to fulfill Nancy's various requirements for the proper atmosphere for lovemaking. Fielding finally gets into bed; Nancy then crosses to the left and exits the frame from the rear as she enters a bathroom adjoining the bedroom. The shot continues without a cut as Fielding, now alone in the frame, indulges in another performance as he hurriedly and carelessly douses his body with talcum powder in preparation for Nancy's return. The shot continues as Nancy reenters the bedroom and resumes her place in bed. There is then a cut to a close-up of Nancy and Fielding at last embarked on their hardly spontaneous act of love. Here is a rare instance in *Bananas* in which Allen's mise-en-scène makes the dialogue of the scene superfluous. The composition of the scene, crucially abetted by Allen's decision to sustain the initial shot, supplies the essential (and genuinely funny) information: Nancy is inertly at the center, Fielding frantically on the periphery; Nancy, as she has before, walks in on Fielding's elaborate performance, a performance that is supposed to be only a warm-up for the *real* performance in bed but that, judging by Nancy's renewed inertness as the scene ends, will probably prove to be more lively and inventive than the main act.

After an entirely detachable and visually trite segment showing Fielding with his psychiatrist, there is a sequence that features Fielding and Nancy in Central Park. This sequence (which runs the magic four minutes) is one of the weakest in the film and one of the clearest demonstrations of Allen's willingness to use the stylistic options available to a director in a way that recalls television's penchant for "technical events" designed to impart visual excitement to a scene.

The sequence begins with a medium shot of Fielding, who is facing the camera, and Nancy, who is three-quarters turned away from it. They are sitting atop a low wall, and Nancy is trying to explain her decision to break off the relationship with Fielding. There is a cut to a more distant shot: Nancy is at the center of the frame, Fielding at the left; the camera is placed behind a tree, so they are framed by leaves. There is a cut to what is now a full-fledged long shot; the camera angle has also changed, placing both Nancy and Fielding in the background-left of the shot. There follows a cut to a two-shot of them against an undefined and blurred blue background.

There is a cut, and the camera tracks left with Nancy and Fielding as they stroll across a bridge. A cut to an overhead shot of them walking is followed by a cut to another overhead shot from a slightly altered angle. There is then a cut to a long shot of them walking down a flight of stairs toward the camera, followed by a cut to a tracking shot in which Nancy and Fielding are partially obscured by the branches of the trees lining the path they are walking on. There is then a cut to a long shot of them slowly walking toward the camera. This is followed by a cut to a two-shot; Nancy, who has finally finished her attempt to explain why she wants to break off with Fielding, then exits the frame. The final shot of the sequence is a medium shot of Fielding being rather theatrically distraught over his loss of Nancy.

What is seriously wrong with this sequence is that Allen's mise-en-scène seems totally arbitrary. The cuts appear to occur randomly throughout the ongoing dialogue. What can be the meaning, given what is happening in the Nancy-Fielding relationship, of the use of leaves as a romantic framing device? Does the early two-shot indicate restored intimacy? It does not appear to, given the overall context of the sequence. What, if any, is the significance of the overhead shots? Allen's directorial choices in this sequence seem motivated only by a desire to impose visual variety on a sequence he presumably felt would be boring without all the stylistic variations. The sequence thus reflects a kinship with the stylistic hyperactivity of television, which is typically intended not to convey meaning but to create an ephemeral sense of excitement.

Fielding and Nancy's breakup in Central Park is followed by a series of no fewer than twelve very brief segments, an astonishing display of Woody Allen's fondness for television's quanta structure. At least two of the segments—one in which Fielding (who is leaving for San Marcos to demonstrate his political commitment to Nancy) says farewell to his parents, both of whom are inept surgeons; and one in which Fielding has a dalliance with a voluptuous female rebel in San Marcos—are entirely detachable, freestanding gags that contribute virtually nothing to the film's coherence or to the development of its characters. Six of the segments feature full-stop shots, which only underline the segments' resemblance to television quanta. As far as plot is concerned, the series

begins with Fielding's arrival in San Marcos to join the rebels and concludes with his ascendancy to the presidency of the country.

Only two of these segments seem to merit specific comment. In one,
Fielding is seen dining at the presidential palace, a guest of the dictator
he and his rebel colleagues will eventually overthrow. The segment is
notable for being another blatant example of Woody Allen's affinity for
the "technical events" approach to filmmaking. Although it is a relatively
brief segment, it contains a number of seemingly arbitrary cuts, as well
as overhead shots, tracking shots, and shots from behind various items
of decor in the dining room; in all of the shots, camera placement and
movement seem to have no point, other than to give the segment visual
variety. In general, the shots in the segment isolate and emphasize bits
of comic business at the expense of the overall coherence of the segment;
once again, it would appear that Allen, apparently fearing viewer
boredom, has made a series of stylistic decisions whose arbitrariness
recalls the pointless, technical displays of television.

Another segment shows Fielding, now the president of San Marcos,
arriving back in New York on a mission to raise funds for the impoverished
country he now leads. He is greeted at the airport by an official of the
United States government. As he and Fielding, both speaking English,
exchange stilted pleasantries, a "translator" repeats — in English — what
each of them has just said. This translator routine is amusing enough;
what is notable here is that the full-stop shot that concludes this segment
is genuinely funny and, more important, *visually* funny. As Fielding and
the official continue their exchange of greetings, two hospital orderlies
carrying enormous butterfly nets enter the frame from the right. When
the "translator" sees them, he flees; Allen sustains the shot as the
"translator" and the pursuing orderlies recede into the background while
Fielding and the official, both of whom seem unable to communicate
without their "translator," stand silent in the foreground. In this shot
Allen achieves the note of absurdism that has mostly eluded him in
Bananas; the shot seems less a crude device for ending a segment than a
clever recapitulation of the absurd situation Fielding finds himself in.

With Fielding back in New York, *Bananas* improves, possibly
because Woody Allen-the-actor reassumes the nervous New Yorker persona he had abandoned in the San Marcos section for an unstable
amalgam of a naïf caught up in large events beyond his understanding
and a Bob Hope-type figure wisecracking his way through a comically exotic foreign environment.

Soon after his return to New York, Fielding is reunited with Nancy
in a brief, well-directed scene. It begins with a close-up of Fielding, who

is wearing an absurd red beard because he does not want the FBI to know that the visiting president of San Marcos is in fact the Fielding Melish who is wanted in the United States for subversive political activities. After the initial close-up, the camera tracks right with Fielding through the dark corridor of a seedy hotel. The tracking ends when Fielding pauses at the door of his room. A hand enters the frame from the left, and Fielding looks in that direction. There is a cut to a medium shot of Nancy, who does not recognize Fielding in his "disguise" and has come to express her admiration for the new president of San Marcos. After a series of alternating medium shots of Nancy and Fielding, the screen goes black, with Nancy and Fielding's dialogue continuing as a voice-over. A light then goes on, and Fielding (still wearing the beard) and Nancy are seen in bed. He announces his true identity and removes the beard; Nancy reacts with wry resignation to having spoiled yet another of Fielding's performances. The scene ends as the lovemaking resumes.

A highly problematic sequence follows. Fielding, it seems, has been arrested and is now on trial. The trial sequence, which runs for six minutes, is an incoherent collection of freestanding, television-like sketches that contribute nothing of significance to either the narrative continuity of the film or to the absurdist tone it erratically strives for (the worst of the bits is a mock television commercial that probably would not even be acceptable as a television sketch).

The trial sequence, however, does have one good moment. Fielding, who is acting as his own counsel, has been ordered bound and gagged by a judge who has wearied of his irregular courtroom tactics. In this condition, Fielding cross-examines a very hostile witness. He drags himself in the chair to which he is bound to a position near the witness stand and poses questions that are, because of the gag covering his mouth, merely a series of unintelligible grunts and groans. The witness mysteriously — and hilariously — understands the noises Fielding emits; under his relentless cross-examination, she breaks down and admits her previous testimony was a lie.

This bit, like the earlier translator gag, makes a genuine connection with the sublime absurdism that runs through but only occasionally surfaces in *Bananas*; and, again like the translator gag, it makes a specific and amusing comment on language, which is the only reliable weapon Fielding has in his encounters with an absurd world.

After the trial (Fielding is given a suspended sentence), Fielding proposes to Nancy. This sequence suffers from the same flawed direction that marked the earlier Central Park sequence. Again, Woody Allen makes choices with regard to montage, camera movement and camera place-

Sublime absurdism runs through, but only occasionally surfaces, in *Bananas*. Miguel Suarez, Woody Allen, *Bananas* (United Artists, 1971).

ment that does not generate any clear meaning and whose only purpose seems to be to give the sequence some visual excitement.

This sequence, however, is not a total failure. It has two features of considerable merit.

First, Allen makes subtle use of lighting and the details of setting to reiterate the contrast between romanticism and practicality that has been the film's one notable thematic preoccupation (albeit a fitfully asserted one). The lighting of the sequence is noticeably more subdued than that of the rest of the film, giving the sequence a romantic cast that suggests Fielding's perspective on this surely momentous juncture in his life. The romanticism is reiterated in the setting, but only up to a point: Fielding proposes to Nancy as they walk along a river bank, but the most prominent feature of the setting is an ungainly, highly unromantic construction crane looming over the landscape. That detail of setting undercuts the romantic connotations of the lighting and injects into the proposal sequence the perspective associated with Nancy, who has consistently opposed a rough practicality to Fielding's tendency to make life a romance or a performance.

Second, the sequence includes a full-stop line that transforms the full-stop device into a brilliant trope. After Nancy accepts Fielding's proposal, he launches into a verbose monologue full of pretentious observations on their relationship. She listens awhile, occasionally mumbling vague assent to something he says, and then puts a stop to his monologue — and the sequence — by asking, "Do you have any gum?" Here, surely, is a full-stop line that transcends its category; it does not merely end a sequence but points forward to an endless succesion of sequences in which Nancy's unyielding practicality will clash with Fielding's romantic posturing.

Bananas should have ended with that line, but unfortunately it does not. It concludes with an epilogue in which Howard Cosell reappears to provide his television audience with bedside coverage of the consummation of Fielding and Nancy's marriage. The epilogue is another detachable segment, a television-style sketch that considerably lessens the impact of the preceding sequence and its brilliant concluding line. *Bananas* thus ends as it began, with a heavy-handed reminder of Woody Allen's infatuation with television and its aesthetics.

While *Bananas* was a pointedly unambitious throw-away comedy, it had, I believe, significant influence on the comedy films of the New Hollywood, an influence that was probably due as much to the growing critical reputation of Woody Allen as it was to the film itself. It contributed to the establishment in the New Hollywood of the fallacy that television aesthetics could be successfully transferred to film. If one reflects for a moment on later comic films of the New Hollywood (*Animal House* and *Porky's* come immediately to mind), one can see in their lack of continuity, their neglect of character development, and their frequently arbitrary direction a clear relationship to television. On the whole, the television fallacy has led to a decline in film comedy. This is the legacy of, among other films, *Bananas*.

The very inconsequentiality of *Bananas* makes it an imperfect example of the television fallacy in the films of the New Hollywood. The full impact of the fallacy begins to emerge when one considers films marked by the television fallacy that received the kind of critical scrutiny and respect that was denied an unambitious film like *Bananas*.

Robert Altman's *Nashville* (1975) has been perhaps the most critically acclaimed of the New Hollywood films featuring a strong directorial commitment to the television fallacy. *Nashville* may be the ultimate "technical event," a film in which virtually every aspect of directorial style has nothing to do with the communication of coherent meaning, everything to do with the creation and maintenance of the impression that something —

anything—is happening, moving or changing. *Nashville* may also be the ultimate tribal comedy, a film in which twenty-odd characters react—or fail to react—to a series of situations that are strung together like beads on a string. It is just barely possible that Altman had parody in mind, that he directed *Nashville* as he did to show that, ultimately, the premises and aesthetics of television will lead a television-pervaded culture into a meaningless box without exits and without windows onto the real world. But if Altman constructed the elaborate box called *Nashville* only to demonstrate that television-saturated audiences live in a box and probably *like* it in there, then he has created a nasty, mean-spirited work that has little to do with the expansive, liberating ends of art.

George Lucas's *American Graffiti* is another New Hollywood tribal comedy that enjoyed considerable critical favor.[6] While *Graffiti* is not the extended exercise in no-meaning that *Nashville* is, Lucas's evident commitment to television aesthetics, like Altman's, prevents his film's overcoming the limitations of the confining structure he has set for it.

At the outset it should be said that *American Graffiti looks* very good indeed, far better than almost anything likely to be offered on commercial television. Lucas, no doubt with the valuable assistance of Haskell Wexler (who is credited as visual consultant), uses color and lighting effects to give his film a visual richness that might seem, on initial reflection, to distinguish it decisively from television programming. That, however, proves to be too simplistic a view: a closer look reveals that Lucas typically uses color and lighting effects to achieve a sense of immediate excitement, not to convey nuances of theme or feeling. Even in that respect then, *American Graffiti* manifests the television fallacy.

The importance of lighting and color in the film (to my mind they are as important as the much praised rock-and-roll soundtrack that Lucas and sound editor Walter Murch designed for the film) is evident from its first moment. The initial total blackness of the screen is pierced by a glowing splash of color whose dominant tone is yellow-green. As the blackness fades, the color is seen to be the neon glow from a sign that spells out "Mel's Drive-In." An establishing shot of the drive-in and its encircling parking area reveals that the time is early morning; the pinkish-gray color of dawn is perfectly achieved, and the enveloping dawn softens the effect of the neon colors at the center of the shot.

This early morning sequence, seen in light of the film as a whole, functions as a kind of statement of thesis: it establishes Mel's as the film's central setting, it introduces the main characters, and it states the one idea that stands out amid the film's anecdotal events.

Terry (Charlie Martin Smith) rides into the establishing shot of Mel's on his Vespa. We are then introduced to Steve (Ron Howard) and Curt (Richard Dreyfuss). Laurie (Cindy Williams), Curt's sister and Steve's girlfriend, then arrives at Mel's. Curt and Steve have recently graduated from high school and are due to leave the following day to attend college somewhere on the East Coast; Laurie and Terry are seniors at the high school from which Curt and Steve have graduated.

Alternating close-ups of Curt and Steve end with a cut to John (Paul LeMat) pulling into the drive-in. Steve's saying to Curt, "You can't stay seventeen forever" is heard as a voice-over as the camera stays on John sitting inside his parked car. The aural overlap is significant, for it soon begins to be clear that John is indeed trying to stay seventeen forever. John's car, a beautifully reconditioned older model in mint condition, also serves to locate his character: its color is a brilliant, dazzling yellow that stands out from the subdued early morning color scheme of the sequence.

There is a cut to Curt and Steve, who are arguing about the former's tentative decision to not go East for college after all. The sequence ends with the camera lingering on Steve's car, another automotive work of art featuring a bold red center stripe on a gleaming white background.

A minor premise of the auteur theory that I find persuasive is that some — many? most? — of the greatest films emerge from what appears on paper to be very weak material. It is not subject matter, which may be quite banal or even undeniably pulpy, that determines the quality of a film; it is how the film's director, through the multiplicity of decisions that constitute mise-en-scène, communicates and transforms the material that is the determining factor. In the case at hand, Lucas is clearly working with rather unpromising material — a story of a collection of teenage stereotypes (John is the juvenile delinquent, Laurie the cheerleader, Terry the awkward misfit, Steve the achiever, Curt the dreamer) who confront fairly ordinary teenage situations and problems. Clearly, if this film is to have any resonance, any claim to greatness, it will derive not from its material but from what Lucas makes of the material in his mise-en-scène. Lucas would appear to have only two ways to go with his material: to create a film with mythic overtones about teenage years, or to create a film grounded in realism about a specific group of well-realized and developed teens. In the initial sequence of *American Graffiti*, Lucas moves toward neither of these ends but rather reveals his commitment to the superficiality of television aesthetics.

First, there is the matter of the symmetrical tracking shots Lucas uses in the sequence to link Terry, Steve and Curt. The symmetry suggests an equality of importance among the three boys; but this is thematic nonsense, since Curt and Steve personify the film's one compelling problem — how to start the future, how to break with the past — while Terry is a standard sidekick figure whom Lucas consistently (not to say cynically) uses for comic relief.

Lucas begins the sequence's central dialogue exchange between Curt and Steve as a two-shot of Curt and *Terry*, with Steve entering the frame as a peripheral figure. Again, why the emphasis on Terry? It can be explained in only one of two ways: it is either arbitrary, unrelated to any larger purpose; or it reflects Lucas's determination to give all the members of his tribe equal attention.

The second explanation seems the more likely when two other directorial decisions in the sequence are taken into account. On two occasions, Lucas cuts away from the Curt-Steve dialogue, once to introduce Laurie, once to introduce John. He presumably cuts away to them because he is committed to keeping the film's tribal comedy structure intact, a commitment that prevents his giving the film the variations in emphasis and rhythm that would have given it nuance and significance beyond the inherent limitations of its material. If Lucas really wanted to make his film a sustained, if humorous, look at particular characters at a particular juncture in their lives — to take the specific case at hand — he would have sustained the Steve-Curt dialogue without a cut, thereby giving it the weight that uncut long takes have. The fact that he did cut away — twice — means that he was more interested in maintaining the television-like flow of his film, more interested in keeping his film within bounds familiar from television, than he was in creating a modulated, involving film about individualized characters.

The earlier suggestion that Lucas had two ways to go with his film — toward myth, in which case simplified, archetypal characters would be acceptable; or toward realism, in which case careful, sustained scrutiny of characters would be a requirement — is, by the end of the first sequence, looking like a false dichotomy. Lucas in the first sequence seems to indicate his preference for a third way: a mise-en-scène that rejects both the mythical and the truly realistic in favor of a largely undifferentiated flow of images that works against any sense of intensity and involvement and encourages a superficial, undifferentiated response from audiences.

With the second sequence, set like the first at Mel's Drive-In, the very long night that will last almost the entire running time of *American Graffiti* begins. All of the main characters check in at Mel's in a kind of ritual that marks the official beginning of the night. Curt and Steve, in a nostalgic gesture, are returning to the old high school to attend a hop with Laurie. John, the undisputed king of the local roads, will spend the night cruising the boulevards. In an unexpected gesture, Steve bestows his much-admired car on Terry (who has only a Vespa), explaining that he will not need it while he is away at college. A delighted, properly appreciative Terry sets out for a night of cruising.

The first cruising sequence of the film is representative of both the minor achievement *American Graffiti* undeniably is and the major achievement that Lucas's adherence to an aesthetics borrowed from television prevents it from being.

For this sequence, Lucas abstains from exercising most of the stylistic options that film directors have traditionally used to create meaning and nuance in their films. His mise-en-scène in this instance is almost exclusively a matter of frequent cutting among medium shots of the characters, a stripped-down mise-en-scène that seems designed to achieve commercial television's goals of generating a sense of excitement (the frequent cuts seem to accomplish that) and keeping the primary images front-and-center (assured by the medium shots). For eight minutes Lucas cuts among medium shots of John and Terry in their cars; Steve, Curt and Laurie in her car; and exterior shots of other cars cruising up and down the main strip. Characteristically, Lucas uses only one other element of mise-en-scène, lighting, to any significant extent in the sequence. The boulevard is very brightly lit, and a reddish glow from traffic lights and neon signs illuminates shots that are out of the glare of street lights (perhaps significantly, the sequence's only close-up is an insert shot of a traffic light). The sequence, to reiterate, is definitely a success on its own limited, television terms: it is visually exciting, the central images are not overwhelmed by secondary images, the action is divided into immediately comprehensible quanta.

Yet the sequence is so much less than it might have been. Let me be clear on one point: I am not faulting Lucas for creating a simple mise-en-scène, which would be tantamount to espousing the pointless stylistic displays I have criticized in television. I am faulting him for a mise-en-scène that, by its adherence to television aesthetics, communicates no more than what is communicated in an ordinary sequence in a mediocre television program. The script has already implied that all this cruising, while it may be fun, is ultimately unsatisfying for the cruisers; but Lucas does not convey that ambiguity in his mise-en-scène. John has already said that the strip is not what it used to be, but that interesting note of premature nostalgia is also absent from Lucas's mise-en-scène. Cruising presumably has something to do with male bonding; but Lucas, with his insistence on a montage that fragments the sequence and his reliance on medium shots that isolate the cruisers, does not convey the idea that cruising is a ritualistic activity that unites teenage males. All we get in this sequence is an efficient, even exciting, but stubbornly superficial rendering of young men driving cars up and down a boulevard. The flow continues smoothly, and the characters remain safely within the delimiting tribal comedy structure that Lucas appears committed to.

The first cruising sequence is followed by a companion sequence that catches up with Curt, Steve, and Laurie at the high school hop. In this sequence (which also runs for eight minutes) Lucas relies on panning shots and, again, rapid cutting to convey the high energy and essential innocence of an early sixties high school dance.

From the hop Lucas returns to the strip. The early part of this second cruising sequence focuses on John and Carol (Mackenzie Phillips), a very young girl who has been foisted on John by some older girls he had tried to pick up. Lucas establishes the relationship (which is founded on mutual hostility) between John and Carol in a series of fairly routine alternating medium shots of them inside John's car. Then, in an instance of the too-pat parallelism that is one of the weaknesses of the film, Terry, who is cruising in Steve's car, also is joined by a girl. She is Debbie (Candy Clark), and Terry spots her *walking* (a virtually unheard of activity in this milieu) on the neon-lit sidewalk of the strip. Lucas initiates the Terry-Debbie encounter in an extraordinary series of close-ups of them as Debbie first considers Terry's car, next Terry himself, and then finally consents to ride with him. The close-ups are problematic, for they lend the two characters an importance and weightiness they do not seem to merit. One suspects that Lucas chose close-ups at this point to emphasize Terry's comic awkwardness and Debbie's comic tawdriness. It is an emphasis that is both superfluous (especially in the case of Debbie, who is played by Clark in a manner that constantly flirts with caricature and that certainly does not require visual underlining) and somewhat unsavory, suggesting as it does a perspective on these two characters that seems to sanction laughing at them. The close-ups, in short, recall the overemphasis and the encouragement of inappropriate laughter that are common on television. The danger involved in misusing close-ups in this way is that they will lose their impact (as they largely have on television) and the film director will be denied a time-honored means of giving emphasis to particular characters or particular moments in a film.

The setting of the next sequence is again the high school hop. Steve and Laurie, who have been spatting since he proposed that they date other people while he is away at college, are forced to lead a snowball dance. There is a medium shot of them caught in the glare of a spotlight; the camera then tracks back from them as they walk toward the center of

The high energy and essential innocence of an early sixties high school dance. Ron Howard, Cindy Williams, *American Graffiti* (Universal Studios, 1973).

the dance floor. The camera tracks left then right with them as they dance in the foreground of the frame. As they dance, they are sometimes illuminated by a harsh spotlight, sometimes by softer lighting.

There is a cut to a more distant shot of Steve and Laurie that shows other couples gradually joining them on the dance floor. There is then a cut to an enormous close-up of Laurie's head resting on Steve's shoulder. The camera remains stationary as the dance continues; the stationary camera plus Laurie's movement within the shot result in various parts of her body — her hand on Steve's shoulder, her eyes when she is facing the camera, her hair when she is turned away from it — filling the sustained close-up shot. In contrast to the earlier shots of this scene, a harsh spotlight provides the unvarying illumination of Laurie's prolonged close-up. This scene ends with a cut to a medium shot of Steve and Laurie that is somewhat closer than the initial shot of the scene, hiding more of the background and of the other couples on the floor.

Steve and Laurie's dance, which Lucas's mise-en-scène endows with such importance, does not work — or it works in a way one can only hope Lucas did not intend. I think that in this instance Lucas forgot the adage that the director is the person who must carry the whole film in his or her head at all times. The timing of this dramatic dance is crucially wrong. Had it occurred after rather than before we learn that Steve is considering not going away to college, it might have been a meaningful and moving scene, an apt rendering of the familiar pleasures that might persuade Steve to stay. Coming at this point in the narrative, the dance seems related to Laurie's decision to accept or reject Steve's proposal that they date other people. In that light, the mise-en-scène seems to give disproportionate weight to a relatively minor problem; or one that is minor in terms of the narrative, with its (sporadic) focus on Curt's and Steve's decisions to leave or stay. Lucas's mise-en-scène here is worse than thematically confusing; it also has unpleasant overtones of condescension. He appears to take a mock-serious perspective on Laurie's dilemma, a disturbing impression that is conveyed by the harsh light that is thrown on Laurie throughout her close-up (what happened to the variation in lighting that figured earlier in the scene?) and by the unflattering fragmentation of her body featured in the close-up. Here Lucas is unmistakably caught in the trap of the television fallacy: he is either giving inordinate emphasis to a thematically minor event, something that is a regular occurrence on television; or he is condescending to a character and encouraging audiences to respond to her problem (which is real, if not momentous) with amusement, the kind of response that the pervasive comic perspective embedded in television aesthetics regularly engenders.

The focus of the film now shifts to Curt, who has run into his ex-girlfriend, Wendy, at the hop. After a brief comic segment involving Terry and Debbie at Mel's, Curt is seen cruising the strip with Wendy and one of her friends. From the car, Curt spots an unfamiliar, glamorous blonde in a white Thunderbird, which is stopped at a red light. Curt is instantly infatuated; he makes eye contact with the blonde, who appears to issue an unmistakable invitation to him to follow her. He insists that Wendy's friend (who is driving) follow the Thunderbird, but she soon loses sight of it.

Lucas will return to this elusive blonde, who is a rather trite symbol of something ill-defined but all-consuming that Curt is pursuing. In this instance, however, Lucas emphatically — and wisely — turns away from symbolism. After the Thunderbird has disappeared from view, Curt decides to continue his pursuit of the blonde on foot. The camera tracks left with him as he begins the chase. Then, in an excellent choice, Lucas keeps the camera in a stationary position as Curt pauses, in apparent confusion, amid the insistent reality of the strip — relentless traffic, eerie illumination from store windows, headlights, streetlights. The scene ends as Curt resumes his futile pursuit, the camera tracking right with him. Lucas has here economically conveyed Curt as a reflective loner trapped in a milieu that does not allow for reflection and solitude.

In the next sequence Lucas reverts to a sitcom mode. John and Carol, still cruising and still exchanging insults, have a seriocomic spat and Carol gets out of the car. John, however, pursues her and she is soon back in his car. Meanwhile, Terry, eager to impress Debbie, becomes a near-witness to a liquor store hold-up while trying to buy a bottle of scotch without an ID. This comic set piece is not very funny and runs a rather long four minutes; but it does contain one beautiful, if supererogatory, image. While Terry is in the liquor store, he leaves Steve's car parked near a large sign spelling out "ICE" in bold red letters on a stark white background. The colors precisely duplicate the paint job of Steve's car, and the shot devoted to the car parked beside the sign recalls the finest achievements of the photorealism school of painting.

A series of sitcom fragments similar to the liquor store segment ensues, but cast adrift among them is the best sequence in the film.

It begins with a medium shot of Carol and John getting out of his car and jumping over a high fence. The shot is disorienting: we do not know where John and Carol are, and the scene is very dark, with the only illumination coming from an unidentifiable source that only partially relieves the darkenss. There is a cut, and it becomes clear that the initial disorientation was deliberate, for now we get the establishing shot which should have more logically begun the sequence. The shot is of what appears to be a large lot full of remnants of wrecked cars. The shot is held as John and Carol, in the far background of the frame, emerge from the darkness and walk amid the wrecked cars toward the camera. There is a cut to a medium shot of Carol and John, who are just barely discernible in the darkness. The shot is sustained without a cut as John and Carol continue to walk toward the camera while the camera continues to track back from them; for a moment, they are completely lost in the darkness, with only their continuing conversation indicating their presence. Eventually, they walk back into an illuminated area. There is then a cut to a more distant shot of them that reveals more of the lot. The camera remains stationary as John and Carol walk toward it; they eventually walk out of the frame, lost in the enveloping darkness.

This sequence surely represents film direction at its best. Without unduly interrupting the narrative and without turning to distracting or intrusive stylistic devices, Lucas has here rendered another side of the lives the characters in his film lead. He has made John something more than a stereotyped hot-rodder; and he has even, without being insistent about it, suggested the likely direction John's life will follow. Lucas's direction makes the dialogue, in which John tells Carol about some of the more dramatic car wrecks of his time and muses about the dangers of a life dedicated to cruising and drag racing, all but superfluous: all that John says is communicated, with greater force, by the mise-en-scène. It is, moreover, a mise-en-scène in which the principal elements of television aesthetics are notably absent. The withholding of the establishing shot, the involving movement of the tracking shots, the two sustained shots that allow the setting to convey a great part of the meaning, the use of darkness in a substantively meaningful way — all of these are directorial choices that depart significantly from the tenents of television aesthetics, which insist on fragmented montage, highlighted central images, and attention-getting (or attention-reviving) technique. With this sequence, *American Graffiti* reaches a cinematic peak that casts its television valleys into bold relief.

The next several minutes of the film recount three incidents that play as routine comic anecdotes. The first seems quite detachable, particularly as it is not especially funny: Curt, still on foot and still on his own, encounters three comically tough members of a teenage gang known as The Pharaohs and is forced to accompany them (he eventually helps them pull off a minor robbery). The second shows John and Carol, who have resumed cruising, attacking another cruising car with shaving cream. The third is another set piece in which Terry and Debbie awkwardly try to make love, first inside Steve's car, then outside it. This is played for easy laughs, which is regrettable because Lucas might have achieved something beyond predictable laughter in his rendering of this encounter between a virginal boy and an experienced girl.

Terry and Debbie's tryst takes place in a wooded area near a canal, which is apparently where the local teenagers go for this kind of fun. When Terry realizes that someone has stolen Steve's car while he and Debbie left it unattended, he and Debbie set off on the long walk back to town to report the stolen car. A medium shot of them starting off initiates the single most unsatisfying sequence of the film. The sequence, which ultimately proves so disappointing, begins promisingly. The setting and the lighting establish one of the most honorable motifs of film comedy: the magical night–enchanted forest motif. Films as diverse as *Bringing Up Baby*, *Rules of the Game*, and *The Philadelphia Story* have made effective use of this motif to explore the great comic theme of the transformative power of creative, imaginative play. The suggestion that Lucas will place his comedy within this distinguished comic tradition is soon undermined as Lucas confirms his allegiance to the much less distinguished traditions of situation comedy.

The medium shot of Terry and Debbie gives way to a long shot of Terry on a path in a clearing in the woods. Once again, Lucas has achieved a brilliant color effect, in this instance the peculiar blue-black of a night illuminated by a one-quarter moon. The long shot is held as Debbie enters the frame and joins Terry at its center. There is then a cut to a shot of Terry walking resolutely forward while Debbie comically struggles to keep up. The shot is held as Terry falls to his knees and out of the frame; with Terry out of the frame, the camera holds on Debbie, who is standing and looking about her in exaggerated uncertainty about what to do next.

From the shot of Debbie there is a cut to Laurie's car parked in what is clearly another part of the woods near the canal. The shot emphasizes the blue-black, moonlit night.

There is a cut to a medium shot of Laurie and Steve inside the car, followed by a cut to a close two-shot of them; both of them are slightly illuminated by the bluish moonlight streaming in through the windshield. There is then a cut to the first sustained shot of the sequence. Steve and Laurie are now in the back seat, about to make love. His back is to the camera and it fills the frame as he bends over the reclining Laurie. She, however, is not in the mood; and he abruptly resumes an upright posi-tion, dominating the foreground-right of the frame. Steve and Laurie fight, and there is a cut to a shot of Laurie pushing Steve roughly out of the car. This is followed by a cut to a medium shot, which is held just long enough to give it emphasis, of Steve lying on the ground as Laurie drives away.

There is a cut to a tracking shot of Terry and Debbie walking through thick woods; the moonlight plays on Debbie's platinum hair. The tracking stops when Terry and Debbie, startled by a (perhaps imagined) sound, stop and run left out of the frame. This, the second sustained shot of the sequence, is followed by a cut to a shot of Terry and Debbie running in the darkness. A series of alternating medium shots of Terry and Debbie, now very spooked, follows. Steve then enters the frame in the last of the medium shots of Terry. Debbie soon joins them, and the camera tracks right with them as they walk through the woods, headed for town. There is a cut to a shot of the three of them walking toward the camera, which is now tracking away from them. There is then a cut to a shot taken from the opposite point of view: they are now walking away from the camera, receding into the background of the frame. Terry has told Steve a rather implausible lie to explain the absence of his car.

The sequence makes sense only if seen as an example of situation comedy grounded in the aesthetics of television. That it is Steve who Terry and Debbie meet in the woods makes no thematic or psychological sense, for the character of Steve carries no connotations that would endow an encounter with him in the moonlit woods with particular significance. To have made a deeper kind of sense and carried a deeper meaning, Terry and Debbie should have run into Curt who has been established as a reflective searcher. Meeting Steve, however, does make a sitcom kind of sense: it ensures that Terry will be faced with the presumably hilarious problem of explaining to Steve what has become of his car.

The meeting in the woods takes place after two parallel failed attempts at lovemaking. The implied suggestion that the sequence will in some way treat this double failure within the context of the magical night–enchanted forest motif proves to be misleading. Lucas leaves this possibility unexplored, demonstrating his indifference to the possibilities of a motif he has gone to some lengths to establish.

Several of Lucas's specific choices in the sequence reveal his allegiance to television aesthetics. His distribution of emphasis highlights those moments that are funny in an obvious sitcom way: Debbie comically running after Terry, Terry's comic fall to his knees and out of the frame, Debbie's exaggerated pantomime of confusion after Terry's fall, Steve's comic helplessness after Laurie has pushed him out of the car and left him on the ground. A director interested in realizing the larger possibilities of this sequence would have handled these moments with a light touch;

a director committed to the goals and methods of television comedy, as Lucas apparently was, would emphasize such moments, as Lucas did.

The last shot of the sequence, showing Terry, Debbie and Steve walking away from the woods and toward town, is empty visual rhetoric. Had something truly, if comically, transformative happened to these three in the woods, the shot, with its implications of a return to mundane reality after a semimagical experience in the woods, would have made sense and would have had its (apparently) intended resonance. But Terry, Debbie and Steve are returning to town with their stereotyped essences unaltered; Lucas's mise-en-scène has not suggested that something lying beneath the sequence's surface has taken place. That final shot is an indispensable element of the magical night–enchanted forest motif; Lucas's use of it indicates his movie-wise knowledge of the motif. But Lucas has not earned the feeling the shot is supposed to evoke. He has directed the sequence as situation comedy, and he has earned no more than the typically tepid response situation comedy evokes.

The next section of *American Graffiti* is given over to plot development and another detachable comic segment.

John and Carol meet Bob (Harrison Ford), a brash stranger who wants to challenge John's king of the road title. They agree to meet at dawn for a drag race. Meanwhile, Steve, who has made it back to town from the canal, consoles himself with a soda at Mel's. When Laurie sees him in apparently intimate conversation with one of the waitresses, she decides to defy him by riding with Bob, John's challenger (the logic behind this decision is not immediately clear, but then Laurie is upset and is not behaving strictly rationally). John finally takes Carol home. They have grown rather fond of each other during their long night of cruising, and a note of grudging affection now lies just below the surface of their sarcastic banter. Lucas uses alternating close-ups of them for their farewell scene, a choice that seems appropriate because, thanks largely to the car graveyard sequence, John and Carol have become the most compelling characters in the film.

Finally, the comic set piece, which is genuinely funny, involves Curt's winning the respect of The Pharaohs (with whom he has spent most of the night) by successfully pulling off a caper that destroys a police patrol car.

Curt, freed at last from his semicaptivity among The Pharaohs, walks back to Mel's to retrieve his car. Steve sees him there and walks up to him. A condensed reprise of the Curt-Steve exchange in the first sequence takes place; it is during this second exchange that Steve first reveals he is now considering not going away to college.

The action turns broadly humorous again after the Curt-Steve scene. Terry and Debbie have made it back to town, and they spot Steve's car parked and apparently abandoned. When Terry tries to reclaim the car, the punks who stole it suddenly appear on the scene. Just as they begin to rough up Terry, John appears and, with Terry's help, drives off the punks. Terry — and Steve's car — have been rescued.

Terry, Debbie and John then go to Mel's. The focus emphatically shifts to Terry and Debbie in a series of alternating medium shots of them standing in front of the drive-in's windows. As they begin to walk out of the frame, there is a cut; now Terry is in the background of the frame, sitting on the curb of the walkway that encircles Mel's, while Debbie is partially eliminated from the shot, with only her legs visible in the foreground. With this odd composition, the climactic scene between Terry and Debbie begins. As he begins to confess the lies (the least outlandish of which being his claim that Steve's car was in fact his) he has been telling her all night to impress her, there is a cut to a medium shot of Debbie listening to Terry's confession. There is then a return to the previous shot: Terry sitting on the curb with Debbie's legs dominant in the foreground. Debbie exits the frame but her words continue as a voice-over as the camera holds on Terry. There is a cut to a shot of Debbie, her back to the camera, talking to a group of boys standing nearby. This is followed by a cut to a shot of John standing by his car, a shot that undermines the momentum of the Terry-Debbie interaction. There is then a cut to a medium shot of Terry, still sitting on the curb. Debbie's legs and skirt enter the frame at the right. She sits down next to Terry, and the resulting composition is a medium shot of the two of them. As she begins to admit her night with Terry was fun and that she rather likes him in spite of everything, there is a cut to a closer two-shot of them. Debbie then exits the frame, after having agreed to go out with Terry again. The sequence ends with the camera holding on the delighted expression that now fills Terry's face.

That last shot of the sequence is the only good one; the rest is pure television. Lucas's misguided direction of the sequence, which is supposed to depict the initiation of an authentic relationship between Terry and Debbie, can be explained only in terms of his adherence to the essentials of television aesthetics. The fragmented montage and fragmented compositions would appear to be rather crude examples of television's "technical events" phenomenon: Lucas presumably thought the frequent cuts and unusual compositions were necessary to forestall viewer boredom with a "talky" sequence. An alternative explanation, even less favorable to Lucas, also suggests the influence of television: the fragmentation of the sequence, particularly the fragmented presentation of Debbie's body, suggests that Lucas has adopted a perspective of comic condescension toward the people and events of the sequence, that he was eager to assure audiences that they too may regard this sequence as just another comic fragment involving two stock comic figures.

The next sequence was presumably intended to be the film's climax, though there has been virtually no preparation for the sequence, which thus lacks the essential coherence of a true climax.

The sequence depicts Curt's encounter with Wolfman Jack, the legendary disc jockey who, thanks to the ubiquitous radios featured in the film, has been a pervasive aural presence in *American Graffiti*. It seems that it has long been rumored that the mysterious Wolfman broadcasts from a station just outside of town, and Curt suddenly decides to track him down. He wants the Wolfman to broadcast a request for the mysterious blonde in the Thunderbird to call him; beyond that, it seems (one cannot be sure of this, given the incoherence of this section of the film) that Curt feels a meeting with Wolfman Jack will somehow relieve the ill-defined angst he has been feeling as his day of departure approaches.

Curt drives off in the predawn darkness to find the radio station where Wolfman Jack reportedly works. A radio tower is soon visible through his car's windshield, and then there is a cut to a panning shot of the tower. Instead of then dissolving to Curt inside the station, Lucas uses a series of brief shots that show him parking his car, finding the entrance to the station, and finally entering it. The effect is to give the sequence, which should convey the sense of predetermination associated with dreams, an overly literal, almost mechanical, tone. Lucas is once again avoiding any mythical suggestions his material might imply. In this case the result is to ensure that the sequence will lack the special emotional power of a cathartic climax.

Inside the station, Curt sees Wolfman Jack (who of course plays himself) through a glass partition separating the disc jockey's small studio from the rest of the station. The first part of Curt and the Wolfman's conversation is a medium shot in which Curt and his reflection in the partition are at the left of the frame, Wolfman Jack at the right. The exact significance of this composition escapes me: the doubling of Curt's image at this point seems arbitrary.

Curt eventually joins the Wolfman in his studio. In a medium shot that is sustained for a considerable length of time, Curt and the Wolfman occupy the extreme left and extreme right of the studio filling the center of the frame. Curt asks the Wolfman to broadcast his request for the anonymous blonde to call him, and the Wolfman offers some hip-avuncular advice about growing up. The lighting of the shot is very bright, almost harsh—Lucas certainly did not use that element of mise-en-scène to suggest a dreamlike encounter with a legendary figure of the teenage subculture. Lucas further anchors the sequence in the literalness of the here and now by following the sustained medium shot with a conventional series of brief alternating shots of Curt and Wolfman Jack as they continue their conversation.

The conversation ends, and the sequence concludes with a series of shots that seems overly complicated and again rather mechanical. The camera tracks right with Curt as he walks through the dark station. There is a series of cuts between Wolfman Jack in his brightly lit studio and Curt in the darkness of the station's record library.

There is a kind of epilogue or coda to this sequence, but its impact is undermined by Lucas's decision to delay its appearance until after he has set up the film's *other* climax, the drag race between John and Bob. Lucas is here playing to his strength as he intercuts medium shots of Bob (still accompanied by Laurie) and John preparing for the race in an open area outside of town. Dawn, announcing the beginning of the day after the very long night that has been detailed in *American Graffiti*, is just beginning to color the sky as the race begins. Before it does, Lucas, in an extreme example of his determination to keep his tribal comedy structure intact, has Steve, who had not known about the race, find out about it in time to arrive on the scene for its finish.

Lucas handles the race itself very well. There are shots of glowing headlights (it is still more night than day at the start of the race) racing toward the camera, a shot of Terry (he has accompanied John to the race: another member of the tribe accounted for) dropping a flag to begin the race, and a long shot of the two cars receding into the background of the frame as they speed down an empty highway. The race ends abruptly when Bob's car overturns. He is unhurt, and John retains his title.

Steve's car pulls into a shot that includes Bob's wrecked car and the observers of the race gathered in stunned reaction to its outcome. Steve's appearance gives rise to the first of the sequence's subclimaxes as he encounters Laurie and they wordlessly embrace in a dramatic medium shot set amid the emptiness of the field adjoining the stretch of highway where the race had taken place.

The second subclimax involves John and Terry. The camera tracks left with them as they walk away from the site of the wreck. Terry is congratulating John on his victory, but Lucas's composition suggests the melancholy John is feeling at this moment. The tracking camera has come to a stop and Terry is now out of the frame; John is at the right of the frame, with the center dominated by his car and the empty field, which is illuminated by a dawn that seems to cast an unnaturally harsh white light on the scene.

This shot is followed by the last act of the Steve-Laurie reconciliation: they are seen embracing and walking toward the camera in a shot whose lighting suggests a rosier, more benign dawn than that seen in the preceding shot of John. Lucas's artful use of color and lighting in these two shots represents his best use of those two elements of mise-en-scène for a thematic, rather than a merely decorative, purpose.

The coda of the Curt–Wolfman Jack sequence follows the Laurie-Steve shot. A close-up of Curt finds him in the phone booth in Mel's parking lot. His mystery woman has heard Wolfman Jack's message and has called Curt. What she has to say is deeply disappointing — just a flirtatious hint to Curt that if he wants her he will have to catch her some night when she is cruising. The camera holds on Curt standing in the phone booth after he has hung up. Presumably, he has undergone a major experience; but neither Lucas's direction nor Richard Dreyfuss's acting successfully conveys the nature or depth of the experience.

The scene then shifts to the town's small airport. Curt is leaving for the East after all; Steve has decided to stay. This is a rather surprising decision; but then Steve has been such a one-dimensional character that it does not much matter — in other words, Lucas's handling of the character of Steve has not *made* it matter.

In a (surely, unintended) parody of the structure of his film, Lucas lines up the main characters and has Curt say goodbye to each of them one by one. The linearity of the composition is emblematic of the confining structure Lucas has imposed on the film; and the words each of the characters says at this moment confirm Lucas's failure to bring any of them (with the arguable exception of John) to a point significantly beyond their stereotyped origins. The final shot of the film, taken from Curt's point of view in the plane as he looks down on Steve's car moving through the flat landscape below, is a doomed last-minute attempt to give *American Graffiti* the emotional resonance and broader significance that Lucas's direction has denied it at virtually every turn.

The smaller scale and more homey subject matter of *American Graffiti*, compared to Lucas's later projects, have led some to regard it as Lucas's "personal" film. That, in my judgment, is a seriously inaccurate label. Far from contributing to the commercial and critical standing of personal filmmaking in the New Hollywood, *American Graffiti* contributed to the legitimation of a New Hollywood directorial style whose reliance on some of the fundamental aesthetic principles of television resulted in films whose adherence to an artificially confining structure and unfelt manipulation of stereotyped characters make them almost precisely the opposite of personal.

Notes

1. The "signal/noise" phenomenon is treated in detail in Jerry Mander, *Four Arguments for the Elimination of Television* (New York: William Morrow, 1978), pp. 267–69.

2. The concept of "flow" is elaborated in James Monaco, "The Televison Plexus," in Carl Lowe, ed., *Television and American Culture* (New York: H. W. Wilson, 1981), p. 19.

3. Mander, *Four Arguments,* p. 303.

4. See chapter 1, n. 5.

5. Michael Malone, "And Gracie Begat Lucy Who Begat Laverne," in Les Brown and Savannah Waring Walker, eds., *Fast Forward: The New Television and American Society* (Kansas City: Andrews and McMeel, 1981), p. 193.

6. Vincent Canby put *American Graffiti* on the ten best list of the *New York Times* for 1973, a distinction *Time* also accorded the film. Critics Stephen Farber, Diane Jacobs and Richard Schickel were among those who named it one of the ten best films of the seventies in a *Take One* critics survey.

3

The Literary Fallacy

All That Jazz (1979)
Apocalypse Now (1979)

The literary fallacy in films has long been with us, and it has been at least implicitly cited over the years as the principal reason for the relative failure of a not inconsiderable number of films. It is a fallacy grounded in confusion about the relationship between the cinema and ideas.

In film as in the other arts, meaning is contained in style; the ideas of a film — its "content" — cannot exist apart from the stylistic elements that constitute a film — its images, its sense of space and time, its background details, its color, its sound, its editing. If the ideas are not present in the totality of a film's mise-en-scène, they are not successfully or satisfyingly communicated.

Now the same is undoubtedly true of the very greatest works of literature: their ideas are imbedded in their rhetoric, their rhythms, their perspectives, their settings, in the behavioral qualities of their characters; as a result, their ideas are communicated with a coherence, completeness and force that account for their greatness.

Literature, however, because of the nature of literary communication, can achieve another effective (though, at least in the American novel of recent years, seldom attempted) kind of communication: in the so-called novel of ideas, the author conveys a sense of ideas in interaction, achieved through the exploration of ideas communicated directly through dialogue passages or suggested by the structure of the novel or personified in its characters. This mode of communication can be effective and often deeply pleasurable, and it is the mode that has been used in novels as diverse as those of Thomas Peacock and John Steinbeck's *The Grapes of Wrath.*

The literary fallacy in film has traditionally manifested itself as an attempt to make films communicate in the manner of novels of ideas. Ideas

44

are conveyed through means associated with literary communication: the narration of the film by one of its characters, the use of monologues, the conversion of characters into representatives of certain abstractions, and the structuring of events so as to point to a moral or concluding thematic statement. While some critics have inexplicably praised the "seriousness" of such films (as if films that use *all* the elements of film to communciate ideas, films that communicate *as films*, are somehow frivolous), others have condemned them as "static" or "talky." It is, as I have said, not a new phenomenon: the literary fallacy can be found in some of the later films of Chaplin, the more relentlessly "classic" films of Ford, the more over-written films of Sturges and Mankiewicz, very nearly all the films of Sidney Lumet.

It is worth reiterating that not everyone agrees that regarding film as a kind of literary subgenre is an aesthetic fallacy. Gore Vidal, for one, thinks this is precisely the attitude that should inform filmmaking:

> Since the talking movie is closest in form to the novel ... it strikes me that the rising literary generation might think of the movies as, pecu-liarly, their kind of novel, to be created by them in collaboration with technicians but without the interference of The Director, that hustler-plagiarist who has for twenty years dominated and exploited and (occa-sionally) enhanced an art form still in search of its true authors.[1]

Among New Hollywood films, Woody Allen's *Manhattan* (1979) would appear to be just the kind of "talking movie" Vidal would approve of, a novel cast in the form of a film, presumably to accommodate the con-temporary literate public's fondness for movies. Allen's overall directorial strategy for the film seeks to generate meaning not through the cultivation of visual information but through its reduction, with the apparent aim of giving enhanced prominence to verbal communication; and to convert characters into types who, in the manner of novels of ideas, stand for par-ticular attitudes or temperaments. *Manhattan* certainly demonstrates Allen's movement away from the bumptious fragmentation of *Bananas*, but it is an interesting question as to whether his movement from the televison fallacy to the literary fallacy represents progress.

While *Manhattan* represents a continuation into the New Hollywood era of the traditional literary fallacy, that era has also seen the emergence of a variation on that fallacy that seems traceable to confusion regarding the nature of authorial vision in film and its relation to the modernist aesthetic. The essence of the fallacy remains: an attempt to make film communicate in the manner of novels. But, in this new variation, the model is not the novel of ideas but the canon of literary modernism.

The central precept of literary modernism is the belief that without the validating perspective of a unique authorial vision, the recording of reality and the recounting of experience lack authenticity; the central stylistic device is an elaborate form of direct address, in which the author communicates directly to the reader his or her vision-interpretation of reality and experience, rather than a mimetic rendering of them that is open to a variety of interpretations. As every aspect of the literary work — its sense of time and place, delineation of character, rhetorical tone — is subsumed within the writer's vision,

> the reader may be left helpless, either overwhelmed or repelled, and in either case without the independent material on which his imagination can begin to work.... [The modernist writer] will seem to force the reader to see things as he does, and will leave him too little to do for himself, in finding the connections and implications that are particularly relevant to him.[2]

A second modernist precept holds that "every serious artist, to be worth his salt, must create his own world and style from scratch, for himself and from himself.[3] The resulting emphasis on stylistic experimentation and innovation leads to a third modernist precept: the importance of acknowledging within the work the creative effort that produced it. The aritst, who is of course aware that he or she is creating art, has an obligation to acknowledge that awareness — "the work that made the picture cannot be allowed to have no place in the picture itself."[4]

The modernist aesthetic stands in sharp contrast to the realist aesthetic that has been the informing force in the art of the American film. Modernism aspires to create works which acknowledge that they are the constructs of an artistic sensibility and which assert the artist's all-inclusive and univocal vision; cinematic realism aspires to create works that conceal the presence of the artist and do not overtly impose the artist's interpretation of the work.

The obvious contrast between the modernist aesthetic and the realist aesthetic of film does not in itself explain why the former is unsuitable to film, why the attempt to transfer the modernist aesthetic to film is a fallacious variation on the more traditional literary fallacy.

The explanation is that, Susan Sontag's statement to the contrary[5] notwithstanding, a film audience, unlike the reader of a (modernist) novel, does not expect to follow serially carefully selected and crafted images that express the director's vision-interpretation of a film's material. The camera, with its unique capacity for seeing so much on so many levels of subtlety simultaneously, creates inevitable expectations in audiences that they will *see* the meaning of a film in the totality of what the camera presents, rather than be told the meaning through a series of images that appear to displace, rather than grow out of, the totality of what the camera sees. Such direct-address images certainly succeed in conveying the director's interpretative vision of the material, but the success comes at a heavy cost. First, the modernist device of direct address through interpretative images, which at first glance seems so utterly visual, actually fails fully to exploit the visual properties of film by failing to embed meaning in *everything* the camera can see. Second, applying the modernist aesthetic to film results in the director's preempting the interpretation of a film through the use of univocal images and thus denying audiences the involvement in the discovery of meaning that is embedded in the inevitably ambiguous totality of a fully cultivated mise-en-scène.

Terrence Malick's *Days of Heaven* (1978) is perhaps the purest example of the modernist aesthetic applied to film to come out of the New Hollywood era thus far. Malick at least had the courage of his (to my mind) misguided convictions: his near total indifference to the central realist task of creating meaning in and through a mise-en-scène that achieves a balance of involving credibility and directorial vision assures that the only available source of meaning in his film are the seemingly imposed (in the sense that they do not credibly emerge from the totality of the mise-en-scène) images that he addressses from time to time to passively waiting audiences. Malick's modernism, interesting enough, manifests itself as a commitment to the aesthetic of the silent film: *Days of Heaven* has very little dialogue and features considerable emphasis on facial expressions, pantomimic gestures, sound effects, still-life shots of inanimate objects, and artfully composed tableaux. Malick, in other words, asserts his vision by highlighting certain elements of mise-en-scène, instead of creating his vision through the cultivation of all of them; in the process, he asserts his artistic presence but also distances audiences from involvement in his film.

Malick's modernist purism, however, has been a rarity in New Hollywood films. The modernist variation on the literary fallacy has more frequently appeared in uneasy and destructive competition with both the traditional version of the literary fallacy and an aesthetics rooted in (or at least not opposed to) realism and committed to the ideal of a balance between credibility and expression, written about by V. F. Perkins.

Bob Fosse's *All That Jazz* and Francis Coppola's *Apocalypse Now* are prominent among the New Hollywood films that are fatally undermined by the clash between the literary fallacy and an aesthetics founded in the communicative nature of film.

Fosse begins *All That Jazz* with a rhetorical device highly favored by directors committed to bringing the modernist aesthetic to film. He addresses audiences through multipart images which, because they are detached from a context with which to interact, can only convey the single (and, inevitably, simplistic) meaning their creator intends them to convey. The first image consists of four shots. In rapid succession, a cassette is seen being inserted into a player, eyedrops are applied to a bloodshot eye, Alka-Seltzer tablets are seen fizzing in a glass (the camera zooms in on the tablets), and a hand is seen reaching for the glass. Fosse, evidently feeling that he has sufficiently established both his presence and his control of meaning in his film, now provides a minimal context for the isolated shots. The camera pans right for a medium shot that shows, at the left of the frame, the reflection in a mirror of Joe Gideon (Roy Scheider), and, at the right, a theatre poster mounted on a wall above a sink. Rapid shots of the cassette, Joe in the shower, Joe applying eyedrops, and Joe taking Dexedrine follow.

From another close-up of an eye as eyedrops are administered, Fosse fades to the second image of the film. The fade is to a long shot of a tightrope walker; a male voice is heard relating an adage that compares tightrope walking to life. There is then a cut to a low-angle shot of the tightrope walker; the voice-over is now a conversation between the male voice and a female voice. There is a cut to a long shot of a woman, Angelique (Jessica Lange), dressed in an elaborate and vaguely old-fashioned white gown and a broad-brimmed hat with a gauzy white veil that covers her face; a number of light bulbs in the foreground of the frame give the shot a soft-focus glow. The costuming and lighting establish Angelique as a fantasy figure. There is then a cut to a low-angle shot of the tightrope walker falling; the fall, filmed in slow motion, is captured from various angles in a series of brief shots. With this rather trite image, Fosse has asserted the idea that Joe lives his life on an edge that he is always in danger of falling over, albeit with considerable grace. The falling shots are followed by a cut to Joe standing in his bathroom and saying, "It's showtime, folks" to his reflection. With that shot the second image concludes.

The two opening images expose the nature of the direct-address strategy and reveal its essential weakness. There is, in the first place, the attempt at the immediate communication of authorial vision — that is, the vision is communicated without the mediation of those aspects of mise-en-scène that would bind it to the overall credibility of the film. Second, there is the insistence that an artist has deliberately fashioned this vision, an insistence that is evidenced by the use of the pan, the fade and slow motion, which are among the more obtrusive modalities of film direction. Third and most important, the images are preemptive: they impose interpretation, making it unnecessary for audiences to discover meaning through an involvement in the totality of the mise-en-scène. We know because Fosse's images permit no other interpretation than that Joe is a driven man and that he associates death with an idealized feminine beauty. These ideas have been declared in a fashion that is essentially literary; they have not emerged from audiences' participation in a complex and compelling mise-en-scène.

Fosse follows with a sequence that begins with a small group of dancers, wearing rehearsal clothes, sitting on the floor of what appears to be a large stage. There follows a series of cuts among various knots of dancers engaged in a variety of warm-up activities. George Benson's pulsating rendition of "On Broadway" comes on the soundtrack.

There is a cut to a medium shot of Joe, his back to the camera, squatting in the foreground of the stage. The camera cranes up to reveal that Joe is at the edge of the stage, which is filled by a veritable mob of dancers. A cut to a direct overhead shot of the stage reinforces the impression of Joe trapped in a throng of writhing bodies.

A series of cuts—with the camera variously positioned at eye level on the stage, overhead, and among the seats of the theatre, where some producer types are watching the on-stage activity with a fluctuating level of interest—establishes the chaotic reality of a mass tryout for a Broadway show. One shot is particularly effective in suggesting the precise quality of Joe's involvement in this reality. The camera picks out Joe embedded in the midst of the dancers, then tracks down to show him slumped against a wall in the background of the frame, with the foreground filled with rhythmically moving bodies that appear to be moving in on him and threaten to engulf him.

The sequence ends with Joe, the director-choreographer of the show, making a one-by-one selection of six dancers out of the dozens who tried out. The camera tracks with him from the stage to the rear of the theatre, where he joins his ex-wife Audrey (Leland Palmer) and teenage daughter Michelle (Erszebet Foldi), who have been observing the tryout.

The superiority of the "On Broadway" sequence to the direct-address images that preceded it is, to my mind, evident. The detailed, involving, highly credible mise-en-scène Fosse creates for the "On Broadway" sequence establishes both the tension and the excitement of the Broadway milieu that defines Joe's life; the complexity of the mise-en-scène makes it possible simultaneously to understand that Joe is a driven, perpetually tense man and to appreciate the allure of the source of his obsession, a complexity of meaning that is in contrast to the univocal nature of the initial image of the film. As for Joe's preoccupation with death, which is conveyed in the second of the opening images, that idea is considerably more nuanced and compelling in the "On Broadway" sequence than it is in the tightrope walker image. It may well be that Joe has an obsession with death, but it is not enough for Fosse to assert that idea through a direct-address image. If he wants to communicate it in more than a notional way, he must establish it, as he begins to do in the "On Broadway" sequence, in a way that attaches the idea to the totality of the credible visual experience the camera reveals to audiences.

Fosse next reminds us of his absolute and unpredictable control of his film by cutting from a shot of Joe joining Audrey and Michelle in the rear of the theatre to a close-up of a face in elaborate clown makeup staring into a mirror. In a series of brief shots (all of which are filmed in soft-focus with a bluish filter), the camera tracks in on Angelique and tracks away from Joe, who is now identifiable as the man in the clown makeup. Joe's conversation with Audrey and Michelle in the theatre is then intercut with shots of Joe in clown makeup speaking to someone (presumably Angelique) off-camera about his shabby treatment of women in general, his ex-wife and daughter in particular. After Joe has left the theatre, there are two more shots of Joe-the-clown and Angelique continuing their conversation about Joe's relations with women. With these shots, Fose initiates his use of another device that is a staple of films marred by the literary fallacy: characters in the film comment on and, more important, interpret the actions audiences see (or *should* see) before them on the screen. The device distances audiences from the film and obstructs the communication channels of film by placing a layer of direct interpretation between the visual reality of the film and audiences' perception of it.

The intercutting of Joe's fantasy dialogue with Angelique continues in the next sequence, which is set in a screening room where Joe (who is also a film director) is supervising the editing of his film under pressure from his producers to accelerate the process to meet an already delayed release date. Joe is editing a sequence of the film in which Davis Newman (Cliff Gorman), playing a Lennie Bruce–like stand-up comic, delivers a sardonic monologue on death to a nightclub audience. Fosse goes for a stream of consciousness effect by intercutting the Joe-Angelique dialogue with shots from the Newman monologue in such a way as to suggest a loose association between the bitter remarks about death in the latter and the rueful comments about life and death in the former. My objection to the use of the stream of consciousness device in film is, again, that it is a merely notional kind of communication that inhibits audience involvement in the visual reality of a film. Fosse has an obligation to exploit the communicative modalities of film to make us see and feel and ultimately know on a much more than notional level what Joe experiences as he watches a monologue concerned with the subject of death.

That Fosse occasionally recognizes and fulfills that obligation is evidenced by a shot near the end of the screening room sequence. Joe, taking a break from the tedious editing of the Newman monologue, is seen standing at a widow of the editing studio; he is contemplating (the shot is held for a considerable time) the marquee of a burlesque house on a street that lies several stories below him. Here Fosse achieves the deep, textured communication cinema is capable of through the cultivation of what the camera is capable of showing us. His montage (the shots preceding and following the window shot are of Newman's death monologue) suggests (without insisting on the point) that death is on Joe's mind at this moment; the meditative quality of the shot (achieved through Roy Scheider's acting and the shot's duration) suggests that Joe in his mind is making a connection between death and the tawdry side of show business represented by what he sees below him; the spatial character of the shot suggests that although Joe is at the top of his profession he is never far removed from the bottom, an unpleasant truth that may in part explain his obsessive dedication to his art. This shot means all of this or some of this or more than this: the point is it conveys with the force cinema is capable of more nuanced meaning than Fosse's obtrusive stream of consciousness shots, and it does so without doing damage to cinema's delicate balance between credibility and expression and without denying audiences the opportunity of discovering meaning as they become involved in the film's emerging reality.

The sequence that follows, which is meant to establish Joe's attitude toward women, is another instance in which Fosse, with only one lapse into the literary fallacy, creates a mise-en-scène that contains and effectively communicates meaning.

Fosse cuts from the screening room to a shot of Joe emerging from darkness and walking through a dim corridor of his apartment. The camera tracks in for a medium shot of Victoria (Deborah Geffner), one of the dancers Joe has just selected for his new show. Victoria, who is at first almost totally concealed by shadows, walks into a dimly illuminated medium shot as she enters the apartment. Almost immediately, she exits the frame at the right; the camera holds on Joe watching her enter the living room. This is a fine, suggestive shot: Victoria is seen as a rather shadowy presence, more something to be watched than someone to be acknowledged; Joe has emerged from the darkness of the screening room and the darkness of his apartment to have an encounter with a shadow, and he appears to adopt the same observer-voyeur stance toward Victoria that he took toward his film in the screening room.

There is a cut to a shot of a female arm draped over a male shoulder, an effective suggestion of the rather detached, impersonal quality of this encounter. The camera tilts up for a medium shot of Victoria and Joe dancing. The camera remains stationary as they slowly dance, and then it holds for a medium shot of Joe sitting on a couch as he again observes Victoria. There is then a cut to a shot that surely is meant to suggest Joe's point of view: Victoria, who is seen in a red glow (presumably produced by the candles in the room), first recedes from Joe as the camera tracks away from her, then becomes more reachable as she approaches Joe and the camera. In this single shot, Fosse has used point of view, lighting, camera movement and movement within the shot to communicate some rather complex information about Joe's relationship with Victoria and (through an extrapolation that seems justified by Victoria's lack of specificity as a character) with women in general. He idealizes them, but does not really see them; he does not make real contact with them, preferring to observe them; yet they come to him, giving him what he (presumably) wants.

Victoria is then seen kneeling on the floor beside Joe, who is seated on a couch. The camera tracks in for a two-shot of them; the glow of candles is very prominent in the background-center of the frame. The camera then tracks in nearer for a close-up of Joe and Victoria in profile; the candles are now eliminated from the frame. The camera holds for a moment, then continues its forward tracking. Joe and Victoria become blurs in the foreground of the frame while a luminous digital clock in the background, which had been only an indistinct glow, comes into focus. With this shot, Fosse has relapsed into the modernist fallacy. It is, in the first place, a rather distancing reassertion of the director's presence, a rather arty vision-interpretation of an experience instead of a rendering of the experience itself. Then, too, the shot is visually incoherent: Fosse's play with focus may mean something to him, but the meaning of his stylistic choices at this moment is not at all clear.

Fosse recovers his cinematic sense for the final shots of the sequence, though even here his technique is more obtrusive than in the earlier part of the sequence. There is a series of zoom shots of Victoria intercut with medium shots of Joe. This is followed by a complex crane shot that nicely recapitulates Joe's relations with women. Victoria, who is now naked from the waist up, is seen in the foreground of the frame, standing in the middle of a short flight of stairs; the composition reiterates her role as an object to be observed and admired. Joe is below her in the background of the frame. The camera cranes past Victoria for a shot, the third in the sequence, of Joe observing her; the camera movement, which literally bypasses Victoria, suggests her relative insignificance. There is then a cut to a shot of Joe's more-or-less steady girlfriend Kate (Ann Reinking) approaching his apartment door, her key in hand. Joe's rather detached womanizing is about to cause a real woman some real pain.

Kate discovers Joe in bed with Victoria, but Fosse cuts their confrontation short. He goes instead to a four-minute flashback showing Joe as a teenager working as a tap dancer in a burlesque show. It is a fairly conventional flashback sequence, though Fosse brackets it with shots of the ongoing imaginary conversation between Joe and Angelique.

The flashback is followed by a fade, and then the series of shots culminating in Joe saying "It's showtime, folks" to his reflection is reprised.

Fosse then intercuts shots of Joe and Angelique in conversation about his treatment of Kate with shots of Joe and Kate discussing their relationship in general and his chronic infidelity in particular. Fosse plainly intends the Joe-Angelique exchanges to again function as a commentary on the primary text, a technique featured in many modernist novels. However, in this instance and generally in the film, the Joe-Angelique segments only serve to stunt the development of a compelling, fully realized mise-en-scène; and they impose an authoritarian, univocal interpretation on what we see in the text, preventing the emergence of a possibly more nuanced understanding of Joe.

The Joe-Kate, Joe-Angelique scene is followed by four brief scenes. In the first, Joe and the rest of the company listen to the show's composer sing "Aerotica," a hackneyed (Joe is seen wincing as the song proceeds) number that seems unlikely to be the showstopper its composer hopes it will be. In the second, another Joe-Angelique exchange is followed by Joe's first musical hallucination, a brief cabaret-type number concerning a ménage-à-trois Joe was once involved in. In the third, Joe is seen struggling to work out the choreography of the "Aerotica" number. In the fourth, he is seen back in the screening room, still editing the Davis Newman monologue about death.

Fosse achieves near-perfect coherence in the next three major sequences of the film, in which he creates a richly expressive mise-en-scène that suggests the complex essence of the man at the center of his film.

All three sequences are set in rehearsal rooms, and an important feature of all three is the attention Fosse devotes to the details of their settings. All three involve Joe and one of the women in his life, and the principal idea that emerges from the mise-en-scène of all three concerns the three-way relation involving Joe, women and dance. The sequences seem to be ordered according to the women's ascending awareness of the role dance plays in Joe's relationships, with the variation in each sequence's mise-en-scène suggesting the variations in their awareness.

The first of the sequences involves Joe and his daughter Michelle. The initial shots emphasize their separation and fragmentation (five shots isolate Joe's and Michelle's hands) and the vastness of the dimly lit rehearsal room. Joe is preoccupied with working out the choreography of the "Aerotica" number; Michelle (who apparently is an aspiring dancer) has been enlisted to help him to try out some tentative ideas.

The pattern of separate shots of Joe and Michelle is broken when he walks into a medium shot initially devoted to her. The shot, however, conveys little sense of intimacy: he is in the foreground, surreptitiously popping a few pills; she is in the midground futilely trying to initiate a serious conversation with him.

Intimacy — or what passes for intimacy where Joe is concerned — comes when Joe and Michelle begin to work. Fosse keeps them together on camera throughout a lengthy series of shots showing them working out choreographic moves. Many of the shots feature their reflections in the mirror that fills one wall of the room, a rather neat and unobtrusive reminder that Joe is probably never just "himself," that he is always a preoccupied and self-conscious artist who is perhaps most himself when he is practicing his art. Michelle tries to talk with her father throughout the sequence; he responds, but the major part of his attention is clearly devoted to working out the choreography. Joe is using Michelle, something he is probably (but not surely) aware of; Michelle is being initiated into awareness that the only way to get even momentarily close to Joe is through the mediation of dance.

The sequence concludes with two shots that concisely suggest the nature of the Joe-Michelle relationship and the role dance plays in it. In the first, a tracking shot shows Joe rushing down a narrow corridor of the rehearsal studio, with Michelle's body still wrapped around his in a dance position she has refused to get out of. In the second, Joe is seen standing in the rain as he waves goodbye to Michelle as she is carried away in a car that gradually recedes from the camera.

Fosse, who is never entirely free of the literary fallacy, inserts at this point a scene which distances audiences from the progressively involving credibility of the rehearsal room sequences by declaring directly what the sequences themselves convey in a much more compelling manner — namely, that life and, particularly, relationships are all part of the show for Joe. The scene also reverts to the strategy of addressing audiences with an image whose meaning, because the image lacks context, is not immediately accessible to audiences. In the scene, identical long shots of Joe standing in the background-center of a rehearsal hall bracket a reprise of the "It's showtime" motif, which this time around has been expanded to include brief shots of Joe and Angelique and an almost subliminal shot of Joe on an operating table.

The second of the rehearsal room sequences features Joe and Victoria. In contrast to both the earlier sequence with her in Joe's apartment and the preceding sequence featuring Joe and Michelle, Fosse almost immediately shows Joe and Victoria linked through the mediation of dance. In a shot that is quickly reprised, Joe and Victoria are seen standing at the windows that run along one wall of the room; they are looking out the windows rather than at each other, and they are linked by a section of the barre that runs beneath the windows. After the reprise of the shot, Fosse includes several brief shots of Victoria and the other dancers of the company rehearsing under Joe's demanding supervision. Then, in an excellent reiteration of the idea that the only way Joe can make real contact with Victoria (or any woman) is through the mediation of dance, Joe is seen walking through the crowd of dancers toward Victoria, whom he kisses on the top of her head. There is a cut to a closer medium shot of the kiss, and then Joe exits the frame. Victoria (who has been under considerable pressure from Joe to improve her performance) remains in the foreground of the shot. The shot is held as she breaks into a radiant smile; the camera remains stationary as the other dancers move from the background of the frame to gather around Victoria in celebration of the breakthrough — in more than one sense — she has achieved with Joe.

The third of the rehearsal room sequences features Joe and his ex-wife Audrey. Fosse has Audrey practicing dance movements (she is the star of Joe's show) throughout her conversation with Joe. This is an excellent directorial decision, especially when considered in conjunction with the earlier rehearsal room sequences; for it suggests that the woman who knows Joe best knows he can be reached only through the mediation of his obsession, dance (and then only briefly).

There follows an eight-minute musical number, which is the "Aerotica" number danced to the choreography Joe has finally devised for the song. Fosse's fragmented filming of the number aptly reflects the fragmented, mechanico-erotico style of Fosse's choreography, a style I have never particularly admired.

The dance is followed by another sequence in which the monologue on death from the film Joe is editing is intercut with shots of Joe and Angelique in conversation, the topic this time being Joe's perfectionism, a quality that has already been established in earlier sequences and that therefore does not require the verbal commentary Fosse here attaches to it.

A second musical number follows. Kate and Michelle, to celebrate the apparently successful preview of Joe's film, entertain him in his apartment with a dance routine they have prepared to the music of "Everything Old Is New Again." The routine is delightful, but the sequence ends with a rather too arty image of Joe's bowed head propped up against a top hat; here is another instance of the artist addressing us with an image that asserts a meaning that should have emerged from the total mise-en-scène of the sequence. That image is followed by a fade, in this film a sign that the idea that a self-conscious artist is in control of what we are seeing is about to be reiterated.

The fade is followed, predictably, by a reprise of the "It's showtime" motif, again with variations. The images are blurred and in slow motion; Joe faces the mirror to deliver the line, but we see only gestures, we do not hear the words; the facing-the-mirror image is immediately reprised, and this time Joe says the line while having a severe coughing fit.

Fosse's commitment to the modernist aesthetic is fully in evidence in the sequence that follows. The company is gathered to read through the script of the show. Audrey reads her opening line, and then the soundtrack goes silent. For the remainder of this rather lengthy sequence, we see actors reading from a script and laughing, but we do not hear their words or the sound of their laughter. Only a few isolated sounds — of fingers tapping on a table, of the striking of a match, the snapping of a pencil — are exempted from the ban on sound Fosse imposes on this sequence. Here is the modernist fallacy with a vengeance: the artist has given us not the rendering of an experience but his interpretative vision of the experience. Fosse's direction of the sequence distances us from the experience it depicts and imposes a received vision whose rather simplistic message — all that is happening here seems grotesquely unreal to Joe — hardly seems worth the loss of credibility and audience involvement the imposition of the vision entails.

The last shot of the read-through sequence is one of Joe sitting at a table and facing the camera. There is a dissolve from Joe's bowed head to a shot of Angelique's broad-brimmed gauzy hat. She very slowly turns to face the camera, and lifts the veil of her hat. With that obtrusively cryptic shot, Fosse begins his vision of Joe's heart attack. His editing pattern accelerates as shots of Audrey, Kate and others reacting to the event are intercut with shots of Angelique simply staring at the camera or very deliberately and slowly arranging her hair. We are denied sustained involvement in the experience of the heart attack; instead, we are offered Fosse's none too coherent vision of the event, in which he rather clumsily seeks to reassert the connection between death and Joe's idealized conception of women, as represented by Angelique.

The next several minutes of the film are devoted to a series of brief scenes set in Joe's hospital room, where he holds court and generally breaks all of his doctor's rules. Before this section of the film begins, there is a scene showing the producer of Joe's show feeling out another director (John Lithgow) about the possibility of his substituting for Joe if his condition should force him to leave the show. That in turn is followed by a scene in which Joe is seen observing Angelique through a viewfinder, which she proceeds to cover with her hands; the obviousness of this scene, particularly when it is contrasted with the subtle evocation of Joe's voyeurism in the first Joe-Victoria sequence, makes it one of the film's most egregious instances of Fosse's tendency to address the audience in the manner of an author eager to press home a point of interpretation.

The section of the film centered on Joe in his room concludes with a sustained shot of Joe and Josh (Max Wright), a representative of the producers of Joe's film, walking throuh a hospital corridor while they go over the first reviews of the film. Fosse makes the corridor seem very long indeed by having Joe and Josh walk toward the camera as it continually tracks away from them. Two cuts to low-angle shots of them from behind add to the sense of their slow progress through the corridor. The sense of Joe's confinement in the hospital, the high jinks in his room notwithstanding, is well established.

Joe and Josh reach Joe's room. There is a cut from Josh entering the room to a shot of a woman filling the screen of the television set in the room. She is an influential film critic and is about to deliver her review of Joe's film. The camera zooms in on her image on the screen, and then twice zooms in on Joe's face as he reacts to her negative review. There is then a shock cut from the television reviewer to a medium shot of a nurse. The camera tilts down for a close-up of Joe lying on an operating table. His heart surgery is about to begin.

Fosse attempts to convey both the physical reality of the operation and Joe's perception of it. The former is accomplished through a series of shots that scrutinize the operation with a documentary-like attention to its gruesome details. The latter is accomplished through a scene in which Joe and Angelique watch Audrey and a number of Joe's doctors explain the operation in the form of a cabaret routine, complete with stage lighting and sound effects. Once again, Fosse has failed to fulfill his obligation to fashion a mise-en-scène that allows us to feel, through the mediation of what we see, Joe's emotional reaction to the operation. Instead, he devises an image that seems to suggest, though this surely can not be the case, that he perceives his operation with the detachment of an observer of a brittlely clever cabaret routine. This may be Fosse's interpretation of the experience of surgery, but it does serious harm to the coherence of the film to suggest an identification between Fosse's interpretation and Joe's perception.

There is a cut from Joe and Angelique watching the cabaret act to a shot of O'Connor Flood (Ben Vereen), a second-rate performer Joe and Kate have mocked earlier in the film, performing on television; the cut, besides indicating that the operation is over and Joe is back in his room watching television, also, by juxtaposing the operation and the television show, suggests that the operation is the emotional equivalent of a bad television show featuring an obnoxious MC, another instance in which the director's obtrusive interpretation obstructs an understanding of the protagonist's perception of an experience.

Joe has a second heart attack, which necessitates a second operation. This time we get Fosse's full-blown vision of the operation as rendered by Joe's subconscious. Joe and Angelique's conversation (which is, vaguely, about death) is heard as a voice-over in a shot of Joe being wheeled down a hospital corridor. There is a cut to a medium shot of Joe and Angelique. The camera tracks slowly in for a close two-shot of them. Angelique extends her hands to Joe's head and draws it closer to her. He stops her by grabbing her wrists; a (no doubt significantly large) gap still separates their heads. There is a cut to Joe surrounded by nurses, orderlies and doctors. Several shots featuring the doctors and other hospital personnel are followed by a close-up of Joe wearing an oxygen mask. Close-ups of Joe are then intercut with a medium shot of first Audrey and then Kate.

Fosse next intercuts graphic shots of the operation with shots of the producers of Joe's show in conference with a representative of the insurance company underwriting the show, who translates the outcome of Joe's operation into dollars and cents.

There is a cut to Angelique's gloved hand moving up Joe's chest to his neck; the death monologue from Joe's new film commences on the soundtrack. Fosse then cuts between shots of Joe unconscious and shots of Angelique's hand caressing his face. There is then a cut to a low-angle shot of a tightrope walker falling into a net; a series of very brief shots show the fall, in slow motion, from several angles. With the voice-over of the death monologue continuing, Fosse (1) cuts to a medium shot of Joe, his eyes now open; (2) cuts to a medium shot of Angelique looking down at Joe; and (3) tracks in for a close-up of Joe, which dissolves into a close-up of a nurse speaking to him.

Up to this point in the sequence, Fosse's modernist fallacy has led him to devise an Angel of Death motif that is distancing and rather trite but not seriously offensive. Now, however, the fallacy manifests itself in a segment that is not only overbearing and heavy-handed but also fraudulent.

A healthy, vital Joe is seen directing a film on an enormous soundstage that incorporates the hospital room where a second Joe is confined to his bed. Healthy Joe directs Audrey, Kate and Michelle in three production numbers — "After You've Gone," "You Better Change Your Ways," and "Who's Sorry Now?" — that pointedly express the three women's hostility toward Joe. Between each number, healthy Joe berates dying Joe for his failure to perform his assigned part in each number. This segment, which runs an inordinate twelve minutes, amounts to the most excessive, self-indulgent, and unnecessary (since the idea that these three women feel hostility toward Joe has already been sufficiently established) instance of direct address in the film.

The fraud is perpetrated through the doubling of Joe: here is Fosse simply declaring, in effect, that Joe's self-awareness has reached the advanced stage that the doubling implies. This is a major thematic development that Fosse should have revealed and carefully elaborated through his mise-en-scène, not simply announced as a given element in an overblown direct-address image.

These dreadful twelve minutes are almost — not quite — compensated for by the six that follow, in which Fosse achieves a near-perfect identification of style and meaning as he portrays Joe facing and ultimately transcending the fear of death.

The six-minute sequence, which deals with Joe's escape from his hospital room following his second operation, divides into seven segments. Throughout the first five of these, the monologue on death from Joe's film is a voice-over; in the context of this sequence, which achieves a brilliant balance between credibility and expression, the monologue works as a supplemental aural complement to the visual rendering of Joe's physical-psychological journey.

(1) Joe is initially seen out of focus, obscured by some sort of net. When his image comes into focus, he is seen with his head against a wall. He walks right, out of his hospital room; the camera tracks back from him as he walks through a corridor door prominently labeled "Exit."

(2) A crane shot shows Joe in the hospital boiler room; he is in the background of a shot dominated by gargantuan machinery and empha-

sizing the vastness of the room. The position of the camera and the composition of the shot make him seem small, a man reduced to the essentials.
The floor of the boiler room is covered with water, and the camera cranes
down as Joe, in what plays as a rueful dismissal of his career (as well as
a parody of Gene Kelly's famous solo in *Singin' in the Rain*), dances, skips
across the puddles on the floor. The camera then cranes up again as Joe,
standing in the center of the vast room, looks up and addresses God in
an improvised prayer.

(3) There is a cut to Joe's outstretched hands, in silhouette. The
camera cranes down with his hands to a low-angle shot of Joe lurching
away from the camera as he makes his way through another corridor. The
camera angle restores Joe's stature, suggesting that he has emerged from
the boiler room not only intact but, somehow, enhanced.

(4) There is a cut to a medium shot of Joe. He is in the background
of the frame; the foreground is filled with jars containing various organs
used in the hospital laboratory. There is a cut to a shot of some doctors
as they become aware of Joe's presence. There is then a cut to a shot of
Joe, his face behind a jar, addressing himself to the eyeballs suspended
in liquid in the jar. There is then another cut to the doctors becoming
alarmed about Joe.

(5) An overhead shot shows a narrow corridor with a double set of
stairs. Joe enters the frame at the left and throws himself against a wall
at the right. He is in the background of the frame, which is dominated
by the double stairway. The camera zooms in on Joe hitting his head
against a wall. Recovered from his panic, he begins to climb one of the
stairways; as he does, he is moving toward the foreground of the frame.
Clearly, he has embarked on another stage of his psychic journey, whose
nature is represented by the connotations associated with staircases.
About halfway up the stairs, he pauses for a stationary-camera medium
shot, a shot that seems to confirm and celebrate his emerging wholeness.

(6) The camera is now tracking right with Joe as he drags his head
against a wall, leaving a grisly trail of blood. There is a sustained medium
shot of Joe as he looks into a patient's room. There is then a cut to a shot
of an arm pulling back a curtain to reveal a middle-aged woman who,
though asleep, is clearly experiencing considerable pain. Joe is once again
observing a woman; but, significantly, he does not long remain in the
voyeur stance. The camera tracks forward with him as he approaches the
woman's bed. There is a cut to a medium shot of Joe, followed by a
medium shot of the women. The camera, reflecting Joe's movement,
tracks in for a two-shot of Joe and the woman as he embraces and then

kisses her. Then he begins to back out of the frame. There is a series of alternating medium shots of Joe and the woman, who is now awake and whose face, previously a study in anguish, is now the image of serenity. Joe, for perhaps the first time in his life, has made genuine contact with a woman by giving generously of himself.

(7) In a deep-focus shot, a hospital cafeteria worker is in the foreground, reporting by phone on Joe's whereabouts; Joe is in the midground of the frame, sitting at a table in the empty cafeteria; the background is filled with empty tables. The setting suggests a nightclub after hours, and what follows subtly suggests that Joe has at last integrated his art into his humanity. The camera tracks with the worker as he moves toward Joe. There is a sustained medium shot of Joe and the worker (now seated at the table with Joe) singing "Pack Up Your Troubles in Your Old Kit Bag." There is then a cut to a shot of orderlies in pursuit of Joe getting out of an elevator. This is followed by a cut to a shot of Joe, seated on a chair and facing the camera; and the cafeteria worker, seated on another chair, his back to the camera; they are again singing "Old Kit Bag." There is then a cut to a shot in which Joe and the worker are in the foreground, while the orderlies are seen closing in on Joe as they move from the background of the frame toward the foreground.

It is deeply regrettable that *All That Jazz* precipitously falls from the very high level of achievement represented by this sequence. After a brief scene in which Angelique's "ministering" to Joe is intercut with shots of doctors and nurses attending him, Fosse concludes the film with another inordinately long (ten minutes) musical number that was, I suppose, intended as a culminating vision but that plays as a cumbersome final display of Fosse's allegiance to the modernist fallacy. Joe is seen performing a sardonic variation on the fifties hit "Bye, Bye, Love." Joe's version is called "Bye, Bye, Life"; and during the course of its performance, Joe encounters every character, major and minor, the audience has seen in the film.

This elaborate rendering of Joe as death approaches adds nothing to — if anything, it subtracts from — the understanding of him achieved through the hospital odyssey sequence.

When the number at last concludes, Joe is seen gliding down a hospital corridor toward Angelique waiting for him at its end. This is followed by a shot of Joe's body being zipped into a plastic bag. Ethel Merman's rousing rendition of "There's No Business Like Show Business" comes on the soundtrack as the final credits begin to roll; and *All That Jazz*, a film destroyed by its director's extended lapses into the literary fallacy, comes to an end.

As Bob Fosse did in *All That Jazz*, Francis Coppola begins *Apocalypse Now* with an elaborate direct-address image that reveals his intention to make his film conform to the modernist aesthetic. For just under sixty seconds, a stationary camera conveys a recapitulatory image of the director's vision of war. The vision begins as a middle-distance view of a jungle; the view is partially obscured by what appears to be dust billowing in the foreground of the frame. The only sound is the rhythmic whirring of helicopters; the helicopters themselves pass in and out of the stationary camera's range at irregular intervals. The billowing dust becomes something resembling flames with a distinctly golden hue; The Doors' "The End" begins on the soundtrack. The flames then become more prominent in the frame, almost completely obscuring the jungle; after a series of muted explosions, the flames engulf the jungle.

Coppola then creates an identity between his vision and his protagonist's point of view. The camera pans right, across the jungle in flames, some hovering helicopters, and a great deal of smoke. During the panning movement, a close-up of the anguished face of Captain Willard (Martin Sheen) appears at the left of the frame; the face is upside down. The panning motion stops, and an image of a slowly revolving ceiling fan is superimposed on the upside-down close-up of Willard. The camera then pans left, across the jungle in flames and the close-up of Willard. Coppola again reverses the direction of the panning movement as the camera moves right across an image of helicopters, smoke and flames. The camera then makes a circular motion to create an image composed of a medium shot of Willard (now right side up), a merged image of helicopter blades, the blades of the ceiling fan, and flames.

The camera pans right across a realistic rendering of what appears to be a hotel room and a highly unrealistic image of a close-up of Willard superimposed on a helicopter. The panning ends with a shot of the ceiling fan, which fades into a close-up of Willard, which is again upside down.

There is a cut to a shot of the fan; the camera then tilts down to a shot of a straightback chair. There is then a cut to a close-up of Willard (still upside down), followed by a cut to a shot of venetian blinds. A handheld camera tracks forward toward the blinds. A hand enters the frame and lifts one slat of the blinds; the camera tilts down to reveal the street scene that can be seen through the slat.

Opposite: A cumbersome final display of Fosse's allegiance to the modernist fallacy. Roy Scheider, *All That Jazz* (Columbia Pictures and Twentieth Century–Fox, 1979).

There is a cut to a close-up of Willard (it seems necessary to say that he is now right side up) looking through the slat. His narration begins on the soundtrack; in it he states that the city seen through the slat is Saigon. This shot of Willard is sustained for some time; Coppola follows it with a rapid series of close-up and medium shots of Willard.

There follows an overhead shot of Willard squatting on the floor of his room; the shadow of the revolving fan is prominent in the frame, and its whirring is prominent on the soundtrack. The camera begins to pan left, and then there is a dissolve to a medium shot of Willard assuming various martial arts positions. The camera then pans right across the shadow of the fan and a close-up of Willard; most of his face is in shadow, with only one eye illuminated. There is a dissolve to a close-up of Willard merged with the flames of the burning jungle. There follows a rapid series of shots of Willard going through a series of martial arts stances. He strikes at his reflection in a mirror, shattering the glass; there is now a good deal of blood on his hand and face. There is a cut to a slightly overhead shot of Willard, blood-stained and clearly in agony, sitting on the floor of his room, his back against the bed. This shot is sustained for some time, and it is followed by a fade.

In this eight-minute segment, Coppola has made it all too plain that we are in the hands of a director committed to the modernist aesthetic. The meaning of the segment does not emerge from a credible and involving mise-en-scène but rather through a series of images which declares and even celebrates the artist's presence and which places audiences in the role of passive receptors of the direct transmission of the authorial vision. Coppola's obtrusive technique (the autonomous panning, the juxtaposed images whose linkage is a blatant rejection of realism, the superimpositions) makes it clear that what we are seeing is the calculated creation of a self-conscious artist who wishes to make a statement. The segment is inevitably univocal: by suppressing the ambiguous richness of a credible mise-en-scène, Coppola, like all directors attached to the modernist aesthetic, assures that the only idea that will emerge from the segment is the single one stated and reiterated in his images — namely, that war is a carnival of destruction that can warp the consciousness of a man too long exposed to it. That that idea seems rather anemic when considered in light of the time and technique expended to convey it is inevitable because the direct-address technique uses the modalities of cinema to summarize and assert, a poor use of modalities whose nature is to integrate (the myriad of connotative details the camera sees) and evoke.

Willard acquires a bit of identity as well as a mission in the sequence that follows. He is an intelligence officer who carries out top-secret missions of questionable legality and dubious morality. He gets his new assignment at a lunch attended by a general, a colonel, and an ominously bland CIA representative. The assignment is to locate and assassinate Colonel Kurtz, a much-decorated officer who has gone off the deep end and established himself as the ruler of a private kingdom in a remote Cambodian jungle. There he is served by Cambodians mesmerized by him, and from there he conducts bloody missions at odds with stated U.S. war aims. The sequence in which Willard is given his assignment is fairly straightforward, consisting mostly of, on the one hand, medium shots of the general, the colonel and the CIA man, and, on the other hand, close-ups of Willard. The sequence concludes with a pan from the general to a shot of a window filled with glaring, blinding sunlight; the emphasis on a light that prevents seeing is a subtle visual characterization of the paradoxical nature of the mission Willard is about to undertake. The shot of the window is followed by an abrupt cut to a mountainous landscape featuring a hovering helicopter in the foreground.

Willard is to travel to Kurtz's kingdom by patrol boat, and the next sequence introduces the crew that will accompany him upriver. Willard's narration provides the thumbnail biographies of each crew member: Chef (Frederic Forrest), a volatile cook from Louisiana who has been around and seen it all; Chief (Albert Hall), the by-the-book captain of the boat who resents the irregularity of Willard's mission; Lance (Sam Bottoms), a very mellow surfer who speaks only southern Californian; and Clean (Larry Fishburne), a black teenager who seems only dimly aware that there is a war going on out there. Willard's commentary, which is redundant because we can see or intuit all that he says about each man, is an instance of Coppola's fondness for one of the favored techniques of the traditional literary fallacy. Coppola further weakens the sequence by concluding it with an image that is so obviously contrived to assert his vision (it recalls the too-precious images that mar the work of authors not in complete control of the modernist aesthetic) that it has the effect of distancing the viewer from the sequence, of discouraging involvement in its emerging meaning. The image begins when the Rolling Stones' "Satisfaction" comes on Clean's transistor and preempts the soundtrack. To that musical accompaniment, Lance is seen water skiing in the narrow river while Vietnamese gathered on the banks look on in dumbfounded amazement.

The sequence that follows is one of the most seriously flawed in the film. Simply in terms of narrative continuity, it is an excessively long (twenty-four minutes) digression from the main line of the narrative. In terms of directorial style, some of it is highly effective, a persuasive

rendering of the peculiar reality of this particular war; but too much of it reflects Coppola's commitment to the modernist fallacy, with its mistaken reliance on direct-address images as substitutes for a gradual unfolding of meaning that is embedded in the totality of the mise-en-scène.

The sequence concerns Willard and his crew's encounter with Lieutenant Colonel Kilgore (Robert Duvall) and his Air Cavalry unit. Willard's party comes upon Kilgore's unit while the latter is engaged in the process of mopping up after an air strike on a Vietnamese village. At the beginning of the sequence, Coppola explicitly suspends Willard's point of view by panning from a close-up of him to initiate an extended segment in which the camera tracks with Kilgore — a flamboyant, Patton-type leader — through the bombed-out village. This segment is generally excellent as it contrasts the strutting, vainglorious Kilgore with the chaos and agony of a village in its death throes. Coppola's compositions and camera angles wittily emphasize Kilgore's stature by setting him against the reduced "skyline" of the village, and the cumulative effect of the extended forward tracking is to suggest inexorable movement toward increasing (but always credible) absurdity.

Coppola, however, cannot long suppress his penchant for imposing meaning through the use of preemptive images that assert the controlling presence of the artist's vision. He cuts from Kilgore to a medium shot of Willard staring vacantly off-camera; Willard's point of view is thus restored, which means Coppola, thinly disguised as his protagonist, can resume transmitting direct-address images. There is a cut to a shot of a cow being lifted out of the village by a helicopter. Ater a cut to another medium shot of Willard (to reiterate that the view of Willard-Coppola is controlling), there is a cut to a shot of a priest, dressed in camouflage, conducting religious services in the midst of the occasional explosions (with their accompanying pervasive smoke) of (presumably) napalm bombs. After a cut to a somewhat closer shot of the priest, there is a cut to a sustained shot of the cow suspended in the smoke-filled sky; the camera tilts up and then zooms in on the cow, two movements that (needlessly) make more emphatic an image that has already overwhelmed the sequence. The relatively complex and entirely convincing meaning of the tracking segment, which evoked the tragedy and absurdity of this war, has been reduced in the cow shots to a contrived metaphor of absurdity that lacks force because it is too obviously contrived.

Opposite: **The absurdity of religious services conducted by a priest in camouflage while the Air Cavalry mops up a Vietnamese village devastated by an air strike.** *Apocalypse Now* **(United Artists, 1979).**

There is a cut from the cow to a panning shot of a stretch of terrain where a kind of beach party is in progress. It is night, Kilgore is playing a guitar, and steaks from the slaughtered cow are being cooked over open fires. Willard's narration resumes on the soundtrack as he redundantly comments on the eccentricities of Kilgore. When Kilgore, a surfer, learns that Willard's party includes a well-known surfer (Lance), he insists that Lance and some of the best surfers in his unit try the waves in a nearby, enemy-held area. The beach party scene concludes with a low-angle shot of Kilgore, wreathed in unrealistically blue smoke that is broken by bands of light from an unidentifiable source, declaring that he and his men will take control of the area because "Charlie don't surf." With this shot, the credibility of Kilgore is undermined. The shot thus seems an important mistake on Coppola's part, for it diminishes the horror one feels when entertaining the thought that men like Kilgore and the Vietnam War formed a symbiotic union which produced absurd tragedy and tragic absurdity.

Shots of the helicopters of Kilgore's unit dissolve to a close-up of Willard staring off-camera. The helicopter shots are then resumed; they are seen against the background of a dawn-pink sky, and a choir singing vaguely liturgical music is heard on the soundtrack. There are thus visual and aural signs that we are about to be given another view of the Vietnam War that expresses not so much its reality as the director's interpretative vision of its reality.

The signs, however, in this instance turn out to be misleading: the air strike to make the area safe for surfing is an effective sequence that does not violate credibility for the sake of authorial expression, though the sequence does go on for a rather excessive six minutes. Coppola, using tracking shots, a hand-held camera, and a fast-paced montage, conveys a multiplicity of perspectives on the air strike, an achievement that enhances the compelling visual excitement of the strike.

The area is cleared and Lance and the others get a chance to surf. The sequence concludes with a shot that was probably intended as the perfect visual-verbal recapitulation of the absurdity of a war conducted by men like Kilgore but that, like the earlier suspended cow segment, has the effect of reducing the experience of pervasive absurdity with multiple consequences to the single impression produced by the director's preemptive vision of the absurdity. The camera slowly and pointedly tracks in on Kilgore as he stands tall on the conquered beach and declares to his admiring men, "I love the smell of napalm in the morning."

The three sequences, two of them brief, one rather lengthy, that follow are more of the same: preemptive images that declare the director-author's interpretation of what we see, instead of revealing meaning through a mise-en-scène that is both involving in its credibility and compelling in its complexity.

In the first sequence, Willard and his crew have resumed their trip upriver after the interlude with Kilgore's unit. Chef suddenly gets it into his head that he must have mangoes and that the jungle extending to the edge of the river would be a good place to find some. Willard, against his better judgment, agrees to pause for a mango hunt, and he and Chef disembark. The camera tracks with them through the jungle for a few frames, and then they encounter a strikingly beautiful but distinctly unfriendly tiger, from which they promptly flee. The last shot of the scene is a close-up of Willard staring into the camera; his narration resumes on the soundtrack as the close-up is held. The encounter with the ineffably beautiful but deadly tiger is another instance of a contrived image that might have worked in a modernist novel but that seems too blatant, too obviously a metaphor for the American experience in Vietnam, to be an effective cinematic image.

The second sequence is a brief interlude devoted to an uneventful segment of the journey upriver. Willard's narration tells us more about Kurtz's journey from honored hero to madman conducting a private war. Coppola repeatedly reminds us that what we see reflects the subjective point of view of his protagonist (who in turn reflects the artistic sensibility of the director) by including in this brief sequence several close-ups of Willard's very sweaty face turned either right or left as he gazes off-camera. That what Willard sees is distortingly subjective is suggested by the unreal beauty of the long shots of the sequence, which emphasize the strikingly beautiful indigo night and the patterns of the moonlight on the river.

The third sequence is another sustained application of the modernist aesthetic as Coppola attempts to overwhelm audiences with an elaborate vision that effectively cuts off immersion in a visual experience whose totality reveals its meaning.

The sequence begins as a tracking shot of the river bank as seen from the patrol boat. The bank is illuminated by an extraordinary number of lights: the impression is of a carnival emerging out of the darkness of the jungle.

There is a series of alternating close-ups of Willard and Clean, both of whose faces are illuminated by the lights on the bank, an unrealistic effect, given the distance that separates the boat from the shore.

There is a cut to a tracking-in on the supply base located on the river bank. A fan-like arrangement of lights dominates the foreground of the frame, and more lights can be seen in the background. Two medium shots of Chef observing the bizarre scene follow; in the second, reflections of lights are superimposed on his image. The crew disembark at the base's dock. There is then a cut, and the camera is now tracking left with Willard as he moves through the base's warehouse. The tracking stops when Willard abruptly stops and very deliberately turns to look to his right.

What he sees is, unmistakably, a vision. What appears to be a stadium is illuminated by seemingly hundreds of lights arranged on towering structures that resemble rockets. After a brief return to the warehouse (and reality), Coppola dissolves from a shot of Willard (his point of view is thus reiterated) to a shot of a helicopter emerging from the darkness. The whirring sound of the helicopter dominates the soundtrack, and the play of light emanating from an enormous searchlight dominates the frame.

There is a cut to the helicopter landing on some sort of platform in the stadium; triangular and semicircular arrangements of lights dominate the midground and background of the frame.

A series of shots of cheering soldiers follows the emergence from the helicopter of a man who announces that three Playmates have come to entertain the men stationed at the base. This series is followed by a long shot of the performing area in which lights, which again seem to be in a fan-like arrangement, dominate the frame.

Coppola's montage now becomes notably rapid as he cuts among shots of (1) the wildly cheering soldiers; (2) the Playmates performing; (3) Willard, disgusted by the spectacle, leaving his place in the audience; (4) Vietnamese watching the show from behind a fence some distance from the stadium (a nice metaphor for the distanced relationship Coppola's modernist images establish between audiences and what is happening on screen); and (5) the eerie, distorting effect on the performers of all the lights surrounding the performing area.

The show is just too stimulating for the audience, and a near-riot breaks out as the soldiers rush the stage. A decision is made to end the show early. Coppola goes to an overhead shot of the helicopter preparing to beat a hasty retreat; the shot is dominated by the copiously billowing smoke from the flare that has been set off to keep the onrushing men at bay while the Playmates get into the helicopter. Coppola shoots the takeoff of the helicopter as a long shot with banks of lights in the background and pinkish smoke in the midground-center. He follows this by dissolving from a shot of the helicopter (bearing the Playboy bunny symbol), now aloft in the black sky, to a shot of the stadium the following morning; that shot is a still life of desolation in which wisps of smoke trail artfully across the composition.

The Playmate sequence is a good illustration of the truism that a film is not a novel. A modernist author might well use light and smoke imagery to convey a vision-interpretation of war; a film director who indulges in smoke and lighting effects to the extent Coppola does in this sequence effectively conveys very little because the violation of credibility he commits (by creating such a blatantly unbalanced mise-en-scène) distances audiences and decreases involvement in the sequence. His vision quite literally overwhelms audiences by discouraging their active participation in the sequence. The meaning of Coppola's vision — the Vietnam War was an unreal experience that can be compared to the ephemeral play of light and smoke — registers on audiences (it can not help but register, since this is the single idea allowed to emerge from the sequence); but it inevitably seems rather obvious and trite because nuanced, textured meaning brought about through the realization of a well-developed mise-en-scène has not been achieved or even attempted.

The journey upriver continues. Willard continues to peruse the material about Kurtz he was given in Saigon. His narration reveals the contents of what he is reading; Coppola alternates shots of the material in the Kurtz dossier with close-ups of Willard's eyes (the repetition of the eyeball shots becomes almost laughable).

The Willard party next encounters a sampan on the river. Chief, over Willard's objections, insists that the sampan be searched for concealed weapons. During the course of the search, Clean panics and ends up machine-gunning the entire Vietnamese family on the sampan, which contains no contraband. Coppola undermines the impact of this scene by concluding it with a rather over-determined image of innocence in the midst of war. A white puppy has been found on board the sampan; and Coppola composes a medium shot of Lance, his figure set against the surreally beautiful twilight that is descending on the river, standing on the patrol boat and nuzzling the puppy. Coppola then cuts to a medium shot of Willard observing the scene, thereby confirming that the image of Lance and the puppy is another instalment in the Willard-Coppola vision of the Vietnam War. The sequence concludes with a fade to black that is sustained for a notably long time.

The fade ends with a slow tracking in on a bridge that appears to be illuminated by dozens of lights strung across it. Flares, skyrockets, and explosions create patterns in the blackness of the sky; the lights on the bridge cast pink-white reflections on the river, and flames can be seen in the background-left of the frame. Willard and his party have reached what is in effect the last outpost of American forces in Vietnam; beyond is the uncharted territory of Cambodia — and Kurtz.

The initial tracking shot, with its emphasis on dramatic lighting effects, suggests that this sequence will be a reprise of the Playmates sequence. But the portents are, happily, wrong. In this sequence Coppola uses light and dark contrasts, a tracking camera and compositions that emphasize emptiness to establish in an utterly convincing and evocative manner the idea that the Vietnam War is a nihilistic void into which Willard and his men are inexorably and irreversibly drawn.

As the patrol boat approaches the river bank, the camera tracks left along the bank. Searchlights irregularly fall on soldiers who are jumping from the bank into the river, begging to be taken aboard and taken away from this hell on earth.

Willard decides to go ashore to seek the officer in charge of the outpost; his repeated question to soldiers he encounters, "Who's your commanding officer?" — a question to which no one is able to supply an answer — becomes the nihilistic refrain of the sequence.

The camera tracks left with Willard and Lance as they go ashore. There is a cut to a shot of them in which they are slightly illuminated by a searchlight. There is then a cut to a close-up of Lance (who is wearing elaborate camouflage makeup) caught in the glare of a searchlight. This close-up, with its emphasis on concealment (the camouflage makeup) and disclosure (the searchlight) initiates the motif of identity and its loss that runs through the sequence.

A long, tracking shot follows as Willard and Lance move among mostly invisible soldiers exchanging fire with an unseen enemy. There is a cut to a medium shot of Willard, who is barely discernible in the darkness; a blur of lights shares the frame with him. This is followed by a cut to to shot of Lance, a disembodied silhouette, standing with his back to the camera in the midground of the frame; the rest of the frame is empty, illuminated only by the same indistinct blur of lights featured in the Willard shot. Coppola's compositions here vividly suggest that Willard and Lance are on the edge of nothingness and that their identities, as represented by their palpable presence, are fading away before our eyes.

There follows a sustained stationary-camera shot in a bunker. As Willard questions the soldiers shooting at an enemy they cannot see, he sometimes shares the frame with darkness, sometimes with the faces of the soldiers, who in turn fade in and out of visibility according to the rhythm of the searchlights. A parallel between the soldiers and dark emptiness is thus created, further strengthening the idea that this last outpost is the hellish place where the war finally consumes the remaining individual identities of the men fighting it.

The camera tracks with Willard and Lance as they crawl out of the bunker. The screen is almost totally black at the beginning of the tracking movement; as Willard and Lance move through the darkness, searchlights erratically illuminate the disembodied faces of the soldiers that line the bunker.

There follows a series of alternating medium shots of Lance and Willard, whose faces are irregularly and only partially illuminated by searchlights. In his only questionable choice in the sequence, Coppola composes the last medium shot of Lance in this series so as to feature the white puppy from the sampan, which is half-concealed under Lance's jacket.

Coppola then intercuts medium shots of the gunnery soldiers and Lance, creating unbalanced compositions in which the frame is divided between human figures and dark emptiness, and close-ups of Willard, whose controlling point of view is now undermined by the erratic illumination that plays across his face. A sustained medium shot of Lance, who is seen standing on a rise, is brilliant: first he is barely visible in the darkness, then he is rendered completely invisible as he is obliterated by the glare of a searchlight; finally, he is illuminated by the orange light of an explosion in the background of the frame. Thus is identity lost, and a grotesque pseudoidentity gained, in war.

Coppola continues the pattern of alternating medium shots of the gunnery soldiers with close-ups of Willard. The latter are held long enough for the irregular rhythm of the searchlights to run its complete, paradoxical cycle: total darkness to blinding illumination to total darkness. Coppola has effectively and persuasively undermined Willard's point of view by the end of this series of close-ups; and, as he has in the shots of Lance, suggested the loss, or at least the serious distortion, of Willard's identity.

The sequence ends with Willard and Lance back on the patrol boat. Coppola cuts among medium shots of Willard and the other members of the crew, but only the shots of Willard feature the erratic, pulsating light-dark rhythm that was a motif of the onshore segment. The suggestion is that Willard has experienceed the no-meaning of hell during his time in this last outpost and he is bearing the experience within himself.

Coppola's achievement in the last outpost sequence acquires enhanced stature when one recalls that *Apocalypse Now* is at least loosely derived from Joseph Conrad's *Heart of Darkness*. In this sequence, Coppola has achieved a cinematic equivalent of Conrad's sublime literary achievement by following the Conradian rather than the modernist aesthetic. He has immersed his film in the palpable reality of war and found in it the metaphysical horror of war that Conrad conveyed in his novella. Had Coppola consistently followed this course in his film instead of lapsing into the modernist fallacy, *Apocalypse Now* would almost surely have been a towering achievement, possibly the equal of *Heart of Darkness*.

Improbable as it seems, there was a sack of mail waiting for Willard and his crew at the last outpost. As they continue upriver deeper into Cambodian territory, each of them is seen reading his mail (Willard's is more classified information on Kurtz, including a report on the failure of a previous attempt to assassinate him). Lance, who is now more or less permanently stoned, is seen standing on the boat and igniting flares that produce a distinctly purple smoke; Coppola gives a good deal of emphasis to the trail of purple haze that so fascinates Lance.

There is a sudden attack from the river bank; Coppola covers it with rapid cutting among tracking shots that reflect the movements of both the patrol boat on the river and the unseen enemy on the bank. Clean, the black teenager, is hit; going for a moment of all-out pathos, Coppola has Clean die while a tape he has just received from his mother is heard on the soundtrack.

Evening—very blue—and fog—very white—descend on the river. The scene on the river bank becomes increasingly bizarre as Coppola, using mostly low-angle shots, shows us the wreckage of planes caught in the branches of the trees overhanging the river. The otherworldly white fog occasionally renders everything invisible; the soundtrack is filled with the sounds of groans and electronic screeches. We are plainly being given the artist's rather arty vision of the experience of entering uncharted and hostile territory.

There is a sudden shower of what appear to be sticks launched from the river bank. The sticks turn out to be spears, and Coppola provides brief glimpses of the tribesmen on the bank who have launched the attack. Chief is struck. The soundtrack goes absolutely silent for a sustained medium shot of Chief as he becomes aware he has been fatally wounded. Coppola concludes this sequence with a series of medium shots of Willard attending Chief as he dies.

Coppola next offers an image of death in war that is too over-composed and too laboriously "poetic" to be genuinely moving. The camera tracks in on the patrol boat anchored in heavy fog. There is a cut to a sustained shot of Lance leaning over Clean's lifeless body as he daubs paint on the forehead of the body and then kisses it; the glare from the sun reflected on the river partially obscures Lance's face.

After a cut to a medium shot of Willard at last telling Chef exactly what their mission is, there is a cut to Lance cradling Clean's body as he stands waist-deep in the river. The glare of the sun is now even more pronounced.

There is another cut to a medium shot of Chef and Willard, who are arguing about the mission. The camera tracks right with them as Willard gets off the boat, with Chef following behind. A series of alternating medium shots of them follows.

After this second interruption (the purpose and significance of Coppola's editing strategy here are not clear), Coppola returns to Lance. He is seen in a medium shot releasing Clean's body to float down the river. The camera tracks back from Lance as he approaches it; then the camera movement stops, and the resulting composition is a close-up of Lance climbing onto the boat. The close-up, which is sustained, certainly adds an emphatic note to the scene; but its significance, given that Lance, at least since the last outpost sequence, has been virtually a nonentity, is unclear. Continuing the shot without a cut, Coppola now forcefully and obtrusively asserts the artist's presence. The camera tracks forward for a shot of Clean's face just barely above the surface of the water; the reflected glare of the sun lends a rather trite aura to the face. Since the camera movement does not reflect the movement of anyone in the scene, it constitutes a pointed underlining of the director's presence and thus adds to the sense that the scene is highly contrived. That sense is further strengthened by Coppola's decision to hold the shot of Clean's face for a considerable time, until it at last sinks below the surface and this prolonged image of death concludes.

Apocalypse Now has at this point reached a critical juncture, for Willard and his surviving crew are approaching Kurtz's jungle kingdom and, therefore, the encounter to which the whole film has been building. While, in theory, that encounter might still have the significance and resonance that would justify the long journey toward it, in fact, Coppola's decisions have already made that outcome most unlikely.

The irony here is that the Willard-Kurtz encounter is likely to be a nonevent, not because of some wrong choices made by Coppola but because of some seemingly very effective ones. In the best sequence of the film, the last outpost sequence, Coppola so masterfully showed the destructive effect on Willard of a sustained exposure to the meaningless horror of war that Willard emerged from the experience with a decidedly weakened grip on reality and with a noticeably weakened identity. The film's climactic encounter thus promises to be one between a man of questionable sanity and shattered identity and another man who is almost surely insane and who has created for himself an ersatz identity. The encounter, in short, promises to be an exercise in meaninglessness. Coppola, in the brilliant last outpost sequence, has already plunged his protagonist into the horror of war and shown its devastating effect on him. One has the thought, as Willard approaches his meeting with Kurtz, that perhaps Coppola should have ended the film with the last outpost sequence, that perhaps the coming encounter is one that should not take place. To his credit, Coppola does not attempt to undo what he has effectively done: as Willard approaches Kurtz's compound, Coppola's choices with respect to camera movement, camera placement and transitions confirm and reiterate the idea established in the last outpost sequence that Willard has become a shattered automaton.

After the final glimpse of Clean's face sinking below the surface of the river, the camera begins to track forward with the patrol boat as it moves through the blackness of the jungle night. The tracking reveals an unidentifiable structure in flames on the river bank. Coppola now begins a series of dissolves that suggests Willard's mindless, involuntary movement toward Kurtz.

First there is a dissolve to a shot in which Willard shares the frame with the burning structure on the bank. Then Coppola dissolves twice, once to Chef and once to Lance, both of whom share the frame with the flames emanating from the bank. There is then a dissolve to a shot that seems to suggest the entire river bank is in flames. The next dissolve is to a medium shot of Willard; as if to suggest that time has lost its significance, sunlight now fills the screen. There is then a dissolve to human skulls lining the river bank, followed by a dissolve to a shot in which Willard shares the frame with the skulls (an outrageously blatant direct-address image). Willard is seen tearing up the Army Intelligence dossier on Kurtz. His narration, now more impressionistic than expository, resumes on the soundtrack. There is then a dissolve to a shot of the scraps of paper that once were the Kurtz documents; they are floating on the river, moving, somehow, in the opposite direction from the patrol boat. This is followed by a dissolve to a tracking shot of the patrol boat gliding effortlessly through heavy fog. Next there is a dissolve to a shot that suggests that Lance, like Willard, has become a mindless zombie: Lance, enveloped in mist and standing on the prow of the boat, is seen going through the unvarying series of martial arts positions.

Chef has not yet been reduced to the mindless state of Lance and Willard, and Coppola emphasizes this by ending the series of dissolves with a cut from Lance on the prow to a shot of Chef steering the boat. Then, as if to show that Chef's normality counts for little here, Coppola resumes the dissolves. The boat (set against an unnaturally vivid pink-red sky) is seen passing through a narrow point in the river. There is then a dissolve to a medium shot of Willard, now in full sunlight, looking through binoculars. Coppola immediately undermines the apparent re-emergence of Willard's controlling point of view by tracking away from him, instead of tracking forward to reveal what he sees through the binoculars.

The undermining of Willard continues in the shot that follows. Willard at first dominates the shot: he is seen in the foreground of the frame, sitting on the prow of the ship; in the midground, tribesmen gathered on the shore are seen; the background is lush jungle. Coppola than reduces and eventually eliminates Willard by craning up to fill the frame with the gathered tribesmen. The camera, reflecting the inexorable movement of the off-camera boat, then tracks forward into the midst of the gesticulating, seemingly hostile natives.

After a shot of Lance vacantly observing the scene, there is a cut to the natives, their bodies painted a ghostly white, rowing out in their canoes to greet (attack?) the patrol boat. There is a series of shots of the boat docking and of Willard observing the scene on the river bank. Then the camera, again moving autonomously, without reference to the movement of anything or anyone on-screen, tracks left across the river bank, revealing a jungle compound full of monumental statuary and an elaborate ceremonial staircase on which a mob of tribesmen has gathered to observe the arrival of the boat. The sequence ends with a series of brief shots of Lance, Chef, Willard and an American (Dennis Hopper) who is among the tribesmen gathered on the shore.

The American is a photojournalist who has joined the Kurtz cult. He greets Willard in a shot in which he is at the left of the frame, Willard at the right, and a naked body hanging from a tree is at the center. As the unnamed photojournalist leads Willard through the compound, Coppola covers their progress with a mix of tracking and stationary-camera shots. Willard's point of view, which had been repeatedly asserted earlier in the film through close-ups of him, is notable here by its absence. The suggestion is that Willard now does not *have* a point of view.

The rest of *Apocalypse Now* is an unusual, perhaps unique, example of both variants of the literary fallacy coming together to destroy a film. Coppola abruptly attempts to turn his film into a novel of ideas, in which one character (Willard) serves as a sounding board for the monologues of another character (Kurtz). The play of ideas, however, is distinctly lethargic, since Willard has become a nonentity and the ideas conveyed through Kurtz's monologues are obscure or pretentious or both. At the same time, Coppola, laboring under the modernist fallacy, attempts to transmit directly his vision of the meaning of the Willard-Kurtz encounter; he does not (as he did so brilliantly in the last outpost sequence) locate the meaning in a mise-en-scène of sufficient coherence and credibility to create an effective interaction between audience and the meaning he tries to convey.

Before Willard has his fated encounter, Coppola reiterates the diminution and disintegration Willard has undergone on his way to the encounter. Willard is taken prisoner by Kurtz's minions, and Coppola films his capture by moving the camera in a vertiginous circular motion as Willard is thrown roughly to the ground by his captors. He is thrown into mud, and Coppola emphasizes his humiliation by remaining on his mud-covered face and body.

Willard, who is literally a captive audience for Kurtz, is next seen in silhouette, kneeling before a doorway that is illuminated by a notably bright orange light; the rest of the frame is in darkness. We hear Kurtz's voice before we see him. The camera, is if compelled to seek out the source of the disembodied voice, tracks in through the doorway and then right through the interior of a nondescript structure. The tracking camera finds Kurtz (Marlon Brando) lying down. Most of his body is invisible in the darkness; only one of his hands (what significance, if any, this lighting scheme has I do not profess to know) is illuminated. Kurtz rises slightly; the camera, is if responding instantaneously to his movement, tracks in on him. Part of his shaved head is illuminated by an unidentifiable light source; his face remains lost in darkness. The camera remains stationary for Kurtz's monologue, a rather self-conscious mixture of reminiscence and cryptic aphorism that seems only incidentally directed at Willard.

Coppola seems to envision this encounter as a vaguely religious one in which Kurtz assumes the sacerdotal role to Willard's empty vessel waiting to be filled with the grace or wisdom Kurtz dispenses. Coppola's pattern in the next segment of the sequence is to cut between Kurtz, who is seen either in enormous close-ups featuring chiaroscuro lighting or performing vaguely ritualistic acts such as washing his hands and head, and Willard, who is seen eight times in precisely the same medium shot. Kurtz's monologue continues throughout the intercutting; but his words are almost laughably cryptic and, in any case, are only words, a rather anemic, ephemeral form of cinematic communication. As for Coppola's visuals, his insistence on a mise-en-scène consisting of close-ups, a reiterated medium shot, and arty lighting makes his vision monotonous and uninvolving, a typically superficial communication from a director pursuing the modernist illusion of the direct transmission of a univocal vision of reality we should be allowed to experience for ourselves.

From Willard's audience with Kurtz, Coppola goes to a brief scene in which an imprisoned Willard has a conversation of sorts with the American photojournalist, whose words are a Kurtz-like blend of vaguely mystical mumbo jumbo. The shots of Willard in this scene are all close-ups; but they do not serve to restore him to prominence because all of them emphasize the bamboo bars of the cage in which Willard is imprisoned and therefore underline his severely diminished status.

Coppola, in seeking to convey the meaning of the Willard-Kurtz encounter, first tried, in the initial meeting of the two men, the old-fashioned literary route, with Kurtz in effect delivering an extended monologue to Willard, whose reduced presence barely disguised Kurtz's direct-address stance vis-à-vis the audience. Now, for the second Willard-Kurtz meeting, Coppola resumes a full-fledged modernist stance as he attempts to achieve a culminating image metaphor that conveys the essence of his vision of Willard's seemingly fated encounter with Kurtz.

The second Willard-Kurtz meeting begins with the camera tracking left with a pair of feet walking through mud. There is a cut, and now the camera is tracking in on Willard's bound body, which is illumianted by a peculiar orange light. The camera tracks up his body to his face. Willard, who is tied to a stake in the ground, looks up, turning his face toward the light.

The source of light is, of course, Kurtz. Reiterating the idea that Kurtz is standing in mud (the mud of experience that is the foundation of wisdom?), Coppola pans up from Kurtz's feet to a medium shot of his face. His face, in striking and startling camouflage makeup, is well illuminated. The medium shot of Kurtz is held for a considerable time and thus acquires considerable weight.

There follows a series of two brief close-ups of Willard alternating with sustained medium shots of Kurtz. In the last of the medium shots, Kurtz begins to move left, and the camera tracks with him.

There is then a cut to a medium shot of Willard. The severed head of Chef (who had remained on the patrol boat with orders to radio for an air strike at a prearranged time) is dropped into Willard's lap. Shots of Chef's head are not intercut with shots of Willard screaming in horror at its sight. There is then a cut to a more distant shot of Willard (whose hands and arms are bound) trying to dislodge the head from his lap. After a shot of Willard's horrified face, there is another shot of Chef's head, now lying in the mud near Willard's boots. After one more medium shot of Willard screaming, the sequence ends with a dissolve to a shot in which the camera is craning down on Kurtz's compound at sunrise.

And that — a hackneyed scene that recalls countless horror films — is the visual expression devised by Coppola to convey, one supposes, the ineffable horror of war. In fact, Coppola has conveyed, to understate the matter, rather less than that and rather less than Conrad conveyed; more important, he has conveyed a good deal less than he himself conveyed in the last outpost sequence. This second Willard-Kurtz meeting must be counted among the major casualties of the modernist fallacy in the New Hollywood era, a notably clear cautionary example of what results when a director attempts to convey meaning through a single image metaphor instead of through a well-realized mise-en-scène.

The mise-en-scène Coppola fashions to transmit the next instalment of his vision is rather incoherent; the only clear idea I derive from it is that Willard, temporarily at least, has somehow regained a measure of wholeness through contact with Kurtz.

Coppola begins the third Willard-Kurtz sequence with a close-up of Willard, whose narrations resumes at this point. After a series of shots showing Kurtz's uniforms, medals and books, there is a series of close-ups of Willard in which his face is either evenly divided between light and shadow or illuminated so as to highlight selected facial features, a lighting pattern which may be intended as a visual rendering of Willard's tentative reemergence as an integrated personality.

In the last close-up of Willard in the series, Kurtz speaking of "the horror" (of war, of life) is a voice-over. Willard looks left, presumably toward Kurtz. There is then a cut to a totally dark screen; the suggestion, contradicted by Coppola's direction of later segments of the sequence, is that Willard should not look to Kurtz, as others have, as a source of enlightenment. Kurtz emerges from the darkness, but just a small part of his head is illuminated. The camera, presumably tracing his movement, tracks right through the darkness.

There is a cut to a close-up of Willard, but he quickly moves left out of the frame. Then, in a reiteration of the thematically confusing association between Kurtz and darkness, the screen once again goes totally dark, with Kurtz's monologue a voice-over. He emerges into a chiaroscuro close-up as Coppola continues the muddled light-dark, whole-fragmented motif.

There follows a series of sustained alternating close-ups of Willard and Kurtz, with Kurtz's monologue continuing throughout the series. In his close-ups Kurtz moves in and out of the light; they may be Coppola's way of visually representing the idea of the identity of good and evil, which seems to be the theme running through Kurtz's monologue. At one point, Coppola dissolves from a close-up of Willard to one of Kurtz; this amounts to an initial suggestion of the identity of the two men, a major addition to the thematic stratum of the film that one rightfully expects Coppola to develop fully and convincingly in his mise-en-scène.

After the dissolve, the camera tracks back from a close-up of Willard to create a new composition in which Willard is seen from a more distant point. There is then a dissolve to Kurtz in the doorway of what appears to be some kind of temple. In the background of the frame, a cow is being prepared for a sacrificial ritual; the shot's color pattern is a combination of orange and pink, and smoke pervades the frame.

Coppola now intercuts shots of Willard preparing to kill Kurtz with shots of the preparation of the cow for slaughter (so much for any hope that Coppola's modernist fixation might allow for a bit of subtlety). In a reiteration of the mud motif that has been associated with both Willard and Kurtz, Willard's face is seen emerging from a muddy river in a shot whose dominant red is criss-crossed by wisps of blue smoke.

Willard, in silhouette, emerges from the mud in the foreground of the frame; in the background, the ritualistic slaughter of the cow continues; and The Doors' "The End," first heard at the beginning of the film, comes on the soundtrack.

There is a cut, and Willard is seen moving through a black emptiness that is broken, rather too artfully, by one flash of very blue lightning. Willard is not at the right of the frame; Coppola fills the center with another hackneyed image: infinitely receding doorways, illuminated by the orange light that has become a motif in the film, though its significance is not at all clear.

Willard has now approached Kurtz's inner sanctum. There is a shot of the knife, its blade gleaming in the darkness, he will use to kill Kurtz. This is followed by a medium shot of Willard barely visible in the shadows that engulf the area just outside the room where Kurtz is dictating some cryptic thoughts into a recorder. Willard emerges into the light surrounding (emanating from?) Kurtz. There is a cut, and now the camera is tracking in on Kurtz; whether this reflects Willard's movement is not clear.

Coppola now reasserts his vision of the identity of Willard and Kurtz through identical low-angle shots of each of them. The idea is underlined by a pair of medium shots that show each of them emerging from darkness. Coppola's insistence in this particular shot on the idea of Willard emerging from darkness apparently is meant to suggest that his killing of Kurtz finally brings him a degree of revivifying enlightenment; but the idea that killing Kurtz somehow accomplishes Willard's spiritual salvation is one we can only passively register, for Coppola has not developed it in the overall mise-en-scène of this sequence.

Willard's slaughter of Kurtz is, predictably, intercut with the slaughter of the sacrificial cow; the implication that both acts are somehow religious is another idea that Coppola has asserted but has not coherently developed in his mise-en-scène.

Coppola devotes three shots to Kurtz's death. The first is a close-up of him as he utters his last words: "the horror, the horror." There is then a sustained close-up of Willard, whose face is now, confusingly, once again in shadow: apparently his destruction of Kurtz has not brought him enlightenment after all. The last shot is a dramatic but essentially meaningless shot of one of Kurtz's hands.

Kurtz's army of devoted tribesmen somehow sense that Willard has killed their king. They stop their ceremony and allow Willard and Lance (who emerges from the crowd) to pass unharmed through their midst. A series of dissolves brings Willard and Lance back to the patrol boat. The final dissolve is to a shot of Willard's eyes, which share the frame with the huge eyes of one of the statues that are on the river bank; the meaning of this composition, if indeed it has any, is, to say the least, obscure. The presence of a helicopter in the shot suggests that Chef had called in an air strike after all. Willard's voice is heard repeating "the horror, the horror," the Conradian refrain associated with Kurtz. That final referencee to Conrad is almost offensive; for *Apocalypse Now* has appropriated the great Conradian theme of the torment of men exposed to the horror of men's cruelty only to diminish it through association with the incoherence resulting from Coppola's attempt to ground his film in an essentially literary aesthetic.

The oft-postponed release date of *Apocalypse Now* and the running accounts in the press of Coppola's agonizing over its final form made it the most anticipated American film of the late seventies. The mixed critical response it received when Coppola finally released it and its rather disappointing (in relation to its cost) grosses did not, however, make it the film that ended the New Hollywood's infatuation with the modernist aesthetic.

The year following the release of *Apocalypse Now* saw the release of two more modernist extravaganzas. Paul Schrader's *American Gigolo* is a truly schizophrenic experience, a film in which Schrader's initial vision of both his material and his protagonist (played by the ineffably inert Richard Gere, who also starred in Terrence Malick's *Days of Heaven*) as a matter of flat, color-coordinated surfaces devoid of substance was at war with his later attempts to fashion a mise-en-scène that conveyed the emotional resonance of the material and the pathos of the protagonist. Woody Allen, moving on from the older literary fallacy that informed *Manhattan*, gave us *Stardust Memories*, a film that was probably supposed to be in the manner of Fellini but that was ultimately only another casualty of the modernist fallacy because Allen could not duplicate Fellini's achievement of securely embedding his vision in every element and nuance of his mise-en-scène, a failure that is more than understandable given that Fellini himself has not consistently succeeded in accomplishing that difficult feat.

The following year, 1981, saw the release of Michael Cimino's *Heaven's Gate*. Cimino, with a willfulness bordering on perversity, systematically undermined anything that was credible and involving in his film by opposing to it his modernist rendering of the material, which seemed extraordinarily excessive in terms of the (mostly incoherent) meaning it conveyed. The result was a failure on a scale that recalled Griffith's *Intolerance*: a big studio, big budget, big director film that was almost literally unwatchable. *Heaven's Gate*, however, will not have been in vain if (it is still too early to be sure) it proves to be the film that marked the end of the New Hollywood's destructive tendency to impose a literary aesthetic on film.

Notes

1. Gore Vidal, "Who Makes the Movies?" in *The Second American Revolution and Other Essays (1976–1982)* (New York: Random House, 1982, p. 147.
2. Stuart N. Hampshire, *Modern Writers and Other Essays* (New York: Alfred A. Knopf, 1970), pp. 45, 159.
3. A. Alvarez, *Beyond All This Fiddle: Essays 1955–1967* (New York: Random House, 1968, p. 4.
4. Hampshire, *Modern Writers*, p. 149.
5. See chapter 1, no. 9.

4

The Hitchcockian Fallacy

Carrie (1976)
Taxi Driver (1976)

The perverse alchemy practiced in the New Hollywood that has turned the towering achievement of Alfred Hitchcock into the Hitchcockian fallacy is an unusually clear and particularly regrettable example of a new generation of artists apparently misunderstanding and ultimately abusing the legacy of an esteemed master.

The Hitchcock criticism of the past twenty years has certainly contributed to the distortion of the legacy. David Kehr's recent reflections in *Film Comment* may be taken as representative of the period's prevailing critical line on Hitchcock. Kehr begins with a perhaps rhetorical question: "Is Alfred Hitchcock an artist?" That question, he claims (rightly, in my view), is "the fundamental question of film criticism in this half of the century—the question that, when it was first raised by a group of young French critics in the early fifties, touched off a revolution in the way movies were watched, discussed, and eventually ... made."[1]

Then Kehr goes on to reassert the false dichotomy that has been at the heart of the Hitchcockian fallacy. The Hitchcock question is

> the question that divides film aesthetics, separating critics who believe in the expressive power of popular filmmaking from those who see art only in the high-brow asceticism of a Bergman or an Antonioni, separating those who believe that film has its own artistic properties and potentials from those who measure achievement only by older, more established values.[2]

Kehr, by aligning, on one side, the "expressive power" and "artistic properties" of film and, on the other, "high-brow asceticism" and "older, more established values," expresses the essence of the Hitchcockian fallacy, which detaches the technique and expressive power of film direction from considerations of such "older" values as thematic coherence.

Hitchcock himself was another contributor to the creation of the fallacy through his reiteration in interview after interview of his belief in "pure cinema," a problematic term with a long and troubled history that has come to connote, among other things, that the evaluation of a film begins and ends with an evaluation of its director's exploitation of the unique communicative properties of film.

The irony is that a cogent response to the Kehr–pure cinema line has long been on record. Robin Wood has stated it with notable clarity:

> The meaning of a Hitchcock film is not a mysterious esoteric something cunningly concealed beneath a camouflage of "entertainment": it is there in the method, in the progression from shot to shot. A Hitchcock film is an organism, with the whole implied in every detail and every detail related to the whole.... [Y]ou will find themes of profound and universal significance ... and you will find these themes expressed in the form and style of the film as much as in any extractable "content."[3]

Wood has elaborated what might be called the organic position on Hitchcock, while Kehr and like-minded critics have asserted what might be called the virtuoso position. The former sees in the Hitchcockian *oeuvre* an exemplary demonstration of thematic significance contained in directorial style, while the latter sees in it a triumphant demonstration of a mastery of cinematic technique so complete as to make questions regarding thematic substance and coherence quite beside the point.

The zeitgeist of the New Hollywood era probably made the triumph of the virtuoso position all but inevitable: self-conscious artists setting out to revolutionize American filmmaking would predictably be attracted to an idea that seemed to set the unique expressive power of film against established values tainted by association with the other arts, particularly literature.

The Hitchcockian fallacy, which holds that the display of directorial virtuosity is the preeminent goal of film direction because it implies a full appreciation and cultivation of the power of film, was surely also propagated in the film schools that produced a number of New Hollywood directors and writers. One suspects that the pronounced technical orientation of the film schools contributed to the New Hollywood directors' embrace of the virtuoso view of Hitchcock, whose mastery of both montage and mise-en-scène has made his work a nearly indispensable case study in classes on film direction.

The hypothesis of a link between film schools and the Hitchcockian fallacy is somewhat strengthened by the fact that two of the leading exemplars of the fallacy in the New Hollywood are both film school graduates: Brian DePalma (Columbia) and Martin Scorsese (NYU).

While the work of DePalma and Scorsese can be linked by both directors' affinity for the Hitchcockian fallacy, that is not to say that their films can be equated on the level of achievement. In DePalma's work one sees a crude but persistent commitment to thematically empty virtuosity, while Scorsese has made thematically ambitious films which are seriously flawed by his lapses into mere virtuosity.

Critics of Hitchcock frequently fault him for having worked with pulpy material, a charge admirers like Wood have refuted through persuasive analyses of Hitchcock's success in coaxing themes of considerable profundity from seemingly unpromising material. In *Carrie*, Brian DePalma's breakthrough film, this process is reversed: working with material that is arguably no more pulpy than that of several Hitchcock films, DePalma fails to bring out what is valuable in the material and indeed highlights its pulpiest aspects. *Carrie* is thus a thoroughgoing perversion of the Hitchcock legacy, and its success no doubt importantly contributed to the wave of (often) technically impressive but (usually) thematically empty horror films that has washed over the New Hollywood, to the despair of so many critics.

DePalma's failure is rooted in the Hitchcockian fallacy: in his pursuit of virtuosity, DePalma fails to establish a tone and point of view for his film, uses the major visual motifs of the film in an incoherent fashion, and shapes the film in such a way that the thematically interesting aspects of the film are lost in a muddle of misplaced emphasis.

Carrie opens in a mood of cool detachment. After an initial overhead shot of teenage girls playing volleyball, the camera, reflecting the omniscient point of view of the director, cranes down to isolate one of the girls, Carrie White (Sissy Spacek). The camera holds on Carrie, effectively establishing her alienation from her peers.

The tone of clinical detachment is radically altered in the next shot, in which DePalma's mindless pursuit of virtuosity makes a muddle of both tone and point of view. The shot is in slow motion; and the camera, moving without reference to the movement of anyone on the screen, tracks through a narrow locker room lined with girls in various stages of undress. The autonomous tracking camera is a well-established code for the stalking of an invisible, threatening pursuer; and the sense of unidentified menace closing in on an unknown object of pursuit is strengthened by DePalma's decision to suppress dialogue and sound effects for the duration of the tracking movement, thereby adding eerie silence.

The success of *Carrie*, a thoroughgoing perversion of Hitchcock's legacy, led to a wave of thematically empty horror films. Sissy Spacek, *Carrie* (United Artists, 1976).

The camera tracks in on a steam-filled shower room to reveal Carrie amid the steam. She would appear to be the object of the invisible stalker, but at this point DePalma switches from the suspense code to the aesthetic of pornography. Continuing in slow motion, DePalma turns to a montage that fragments Carrie's naked body in a series of brief shots. Apparently, the technically impressive tracking shots was more related to voyeurism than suspense, since the tracking camera (which apparently was meant to represent the audience's point of view, rather than that of an invisible stalker) has come to rest for a detailed examination of Carrie's exposed body. DePalma's decision to continue in slow motion, which had made some sense when it appeared to be an element in the invisible-stalker tracking shot, only serves to underline the leering tone of the shots in the shower.

DePalma alternates several shots of blood dripping down Carrie's thigh with shots of her hysterical reaction to her first experience of menstruation. He then further muddles the meaning of the elaborate tracking shot by creating a composition in which the girls, lined up in the locker room in seemingly united hostility, are seen from the point of view of Carrie, who is lost in the infernal steam of the shower; the invisible, relentless menace of the initial tracking shot has not been replaced by the familiar hostility of teenagers to the outsider among them. DePalma now confusingly identifies Carrie's point of view with the audience's as the camera tracks forward with her through the gauntlet of jeering girls in the locker room. The identification is strengthened as the camera tracks back with Carrie as she retreats under the onslaught of the girls, who are pelting her with items from their lockers; the extended tracking interacts with the distribution of the actors to create a series of extreme close-ups of the girls as they assault the hysterical Carrie. DePalma's mise-en-scène has thus created a ludicrously exaggerated image of Carrie — and the audience — under attack by teenage harridans.

Shots of Carrie cringing in the shower are intercut with enormous close-ups of the girls as they hurl various objects at her. DePalma then indulges in more thematically misleading technique by tracking through the locker room (the movement is again autonomous, since no one on the screen is moving in this direction) to an office lcoated at the end of the room; the gym teacher, Miss Collins (Betty Buckley) can be seen through the glass wall of the office. The emphatic tracking in on Collins seems to promise rather more than what actually occurs. Collins breaks up the attack and comforts Carrie, but she conveys some sympathy with the girls' contempt for Carrie's overreaction to menstruation. The sequence concludes with a medium shot of Collins embracing Carrie, who is still sobbing uncontrollably.

This opening sequence gets *Carrie* off to a most unpromising start. DePalma's series of stylistic choices have replaced the initial sense of a detached study of an outsider, which was in turn briefly replaced by the sense of an unseen and then visible menace, with the identification of the audience with Carrie, an identification that seems unsustainable, given the very particular and seemingly temporary circumstances of Carrie's situation. The sequence makes sense only if seen in terms of the Hitch-cockian fallacy. DePalma has created a quite cinematic sequence: the tracking shots, close-ups, slow motion, and fragmented montage result in a visually compelling and uniquely cinematic experience. The style of the sequence, however, seems so indifferent to the creation and maintenance of a coherent tone and a consistent point of view that one suspects that style, not meaning, is the point of the sequence. One suspects, in other words, that DePalma, in the grips of the Hitchcockian fallacy, has set out to create an object of "pure cinema" which does not require validation in terms of thematic coherence.

The next sequence is a thematic muddle. DePalma at first seems to pick up the previously discarded view of Carrie as the alienated outsider by creating and then repeating a three-part series of shots in which (1) Carrie is seen in the waiting room of the principal's office, a window with closed blinds behind her; (2) Miss Collins and the principal are seen discussing Carrie in the latter's office; and (3) students passing through the corridor near the office are cast in apparent opposition to Carrie, who is seen sitting alone through the open outer door of the office.

The idea of Carrie as abused outsider is, however, dropped once Carrie enters the principal's office to talk with him and Miss Collins. As Carrie stands in front of the principal's desk, DePalma uses a series of eight low-angle shots of her, intercut with medium shots of the principal and Collins, that suggest Carrie's superiority rather than her vulnerability. It is with this series of shots that Carrie's power of telekinesis (she levitates an ashtray on the principal's desk) is introduced. The suggestion of the low-angle shots is that Carrie's unusual power is the basis of her superior-ity. That is an entirely acceptable idea; the only problem with it is that stylistic choices DePalma makes later in the film undercut it. While it is admittedly difficult to integrate an idea as gimmicky as the protagonist's possession of preternatural power, DePalma should at least treat it con-sistently. He should not, as he does, present it sometimes as the source of Carrie's superiority, other times as a manifestation of her profound alienation and isolation.

A brief scene involving Carrie's mother, Margaret (Piper Laurie), and the mother of one of Carrie's classmates follows. It establishes Margaret as a mentally unstable, religious fanatic who deeply disap-proves of even nonsexual relations between teenage boys and girls.

The next sequence begins with an establishing shot of a white Vic-torian house; a "For Sale" sign is in the foreground-left of the frame. Margaret enters the frame from the left and walks toward the house; as she begins to move, DePalma, suggesting that Carrie is as in control of her home environment as she was in the principal's office, zooms in on Carrie looking out of a window on the uppermost floor of the house.

There is a cut to Margaret entering the house and walking past the camera toward the background of the frame. In his first assertion of religious imagery, DePalma composes a shot in which Margaret is centered in front of a tapestry of "The Last Supper" that dominates the background of the frame.

After a cut to a shot of Carrie pacing diagonally, from the background-left to the foreground-right, across a room that appears to be the attic of the house (the composition suggests that Carrie, far from being in control, is in effect a prisoner), there is a cut to Margaret on the first floor. As she moves toward the camera to answer a telephone in the foreground of the frame, the camera tracks in on her. The composition places her in the center of an arch, separating the hallway from the living room, that recalls the arches of a gothic cathedral; in addition, the composition places Margaret among the figures of the "Last Supper" tapestry, which is at the center of the foreshortened background of the frame. With this shot, DePalma appears to commit himself to the elaboration of a religious motif in his film; it is, regrettably, a commitment he keeps in a rather incoherent fashion.

There is a cut to an establishing shot of a stairway with doors on either side. Carrie enters the frame and sits down on one of the upper stairs. DePalma continues the play on the spatial estrangement of Carrie and Margaret by intercutting several shots of Carrie in her elevated position on the stairway and Margaret below, speaking on the telephone. The series of shots ends with a middle-distance view of Carrie on the stairway that emphasizes the closed doors on either side of her. The sense of Carrie's entrapment is strengthened by the shot.

DePalma brings Carrie and Margaret together in a shot in which Carrie occupies the midground-left and Margaret the background-center; Margaret is placed in the center of the cathedral-like arch that separates the hall and the living room, so DePalma's mise-en-scène again associates Margaret with the power (or at least the symbols) of religion. There is movement within the shot as Carrie walks away from the camera toward her mother in the background. The camera tracks in on them, increasing the sense of an imminent confrontation between mother and daughter. The tracking results in a composition in which Carrie, her back to the camea, is in the foreground of the frame; and Margaret, facing the camera, is in the midground. In the film's first chilling moment, Margaret suddenly bursts out of her archway and lunges at Carrie and the camera.

DePalma now emphatically reiterates Carrie's victim status as he alternates overhead shots of Carrie, thrown to the floor by the blow her mother has dealt her, with low-angle shots of Margaret looming over her. After two sustained medium shots of Carrie and Margaret on their knees praying for Carrie's salvation (the call Margaret received was from the school, and she has interpreted the incident involving Carrie's menstruation as the beginning of Carrie's slide into perdition), the camera tracks right with them as they enter the kitchen. Margaret forces Carrie through a door in the kitchen, closes it, and then assumes a position against the closed door that suggests she has been crucified on it.

There is a cut to a sustained overhead shot of Carrie in a very small room, not much bigger than a closet. A shot of Carrie lighting a candle is followed by one of her praying. She is praying to an image of Saint Sebastian, a notably grotesque image that emphasizes the bloody wounds caused by the arrows protruding from the figure of the martyr. There is then a dissolve to an exterior shot of the house at night.

The dissolve ends with a shot of Margaret in the extreme foreground of the frame and Carrie in the background. Carrie exits the frame without speaking to Margaret; the camera holds on Margaret's troubled face.

There is then a dissolve to Carrie standing in front of a small mirror in her attic room; the religious motif is reiterated through the reflection in the mirror of an image of Christ wearing the crown of thorns. The camera zooms in and out on the mirror as grating electronic music rises on the soundtrack. After a cut to a close-up of Margaret, there is a cut to a shot of the mirror shattering under the force of Carrie's exercise of her telekinetic power. The inclusion of the shot of Margaret here creates ambiguity: it is not clear if Carrie's power is somehow derived from Margaret (the reassertion of the religious motif would seem to support that idea) or if the exercise of Carrie's power is in response to Margaret's oppressive hold on her daughter. The ambiguity is not resolved by the last shot of the sequence, in which the camera, following Carrie's gaze, pans across the attic to the cracked mirror, which again reflects the face of Christ wearing the crown of thorns.

While DePalma's insistence on the crown of thorns reflection is probably another instance of his sacrificing coherence for virtuosity, the Carrie-Margaret sequence is, on the whole, an effective one. DePalma's direction of it suggests that the film will focus on Carrie's efforts to break free of her mother's hold on her, a perverted domination founded on religion and an aversion to sex.

It is only in the context of the film as a whole that the sequence seems a turning point, the moment when DePalma decisively turned away from thematic coherence and toward empty virtuosity. The amount of time (seven minutes) and calculated technique (the compositions establishing the religious motif, the play of low-angle and overhead shots, the problematic but technically effective crown of thorns shots) DePalma devotes to this sequence would seem to establish the primacy in the film of the Carrie-Margaret relationship. De Palma's pursuit of virtuosity, however, eventually undermines the centrality of this promising (and, parenthetically, very Hitchcockian) relationship. As a result, the sequence, seen as part of the film as a whole, seems only a display of virtuosity, a self-justifying exercise demonstrating what a technically proficient director can accomplish through the exploitation of the spatial and decor components of mise-en-scène.

DePalma follows the Carrie-Margaret sequence with more than twenty minutes of trite plot development. He devotes seven minutes — running time equal to that devoted to the Carrie-Margaret sequence — to Miss Collins's punishment of Carrie's classmates for their locker-room assault on Carrie. The reason for giving such weight to this sequence was, presumably, to establish motivation for the elaborate revenge on Carrie as one of the girl's plans.

DePalma then includes scenes in which (1) Carrie meets the class dreamboat, Tommy (William Katt); (2) Sue (Amy Irving), feeling guilty about her participation in the locker-room incident, persuades Tommy, her steady boyfriend to invite Carrie to the upcoming prom; (3) Chris (Nancy Allen) persuades her boyfriend Billy (John Travolta) to help her carry out a plot against Carrie; (4) Carrie, reluctant because she knows her mother will disapprove, finally accepts Tommy's invitation to the prom; and (5) Billy, Chris and a couple of their friends are seen slaughtering a pig, the first step in Chris's (incredible) plot. After this long series of brief scenes, the tension and involving intensity generated in the Carrie-Margaret sequence have been totally dissipated. It may be that all of this mechanical plot development was necessary, but DePalma should have found a way to accomplish it without doing such damage to the shape of his film. Since he did not, *Carrie* becomes a thematically trite film about an incredible teenage revenge plot and its aftermath, rather than a film centered on the timeless theme of a child freeing herself from a domineering and destructive parent.

When DePalma does finally return to the Carrie-Margaret relationship, he exploits it as a framework for another display of his command of cinematic technique; indeed, he demonstrates his indifference to the thematic significance of the mother-daughter relationship by devising a premature and unsatisfyng climax for the issues embedded in the relationship, thereby making the rest of the film anticlimactic in terms of its most interesting theme.

DePalma begins the second Carrie-Margaret sequence with an exterior shot of their home. It is night and it is raining; the darkness is pierced by lightning, and the sound of thunder dominates the soundtrack. DePalma, it would appear, is susceptible to the pathetic, as well as the Hitchcockian, fallacy.

From the exterior shot of the house there is a cut to a medium shot of the "Last Supper" tapestry on a wall of the dining room; since the only illumination in the room is provided by candles, DePalma has forcefully reasserted the religious motif by creating a distinctly church-like atmosphere. The camera tracks back from the tapestry to reveal Margaret and Carrie seated at the dining room table, the former at the left end of the table, the latter at the right. The near-total darkness of the room seems a palpable presence separating the two women.

It soon becomes clear that, in this sequence, DePalma is most interested in demonstrating the striking images a skilled director can create by exploiting lighting effects. The play of light and darkness in this sequence seems to have no thematic relevance; it is self-justifying, a display of pure cinema.

There is a series of medium shots of Carrie and Margaret, all of which feature the glow of candles and periodic appearances of blue lightning bolts, which are seen through the windows of the dining room. After this series, DePalma reprises the initial medium shot of Margaret and Carrie at the table. Now, however, the room is noticeably darker than in the first shot. This would appear to be without thematic significance, since the ongoing interaction between Carrie and Margaret has not taken a "darker" turn. The increased darkness has only a technical significance: it makes Margaret and Carrie invisible and serves as a better background for the bolts of blue lightning that now streak across the frame, sporadically illuminating the "Last Supper" tapestry.

Margaret, angry and frustrated over her inability to dissuade Carrie from attending the prom, rises from her chair. A series of alternating medium shots of Carrie and Margaret follows; DePalma at this point provides Margaret with a new and unidentifiable source of illumination, which casts her in a red-orange glow. What, if any, thematic significance this latest display of lighting effects has is unclear.

Margaret leaves the dining room, and the camera tracks right with her. A medium shot of Margaret and Carrie is followed by alternating close-ups of each of them. DePalma then inexplicably goes to a low-angle shot in which Margaret towers above Carrie; the choice of camera angle here is thematically incoherent, since Carrie has been successfully resisting her mother and, at least for the moment, has attained equality with her. But this sequence is about lighting effects, and one perhaps should not expect the camera angles to make sense.

There is a cut to a shot in which Carrie is following her mother as the latter moves left. Margaret exits the frame, and the camera holds on a medium shot of Carrie. There follows a rapid series of shots showing all the windows and shutters of the house slamming shut. Carrie has again exercised her special power, though *why* she does so at this moment (she has, after all, successfully withstood her mother's pressure to rescind her acceptance of Tommy's invitation) is not clear. The most likely explanation is that DePalma wanted to put on a kinetic display of his own, a little demonstration of the visual excitement that can be generated through a combination of accelerated montage and special effects.

A series of medium shots of Carrie and Margaret (who has been thoroughly frightened by Carrie's display of power) follows. In the series, each woman is associated with an unchanging element in the composition of each of her shots. Margaret shares her shots with blue lightning bolts, which appear every time DePalma cuts to her; Carrie shares her shots with the tapestry of the "Last Supper." Carrie's gaining control of the "Last Supper" motif seems highly incoherent, suggesting as it does that she has subsumed, rather than defeated, her mother. The more likely explanation is, again, that DePalma in this sequence is interested only in the creation of certain visual effects and is not troubled by any thematic inconsistencies his compositions might cause.

The last shot of the sequence is impressive in a pure cinema sense. Margaret is seen in the midground of the frame, standing in the middle of the kitchen; she is looking with fear and horror at Carrie, who is off-camera. Behind her is a window whose top half is filled with an orange-red glow, while its bottom half is a vivid blue. I have no idea what meaning this color scheme might have, but it is genuinely beautiful, a cinematic equivalent of a color-field painting.

The sequence concludes with Carrie declaring what she has already demonstrated: she will henceforth not feel obliged to obey her mother's every command. Since that declaration of independence would seem to be the climax of the thematically interesting aspect of the film, one gets the uneasy feeling that DePalma, having declared the substance of the film over, will feel even more free to indulge in virtuoso displays of style in the remainder of the film than he has up to this point.

Two brief scenes, which would have had greater impact had their order been reversed, follow. In the first, Billy and Chris are seen placing a bucket on the scaffolding above the bandstand in the gym where the prom is to be held. In the second, a silent medium shot set in the White home suggests that a kind of truce has been declared in the Carrie-Margaret battle. Margaret is in the foreground of the frame, quietly praying (presumably for the salvation of Carrie's soul); Carrie is in the midground, making her dress for the prom, her determination to defy her mother apparently unshaken. Had this scene preceded the Chris-Billy scene, it would have made an effective coda to the climactic Carrie-Margaret sequence.

In the first Carrie-Margaret sequence, DePalma created a study in cinematic space and the connotative use of decor; in the second, he explored the possibilities of light and dark contrasts and lighting effects. Now, in the third Carrie-Margaret sequence, he adds camera angles to his repertory and continues his exploration of the spatial and color properties of film. The sequence is quite beautiful and could, if it were possible, be hung on a wall of a gallery; but it is thematically incoherent, another demonstration of DePalma's proclivity for inorganic filmmaking.

The initial shot of the sequence is suffused with a notably pink glow. Carrie and Margaret are in the former's attic room. It is the night of the prom. Carrie is putting on makeup in front of a mirror (which again reflects the image of Christ with the crown of thorns that hangs on a wall of the attic); Margaret is in the foreground of the frame, observing Carrie.

There is a cut to a medium shot of Carrie from Margaret's point of view. The camera tracks forward with Margaret as she moves toward Carrie; the tracking pauses on a shot of Carrie's corsage, then resumes for a shot of her breasts. Then, in a movement that seems unmotivated, the camera tracks back for a more distant shot of Margaret and Carrie that emphasizes their separation and continues the association of Carrie with the mirror. This shot is sustained and becomes a lovely tableau of the two women illuminated by a soft pink light. Then, at the sound of a car approaching, there is a cut to a shot of Margaret and Carrie approaching the camera as they run to the attic window.

After a shot of traffic on the street below, DePalma cuts to the first highly problematic shot of the sequence.

Margaret and Carrie are seen in double close-up as they look out the window. This seems a curious choice of composition and camera position, given DePalma's earlier and repeated insistence on compositions that separated the two women. Then, as Carrie moves back toward the center of the attic, DePalma tilts the camera to create the impression that the room itself is tilted. Since this is Carrie's room and the shot reflects her point of view, the suggestion that Carrie herself is "tilted" seems quite strong. Yet this makes no sense, since Carrie at this moment is at her sanest, as she moves toward integration with her peers and a permanent break with her mother, both resulting from her determination to attend the prom. DePalma's choice of a tilted camera angle thus seems a blatant example of style detached from meaning.

The tilted room effect continues in the next shot, in which Carrie, again at the mirror, is in the background of the frame; and Margaret is pacing right-left-right in the foreground. The spatial estrangement of mother and daugther is thus reasserted.

There is a cut to a medium shot of Margaret, who walks toward the camera. The resulting close-up of her seems to promise some decisive action on her part, but DePalma then cuts to a shot in which Margaret resumes her pacing and then walks toward Carrie. As she does, the camera is again tilted, reinforcing the idea that Carrie is somehow the cause of the tilt. One begins to suspect that the tilt is to serve as harbinger of another display of Carrie's telekinetic power; if this is in fact the explanation behind DePalma's emphasis on the distorting camera angle, then this is a prime example of DePalma emphasizing the pulpy elements of his material.

There is a cut to a low-angle shot of Carrie (her control of the situation is thus reaffirmed); in a bold display of technique, the shot is taken from a tilted angle, so Carrie is both looming and tilted, whatever that is supposed to signify. Another feature of the shot is the return of the distinctly pink lighting, which had been more subdued in the last several shots. The shot is an altogether impressive display of DePalma's technical daring, but its essential meaninglessness reveals again the detachment of technique from meaning that is the essence of the Hitchcockian fallacy.

From the virtuoso shot of Carrie, there is a cut to a shot of Margaret cringing at the sight of Carrie, whose point of view is identified with the camera's. There is a cut to a shot of Carrie walking toward the window (the camera angle is again tilted and the pink hue is again very pronounced), followed by a long shot of Tommy parking his car in front of the White house. There is then a cut to a shot of Carrie taken from a very distorting angle. The color code has changed: a red-orange glow in the background of the shot has replaced the pervasive pink; the significance of this change is not clear. Carrie, still ignoring her mother's pleas not to go the prom, closes the window; DePalma sustains a shot of her in silhouette seen from the exterior side of the windr '.

There is a cut to a medium shot of Margaret, at the rear of the frame, facing the camera; and Carrie, in the foreground, her back to the camera. A normal camera angle has been restored, although this wouldn't appear to signify any change in Carrie or the Carrie-Margaret relationship.

As she goes to meet Tommy, Carrie pushes Margaret onto a bed and holds her there with the force of her telekinetic power; the distorting, tilted camera angle has returned. Carrie moves toward the camera and then exits the room and the frame. The camera zooms in on Margaret as she watches Carrie leave and mutters something about witches not being allowed to live.

DePalma by this point in the film has directed himself into a most unpromising corner. He has mishandled what was potentially the most interesting strain in his material, the Carrie-Margaret relationship; and he has thrown away the potentially most satisfying climax to his film, Carrie's liberation from the deadly grip of her mother. He is left with only the pulpiest element of the material, the improbable revenge plot against Carrie planned by some of her nastier classmates. Therefore, he is obliged to make the high school prom, during which the plot is carried out, the nominal climax of the film.

The first feature one notices about the prom sequence is the lighting: the color scheme of the sequence is garish, an ugly clash of pink, blue and green, emanating from what must be very large spotlights placed around the gymnasium where the prom is being held. The strong sense of ugliness conveyed by the lighting was probably unintended (DePalma, no doubt, was only interested in seeing what he could achieve with lighting effects); for it is at odds with meaning DePalma (presumably) wanted to convey in the early part of the sequence.

That meaning is, simply, the transcendent, transforming happiness Carrie feels at being at the prom with Tommy. Their first dance initially seems an apt expression of her happiness as DePalma, placing his camera at a low angle, shows them dancing among the glittery stars dangling from the gymnasium ceiling. Soon, however, DePalma's virtuosity makes a muddle of meaning: as Carrie and Tommy move in circles around the dance floor, DePalma moves his camera in a circular motion at such a speed as to create an unpleasant, vertiginous effect. Instead of creating a sense of Carrie's rapturous state, he creates a dizzying, almost sickening effect; in doing so, he diminishes the power of his already unpromising climax, which has no chance of working without the prior establishment of a sense of Carrie's utter joy at this transcendent moment in her life.

DePalma leaves the prom for a brief scene that is one of the film's most blatant examples of technique without (apparent) thematic significance. Margaret is seen in an overhead shot in the kitchen of her house. She picks up an absurdly large knife and proceeds to chop carrots on a cutting board. With each chop there is a cut to a closer shot of the knfe; by the end of the series, the knife is seen in close-up. The meaning of all this is so difficult to discern that one suspects that there is not any. The scene is probably an instance of DePalma doing something Hitchcock never did: using stylistic options — in this case, an overhead camera and a rhythmic montage — to create a sense of suspense that is unrelated to developments that significantly involve the film's characters and themes.

DePalma returns to the prom for a series of shots in which Chris, Billy and several of their friends are seen preparing their spectacular revenge against Carrie. Part of the plot involves assuring that Tommy and Carrie are chosen king and queen of the prom. DePalma goes to slow motion as Carrie and Tommy approach the bandstand to be invested as the royal couple of the evening. The use of slow motion is, from a thematic standpoint, inexcusable, because it suggests that what is about to happen is a fantasy, a suggestion that only further weakens the film's climax. The decision is justifiable only on grounds of virtuosity, only if it is seen as another display of the variety of expressive devices available to a film director.

DePalma continues the slow motion and adds a few other virtuoso touches for the conclusion of the prom sequence. It turns out that the revenge planned for Carrie is to drench her in pig's blood contained in the bucket that has been concealed above the bandstand. This reprehensible (and farfetched) trick triggers in Carrie a full-force display of her preternatural powers. For four minutes, in slow motion, DePalma shows us the death and destruction Carrie brings down upon the gym and all the people in it. Besides slow motion, DePalma uses a split screen, a spinning kaleidoscope process shot, and a printing effect that drains primary colors from the film to capture Carrie's revenge on her tormentors. The four-minute segment is an altogether stunning display of the power of film and the possibilities of film direction; it is also an excellent example of direction which seems almost laughably excessive when its stylistic components are evaluated in terms of the meaning they generate.

The final shot of the prom sequence is an exterior shot of the gymnasium in flames. In slow motion, the doors of the building open and Carrie walks through them. The slow motion and the effect produced by process photography of the flames engulfing the gym give a most unreal look to the shot, reiterating the confusing suggestion that what has happened at the prom is a fantasy.

Carrie is next seen walking zombie-like along a road. She encounters Chris and Billy, who have escaped the destruction wrought in the gym, fleeing in the latter's car. Calling once again on her special powers, Carrie causes the car to overturn and go up in a burst of flames.

There is a dissolve from the burning car to a shot of Carrie approaching her house. DePalma composes a masterful shot of the house, which could have been the focal point of a truly interesting film. In a sustained long take, we first see Carrie in the foreground of the frame; two windows of the house, aglow with, presumably, candlelight, are in the background of the frame. The camera then tracks left with Carrie, and the new compositon emphasizes three windows and the front door of the house, all of them aglow with a light from within. The camera tracks back as Carrie approaches the house, and it tilts up to reveal that the window of her attic room is also aglow. Unfortunately, this effective evocation of the oppressive, mysterious house seems wasted; for, after the excessive extravaganza of the sequence at the prom, everything seems anticlimactic.

The camera follows Carrie into the house, which is filled with seemingly hundreds of small candles. An overhead shot of Carrie climbing the stairs to the attic is followed by a shot in which the camera tracks into a bathroom with Carrie. As Carrie turns on a light in the bathroom, Margaret, who had been concealed by the darkness of the attic, suddenly is revealed hiding in a corner of the room.

When Carrie exits the bathroom, Margaret emerges from her hiding place. In a series of shots that might have carried considerable impact had DePalma not preceded them with the excesses of the prom sequence, Margaret is first seen embracing Carrie and then, in a series of overhead shots that reflect Carrie's point of view, she is seen kneeling at Carrie's feet.

There is a cut to a shot of Carrie getting on her knees next to Margaret. The camera holds for a medium shot of them. Then there is a cut to a shot of Carrie's head resting on Margaret's breast. Margaret reaches for a knife lying near her. There is a cut to a close-up of Margaret illuminated by a glaring white light. A series of close-ups of Carrie, Margaret, and the knife follows. There is then a cut to a shot of Carrie, stabbed by Margaret, falling downstairs toward the camera. This is followed by an overhead shot of Carrie lying at the bottom of the stairs, which in turn is followed by a low-angle shot of Margaret (now restored to her superior position) descending the stairs.

There follows a series of alternating low-angle shots of Margaret and overhead shots of Carrie lying on the floor. Carrie then summons her special power and causes every knife and sharp instrument in the house to fly at Margaret. The attack ends with the camera slowly tracking back from Margaret, who, in an image that recalls the Saint Sebastian figure seen early in the film, is seen impaled by dozens of knives against a door in the kitchen. This effective but essentially anticlimactic sequence ends with the house in flames. The film itself ends moments later, after a kind of epilogue in which Sue, who has survived the prom-night massacre, dreams that Carrie has attempted a return from the grave. That—a trite set-piece in which something shocking turns out to be a dream—is a rather fitting conclusion to *Carrie*, a film directed by a man who consistently settled for the thematically trite while pursuing the stylistically audacious.

In *Taxi Driver*, Martin Scorsese's virtuosity (which is genuinely impressive; Scorsese is probably the most technically accomplished of the New Hollywood directors) leads him into the fundamental error that V. F. Perkins identified in a famous film of an earlier era:

> In *Moulin Rouge* John Huston established (and exploited with, for the most part, enthralling results) a system of colour based on the palettes of the Impressionists and therefore owing nothing to naturalism. Yet he had not created a world whose reality could tolerate a room that changed colour in sympathy with its occupant's moods. When the director characterized his hero's jealousy by flooding the set with in the film's own terms, inexplicable green light, he broke down the essential structure of his picture's relationships and thus destroyed the world within which his hero *existed*. A minor, momentary relationship between the hero's temper and a . . . colour was surely not worth achieving . . . at the sacrifice of the fundamental pattern.[4]

In *Taxi Driver*, Scorsese, working with a script by Paul Schrader (another film school graduate), never quite establishes a fundamental pattern that expresses the volatile interaction between his deeply alienated protagonist and the pervasive corruption of New York City because Scorsese's frequent lapses into mere virtuosity prevent the emergence of a coherent pattern. He fails to create a meaningful world for his film; and *Taxi Driver* is ultimately a seriously flawed, if commendably ambitious, work.

Scorsese in effect creates only half a world. He is very good at conveying a sense of the distorting, disfiguring filter of his protagonist's sensibility, a task ideally suited to Scorsese's virtuoso sensibility, which responds to the challenge of creating a visual pattern that suggests a psychotic's highly subjective point of view. His commitment to virtuosity, however, carries over into his rendering of the other component of what should be his film's fundamental pattern, the inescapable sordidness of New York City. Here Scorsese's virtuoso sensibility works against the good of his film; for his tendency to create virtuoso effects undermines a sense of the reality of the film's milieu, which in turn weakens the sense (which is crucial to the thematic coherence of the film) of an interaction between a convincing reality and a susceptible sensibility. It is as if Hitchcock in *Rear Window* had failed to convey a sense that there was something real that existed outside of his protagonist's mind, something with its own existence that triggered a response in one man's unique psyche.

Scorsese's achievement and his failure are both evident in the film's opening sequence. In a series of shots linked by dissolves, Travis Bickle (Robert DeNiro) is seen driving a taxi through urban streets. In this series, Scorsese makes brilliant use of various elements of mise-en-scène to suggest Bickle's unique point of view. Scorsese dispenses with the full color spectrum, so the shots have a drained, decidedly unnaturalistic look. It is raining while Travis drives, and Scorsese makes full use of the visual possibilities of neon reflected in puddles. He also uses slow motion and oddly colored steam rising from the rutted blacktop to emphasize the sense of the controlling force of a subjective point of view. Scorsese makes clear that the point of view is Travis's by twice interrupting the dissolve pattern to cut to close-up shots of Travis's eyes reflected in the rearview mirror of his taxi. These first shots are fine, a representative sampling of Scorsese's virtuoso control of the modalities of film direction.

Yet the sequence also contains the first of a number of crucial mistakes that seem rooted in the same virtuosity. When Scorsese flashes back (appropriately, without employing conventional flashback signals, thereby successfully conveying Travis's necessarily subjective sense of time) to a scene showing Travis applying for work at a cab company, he brings the steam we have seen rising from the streets into the office where Travis applies for employment; well into the scene there are still wisps of steam visible in the office. This seems an incoherent continuation of the steam effect, for it undermines a sense of a real world that exists apart from Travis's perception of it, a world that feeds his psychosis and which should be fully and realistically conveyed if we are to understand Travis and his psychotic reaction to his environment. Scorsese makes a similar but more serious mistake in concluding the sequence. Travis, having gotten the job, is seen approaching the camera as he walks along a sidewalk near the cab company's garage. There's a dissolve, and now Travis is seen drinking from a bottle in a paper sack. Presumably, some time has passed;

The inescapable sordidness of New York City nurtures and eventually triggers acts of individual madness. Robert De Niro, *Taxi Driver* (Columbia Pictures, 1975).

yet it seems clear from the buildings Travis is passing that he has made no perceptible progress since the preceding shot. Here is an instance of Scorsese the virtuoso playing with the space and time possibilities of film. Such play, however, seems inappropriate in this instance; for, again, the effect is to undermine the reality of Travis's milieu and to suggest that we will see only what exists in his mind.

If Scorsese is not going to develop a convincing and compelling world to oppose to Travis's subjective world view, then he cannot coherently develop what is potentially the major theme of *Taxi Driver*: pervasive urban madness nurtures and eventually triggers acts of individual madness. Instead of developing that theme in a well realized mise-en-scène, it appears, on the evidence of the first sequence, that Scorsese intends to make *Taxi Driver* a virtuoso study in the sustained point of view of a psychotic, a kind of Americanized, contemporary *Cabinet of Dr. Caligari*.

Yet the *Caligari* analogy does not consistently hold. In the film's second sequence, Travis's point of view is suspended as the camera, adopting the detachment of an overhead view, observes him in his spartan rented room as he writes in his journal. Travis's voice on the soundtrack tells us what he is writing, and the total effect of the scene is to oppose the realistic rendering of Travis's seedy room with the bizarre, twisted thoughts he is recording in his journal. Had Scorsese achieved and consistently maintained this pattern in his film, *Taxi Driver* would have been the significant study of the interaction between societal madness and individual madness that it had the potential to be.

From the scene of Travis in his room, Scorsese goes to another extended segment showing Travis driving through the mean streets of New York City at night (Travis, by choice, drives at night because he has severe insomnia). In this passage Scorsese achieves neither the excellent balance or tension of the scene in Travis's room nor the *Caligari*-like quality of the first sequence. Travis's point of view is again suspended as the camera observes him driving, but the detached camera's point of view seems as subjective and distorting as Travis's. He is seen facing the camera in a medium shot in which the rain-distorted reflections of neon in the rear window turn his taxi into an odd, psychedelic prison. There is then a cut to a shot in which the camera, moving without reference to the movement of anyone or anything on screen, tracks rapidly forward through streets that are full of neon puddles and billowing steam and that are suffused with a red neon glow. There is a cut; and now the camera is tracking laterally (so it plainly is not reflecting the established forward movement of Travis's taxi) across a ghetto scene so darkly lit as to suggest a crude painting on a velvet background. The cumulative effect of the segment is to suggest a hallucinatory view of New York; but the relevant question is: Whose hallucination is this? Scorsese, even when he has suspended his protagonist's point of view and so can not be going for a *Caligari* effect, insists on undermining an realistic evocation of New York, which seems thematically necessary for his film. One gets the feeling that Scorsese's virtuosity will not allow him to communicate realistically, even when that is what the work at hand calls for. He feels obliged, apparently, constantly to explore and exploit the expressive powers of cinema, even at the expense of the coherence of his film.

The next sequence splits in half. It begins as a realistic rendering of a porno theatre, that refuge of the alienated where Travis spends his days. Scorsese at first seems genuinely interested in conveying the detailed reality of the theatre, and his efforts succeed in achieving a sense of the interaction between the palpable reality of this component of Travis's milieu and his own troubled psyche.

Soon, however, Scorsese's virtuosity gets in the way. He places the camera in the rear of the tiny theatre. As Travis walks toward the camera, the screen behind him becomes a reddish glow, similar to the distorted neon glow that has been featured in the driving sequences; the sense of the sordid reality of this specific place is weakened by this directorial indulgence in a rather showy lighting effect. That sense is further weakened by the shot that follows: the camera pans across the theatre's other patrons, whose faces become blurs and seem to merge with the faces and bodies on the screen; the pan continues past a medium shot of Travis, who is in focus. This is certainly a virtuoso effect, a display of what a director can say through the exploitation of changes in focus. The question that remains is whether what Scorsese is saying in uniquely cinematic language is thematically coherent or merely visually witty.

The next sequence introduces a perhaps necessary plot device. Travis becomes infatuated with a woman, Betsy (Cybill Shepherd), who works at the campaign headquarters of a political candidate. Appropriately enough, Betsy is introduced in a shot that reflects Travis's askew point of view. She emerges from a crowd of pedestrians and then, in slow motion, walks to the left of the frame. As she enters the campaign headquarters building, there is a dissolve to a shot of Travis's crude, childish printing on a page of his journal; his voice on the soundtrack speaks the words we see in the journal. There is then a cut to a slow craning down on Travis as he labors over the journal. Betsy has thus been effectively identified as a creature of Travis's mind, though the significance of this becomes somewhat problematic as the film proceeds.

Travis has a rather tentative meeting with Betsy at campaign headquarters. Scorsese handles their meeting in a fairly unremarkable, realistic, fashion, though he does make choices — an elaborate reverse-zoom shot, somewhat gimmicky point of view shots — that seem rather obtrusive for this realistic rendering of Travis's encounter with the flesh-and-blood Betsy.

The meeting with Betsy is followed by another driving interlude in which Scorsese, as he did in the first scene set in Travis's room, appears to move toward the pattern that seem most promising, in terms of thematic development, for the film. The interlude begins with Travis associated with the now familiar images of rain-distorted reflections of ubiquitous neon lights. As the scene continues, however, Scorsese goes to an increasingly realistic view of the sordid neighborhoods where Travis prefers to work. It seems that Scorsese is belatedly shaping his film to communicate the important theme of the tragic effect of the ugly meanness of New York on an already disturbed sensibility.

The sequence that follows, set at the Belmore Cafeteria, the well known cabbie hangout, does not clearly continue the promising movement of the immediately preceding scene. It is more like the porno theatre sequence, split between an effective first half and a problematic second half.

The sequence begins with a fairly conventional series of medium shots of cabbies sitting at a table at the Belmore. When one of them, Wizard (Peter Boyle), remarks with reference to the city, "It's a fuckin' Mau-Mau land out there," there is a cut to a slow craning up on Travis as he enters the cafeteria. This is one of the best choices Scorsese makes in the film: it juxtaposes in an effectively pointed manner an expression (which is, granted, only a verbal expression, but one that is at least pungent and forcefully delivered) of the reality of New York City with an emphatic shot of Travis.

Scorsese continues with a pair of shots in which he uses a tracking movement and then a pan to link Travis and the other cabbies with a pimp sitting at a table near the center of the cafeteria.

This is another effective choice; for Scorsese has linked Travis with a realistic representation (this time, a visual one) of the reality of the milieu that confronts Travis's fragile psyche.

At this point, however, Scorsese's proclivity for the virtuoso effect again gets in the way of the evolving meaning of a sequence. He cuts to a slightly overhead shot of Travis putting an Alka-Seltzer tablet in a glass; then, in a shot that Bob Fosse was to pick up in *All That Jazz*, Scorsese cranes down into the glass so that the effervescing bubbles fill the screen. This can only be regarded as a blatant display of virtuosity, as a technically accomplished director's celebration of the supple qualities of film language. Unfortunately, the shot deforms the meaning of the sequence and once again tilts the film toward an excessive concentration on Travis's distorting point of view.

A nine-minute segment featuring Travis and Betsy, first at campaign headquarters and then having coffee at a lucheonette, follows. This is a straightforward sequence, notable for Robert DeNiro's excellent portrayal of a troubled man awkwardly groping for an opening toward normality. Scorsese includes only one bravura touch in the sequence. At one point, an unusually long bus can be seen through the window in front of which Travis and Betsy are sitting. Running the length of the bus is an advertising placard that features in large letters a slogan advising us to "Live It Up." That, of course, is a fitting caption for the sequence, which is about Travis's tentative introduction to a more expansive kind of life.

After a brief scene showing Travis buying Betsy a gift in a record store, there is an extended driving sequence in which Travis has two significant encounters. In the first, he picks up Pallantine, the candidate Betsy is working for; he uses his time with Pallantine to vent his anger about the steadily deteriorating state of New York City. In the second, Travis almost gives a ride to Iris (Jodie Foster), a teenager hooker who is fleeing her pimp, Sport (Harvey Keitel); Iris enters Travis's cab, but Sport immediately drags her out of it and dismisses Travis. Throughout this driving sequence, Scorsese uses a reduced color spectrum to give a washed-out, almost sepia tone to the sequence; the effect of this exploitation of the expressive potential of color is, again, to undermine a sense of the reality of the milieu in which Travis functions, since the placement and movement of the camera indicate that the unnaturalistic color is not mean to convey Travis's point of view. The problem is somewhat corrected in the conclusion of the sequence, in which ghetto youths splatter Travis's taxi with eggs. Here is a welcome moment of realism, one that effectively captures the sense of Travis trapped within the pervasive madness of the city.

Travis has a date with Betsy that turns out disastrously because he takes her to a porno movie. He tries to reach her by phone after she has left him in anger. In a scene in which Scorsese's exploitation of the connotative potential of color and space in cinema seems thematically valid, we see Travis on the phone in a medium shot that features the washed-out, near sepia hue of the previous sequence. The camera pans right from Travis on the phone to a shot of a long, empty corridor; Travis futilely pleading with Betsy on the phone is a voice-over. Then Travis enters the frame from the left and walks down the corridor, away from the camera. The shot is held as a stationary camera observes Travis until he has walked almost the entire length of the long, narrow corridor. Scorsese has here created a powerful image of Travis's state of mind at this juncture without violating the realism that should be maintained as a vital part of the fundamental pattern of the film.

Scorsese continues the evocation of Travis's emotional response to Betsy's rejection in the next sequence. Travis goes to campaign headquarters to confront her; and Scorsese chooses a notably bright, almost blinding lighting scheme for their scene together, possibly to create a visual equivalent of Travis's line, heard as a voice-over, "I realized how much she's just like the others, cold and distant." Scorsese's rendering of this sequence seems wrong, an un–Hitchcockian lapse into inorganic direction; for the visual-verbal intensity of the scene suggests that Travis's subsequent behavior is a reaction to Betsy's rejection, an untenable idea given the virtual nondevelopment of Betsy's character.

The next sequence, the second set at the Belmore Cafeteria, continues the extraordinarily bright lighting scheme, this time in the interior of the cafeteria. The suggestion is thus made that Travis is still reacting to his rejection by Betsy.

Scorsese radically alters the lighting scheme when Travis and Wizard step outside the cafeteria for an extended conversation. All of the middle-distance shots of the exterior of the cafeteria and its immediate surroundings have a distinctly pink hue, but the medium shots devoted to Travis have the near sepia look that has become associated with him. The unrealistic color scheme is extended to several shots of a group of black hookers standing near the entrance to the cafeteria. Scorsese thus misses another chance to convey the idea of the unmediated reality of New York in opposition to the distorted viewpoint and pesonality of Travis. By again failing to establish that opposition, Scorsese has failed to serve the thematic needs of the film. He has instead indulged his apparent desire to explore the communicative potential of lighting, even at the expense of the organic development of the film. He has, in other words, again revealed his underlying commitment to the Hitchcockian fallacy.

Taxi Driver has now reached a turning point, for its protagonist is about to move decisively toward the irrational acts that Scorsese has shown to be very near his surface. Scorsese, however, has not yet established a convincing context for Travis's acts because his pursuit of directorial virtuosity and his desire to explore the language of cinema have resulted in his making a muddle of the rendering of the urban madness that is the only credible and thematically interesting context for Travis's acts of madness. Without that context, *Taxi Driver* must be regarded as a study in a madman's perceptions of his environment, something that Scorsese has not rendered with sufficient consistency or rigor; or Travis's acts of madness must be understood as motivated by Betsy's rejection of him, a possibility that would reduce *Taxi Driver* to a rather trivial and implausible story about the extreme consequences of unrequited love.

At this point in the film, however, it is not too late for Scorsese to make of *Taxi Driver* the film it seems to have the potential to be. Indeed, the sequence immediately following the second Belmore Cafeteria sequence contains two of the best—from the standpoint of thematic development—shots in the film. Travis is again driving through one of the meaner neighborhoods of New York; and the camera for a while tracks with him, rendering the scene from his point of view. When, however, Travis spots Iris, the young hooker, crossing a street, Scorsese unmistakably departs from Travis's point of view. In a truly masterful panning movement, Scorsese's camera follows Iris across a stretch of urban landscape that emerges in all of its compelling sordidness. Scorsese then restores Travis's point of view as the camera tracks with Iris. Here is a moment that is in the true spirit of *Rear Window*: the objective reality that is interacting with the unstable protagonist is first established, and then the all-important subjective point of view of the protagonist is reasserted.

Unfortunately, Scorsese does not fulfill the promise of this brief segment. He returns instead to a concentration on the element of his film's pattern that has already been somewhat overdeveloped: the troubled psyche and disturbing behavior of Travis Bickle.

After another scene showing Travis writing in his journal, he is seen buying a veritable arsenal of firearms from a dealer who brings his inventory to Travis's room. The *Caligari*-like subjective point of view is again suspended as Scorsese's camera observes Travis from either an overhead or a detached middle-distance position.

Travis is next seen doing push-ups to get in shape for the still unknown task he is preparing to perform. We see him practicing with various guns, first at a target range, later in his room. Scorsese's fondness for the visually daring gets somewhat out of hand at this point as he composes shots of Travis manipulating guns in front of a mirror, shots that suggest Travis's real aim is to kill himself. Scorsese's accomplished play with mirror reflections (always an irresistible challenge to directors of the pure cinema school) is impressive; but it is inorganic, for the idea that Travis is essentially suicidal has not yet been previously suggested and will not be subsequently developed. The mirror shots are apt illustrations of the filmmaking of a director who has missed the organic lesson of Hitchcock's work and has instead fallen into the Hitchcockian fallacy of positing directorial virtuosity as the ultimate goal of film direction.

It becomes clear that Travis plans an assassination attempt on Pallantine; the rather trite idea that Travis is motivated by anger at Betsy's rejection of him is thus reinforced. In an amusing five-minute scene, Travis goes to a Pallantine rally, where he engages a Secret Service agent in conversation.

From the rally, Travis returns to his room for a lengthy sequence in which Scorsese displays his appreciation for the supple language of cinema but, in the process, sows thematic confusion.

The sequence begins with a medium shot featuring Travis's arm extending into the center of the frame; he is rather playfully twirling a handgun. His upper torso and arm and the handgun are visible in a mirror reflection in the background of the frame. There is a cut to a medium shot of his reflection, a choice that seems to indicate Scorsese's desire to distance what we are seeing from the zone of realism. Without a cut, Scorsese then pans to a medium shot of Travis himself; he is talking to his reflection in the mirror.

After a series of medium shots of Travis practicing his draw, Scorsese cuts to a more distant shot that reveals more of Travis's room, which features Pallantine campaign posters mounted on a wall. Scorsese again undermines the potential realism of the sequence by using two dissolves, one that places Travis in a close, spatial relationship with the Pallantine posters, and a second one that reprises the same shot of Travis but that eliminates the posters. The total effect is disorienting: the point of view is seemingly objective, yet we have little sense of a realistic rendering of an event.

Scorsese further undermines our confidence in the reality of the camera's observations through a bold departure from aural-visual verisimilitude. After the second dissolve, a passage of Travis's narration on the soundtrack is immediately repeated after it is initially spoken; his movement within the shot is similarly reprised immediately after its initial execution. The effect is akin to that of a stuck record, an effect that rather severely reduces the realistic connotations of the shot.

Scorsese has not yet finished with his play on real and unreal. Immediately after the highly unrealistic stuck record shot, he tilts back toward realism by cutting to a shot that repeats the film's most firmly established realistic motif: an overhead shot of Travis lying on his bed amid the utterly realistic decor of his depressing room. This final shot makes of the sequence (which, it should be noted, is distinguished by more superb work from Robert DeNiro) an incoherent passage, an interlude that may be taken realistically or as another instance of the seemingly objective camera in effect subversively conveying the highly subjective point of view of the film's protagonist. The sequence is thus a clear-cut instance in which Scorsese has used his assured command of the modalities of film direction in an inorganic fashion.

The next two scenes, taken together, convey the pattern that Scorsese should have consistently maintained throughout the film. In the first, Travis, while shopping in a convincingly seedy grocery store in a New York barrio, thwarts an attempted holdup by fatally shooting the would-be thief; Scorsese concludes the scene with a chilling, powerful overhead shot of the store owner bludgeoning the lifeless body of the thief. This vignette of the everyday horror of New York City is followed by a scene in which Travis is seen watching television (the program he is watching is "American Bandstand") in his room. The camera tracks from a medium shot of Travis to a close-up of the hazy image on the television screen, then tracks from the shot of the television image to a close-up of Travis. Here is the pattern *Taxi Driver* requires to bring out its deeper theme: a brutally realistic rendering of the madness of New York City balanced against an appropriately subjective rendering of the twisted interior world of Travis Bickle.

From the shot of Travis watching "American Bandstand," there is a cut to the first of a series of four low-angle shots of skyscrapers with Pallantine addressing a rally through a loudspeaker as a voice-over. Travis's trial run of his plan to assassinate Pallantine has begun.

The camera cranes down on the windshield and hood of Travis's taxi. The craning movement stops for a medium shot of Travis, who is seen from behind the windshield of the taxi; he is at the right of the frame, with the left given over to the glare of the sun reflected on the windshield. The voice-over of Pallantine's speech gives way to the voice of Travis, who is composing a letter to his parents in his head.

The letter Travis is composing continues as an aural overlap in the next shot, in which the camera tracks through the crowd at the rally to Pallantine (and Betsy) on the podium. The effect of continuing the voice-over of the letter is to raise doubts about the reality of what is happening, to suggest that this incident is something Travis is fashioning in his mind, as unreal as the life he is creating for himself in the letter he is composing.

A medium shot of a policeman telling Travis to move his illegally parked cab is followed by a tracking shot of Travis driving away. There is then a cut to a shot in which the camera tracks in on Travis, now back in his room. The letter he is composing continues as a voice-over. The voice-over of the letter has thus bracketed the trial run of Travis's plan to kill Pallantine, raising anew questions about the objective reality of the trial run. The possibility that the whole incident may have occurred only in Travis's mind is strengthened by a close-up of Travis that Scorsese composes, in which Travis's face is partially obscured by the card on which he has written the letter we have heard on the soundtrack. That possibility is even further strengthened by the conclusion of the sequence, in which Travis kicks over the television set he is watching, which then explodes. This very fluent sequence, in which Scorsese has made excellent use of both the aural and visual properties of film, is thus harmfully ambiguous: it is not at all clear if Travis has actually made a trial run of an assassination plot or if what we have seen is the fantasy of a troubled mind, as removed from reality as the fantasy life Travis describes in his letter and the escapist programs he watches on television.

There follows a fourteen-minute sequence in which Travis spends time with Iris, the young prostitute he has seen on two previous occasions. The sequence is generally excellent, distinguished by the convincing rendering of the sordid milieu in which Iris functions and by the sensitive acting of Jodie Foster and Robert DeNiro.

Scorsese first establishes the reality of Iris, a significant achievement in film in which the reality of what is seen has become questionable. There is first an establishing shot of a ghetto street. The camera initially reflects Travis's point of view from inside his taxi. Scorsese then, as he did in the last sequence involving Iris, suspends Travis's point of view as the camera pans right and then left with Iris as she makes her way through the ghetto streets. Travis's point of view remains suspended in the next shot, in which he, Iris, and her hooker friend are all seen walking toward the camera. Iris and her friend exit the frame, and Travis then talks business with Iris's pimp, Sport.

Scorsese next establishes the reality of Iris's life and Travis's efforts to enter it. There is a medium shot of a rotting tenement building seen from the opposite side of the street; Travis and Iris can be seen standing in front of the building. The camera tilts up on the building to provide a more detailed look at its utter ugliness. There is then a cut to a shot in which the camera tracks behind Iris and Travis as they walk down an exceedingly dark corridor that almost reeks of decay. The tracking continues for a low-angle shot of a small flight of stairs; Iris and Travis have paused at the bottom of the stairs to deal with Iris's timekeeper, a grotesque character who seems at home in the darkness of the corridor. There is then a cut to an overhead shot that reflects the point of view of Iris, who has climbed the stairs and has paused to look back at Travis, who is still dealing with the sleazy timekeeper. Travis then begins to move toward the camera as he starts up the short flight of stairs.

In an excellent series of shots, Scorsese aptly conveys the difficulty Travis has in making real contact with another person, even Iris, to whom he is strongly attracted. The camera tracks behind Iris as she enters her apartment through beaded curtains hung near the door. There is a cut, and now the tracking is reversed as the camera moves from inside the apartment toward Travis, who is standing at the entrance on the other side of the curtains. There is a cut, and the tracking movement is again reversed as the camera moves toward Iris inside the apartment. This is followed by another cut to a shot in which the camera is once again moving from inside the apartment toward Travis, still standing behind the beaded curtains.

There is a cut to a shot of Travis and Iris, at last together inside the apartment. In a series of medium shots that feature the tawdry seediness of the decor of Iris's apartment, Travis tries to persuade a dubious Iris to abandon Sport and change her life.

After a shot outside the apartment that again conveys the dark reality of the building's corridor and the sleazy reality of Iris's timekeeper, there is a four-minute scene of Iris and Travis in a cheap coffee shop. Travis continues to persuade Iris to give up her way of life, offering to finance an attempt at a new life. Iris remains skeptical and noncommital.

The excellence of this sequence is marred by its concluding scene. The problem is a now familiar one: Scorsese's tendency to create virtuoso displays of dubious thematic significance. In this case it is a scene in which Iris and Sport, in a room filled with purple shadows and illuminated by pink lighting, dance slowly to a lushly romantic song Sport has put on the stereo. Sccorsese times his cuts to the rhythm of the music, and he keeps his camera close in on the shadowy presences of Iris and Sport. The scene does not actually negate the meaning of the sequence it concludes, but its romanticism seems merely and pointlessly weird, a perverse undercutting of the involving realism of the rest of the sequence.

Taxi Driver now takes what in my view are two cruciallly wrong turns, the first attributable to Paul Schrader's screenplay, the second to Scorsese's commitment to the Hitchcockian fallacy.

Travis attempts to assassinate Pallantine at another political rally. Thwarted by the vigilance of Secret Service agents, he vents his murderous rage on Sport and others who, in his mind, are responsible for Iris's degradation. Schrader's insistence on the reassertion of the Pallantine factors muddies the film's waters: it promotes the facile idea that Travis's acts of madness are importantly related to his brief encounter with Betsy; and it injects a political element that, as was the case in Robert Altman's *Nashville*, is at best trite, at worst perversely misleading.

Scorsese concludes the Pallantine sequence with a magnificent, sustained crane shot of Travis fleeing the Secret Service agents through the crowds attending the rally and the traffic in the immediate vicinity. This is followed by a cut to a shot of Travis back in his room.

After the brief scene in Travis's room, the bloody rampage that is the climax of the film begins. The meaning of this sequence — and therefore of the film itself — is fatally undermined by Scorsese's evident commitment to the idea that the primary goal of film direction is the exploitation of the unique expressive power of film. Acting on that premise, Scorsese, as he has done before in *Taxi Driver*, upsets the crucial balance between credibility and expression, creating a climactic sequence whose ambiguity is annoying rather than suggestive.

Scorsese devotes eight minutes to the climactic sequence. It begins with the camera tracking left with a man who approaches Sport, who is standing on the stoop of the run-down building where the first Travis-Sport scene took place. The man pays Sport and then exits the frame; the camera holds on a medium shot of Sport standing on the stoop.

There is a cut to a medium shot of Travis at the wheel of his taxi, a shot that is reprised after a cut to a middle-distance view of Travis's taxi that features the unnaturalistic neon pink coloration that Scorsese has occasionally used in the film's driving sequences. This color effect has previously been used to suggest that Travis's point of view is coloring the passages of the film in which it appears, a suggestion that Scorsese has had some difficulty controlling in a thematically coherent, organic manner.

In a lengthy, uncut shot, (1) Travis's taxi is seen moving toward the camera; (2) the camera tracks right with Travis as he approaches Sport on his stoop; (3) a stationary camera observes Travis shoot Sport after a sustained dialogue exchange; (4) the camera tracks left with Travis as he walks away from Sport, who is seriously wounded; (5) Travis moves to the background of the frame and sits down on another stoop; (6) the camera holds for a sustained shot of Travis as he sits in near-total darkness. During the course of this shot, the color scheme is pointedly altered. When Travis's taxi first pulls into the frame, the shot has the drained, washed-out look that we have seen before; later in the shot, the hue is changed to a muted pink-and-green glow, which interacts with the darkness of the unilluminated street and recalls the lighting of the second Belmore Cafeteria sequence. Scorsese's undisguised play with unnaturalistic lighting effects, added to the intense concentration on a quiescent Travis that concludes the shot, plants the first suggestion of the possibility that the events of the sequence may only be projections of Travis's disturbed imagination, a possibility that makes a muddle of the climactic sequence.

Scorsese's apparent commitment to the pursuit of virtuosity at all costs is in evidence in the next segment of the sequence, and it continues to create thematic confusion. There is a cut to a low-angle shot of Travis climbing the exterior steps of the building where Iris lives and works. There is then a cut to a shot in which the camera tracks behind Travis as he walks down the building's first-floor corridor, which is initially very dark, then an unnaturalistic pink. Iris's timekeeper then approaches the camera. There is a cut to a medium shot of him as Travis shoots him point-blank; the color of this shot is a bold pink. After a cut to a medium shot of Travis's blood-splattered face (the color scheme has now reverted to the drained, washed-out hue), there is a series of three shots in which

Scorsese, apparently interested in creating abstract, geometric patterns with the camera, shows the corridor and its stairways from various angles. The effect of this rather cubist series is to further remove the sequence from the realm of realism.

After a brief shot of Iris in her room, there is a series of shots of Travis shooting the remarkably hard-to-kill timekeeper. Then Travis himself is shot in the neck. As he turns to face the camera, the camera zooms back from him. There is then a zoom in on Sport (who fired the bullet that has struck Travis) shooting at Travis, followed by a reverse-zoom on Travis firing at Sport. Scorsese's choreographed use of the zoom seems inorganic, a display of virtuosity that distances us from the brutal reality of what is happening.

Sport finally dies, but the apparently indestructible timekeeper continues his pursuit of Travis. Scorsese devotes a series of shots to the duel of Travis and the timekeeper; the shots are notable for their continued emphasis on the geometric beauty of the corridor and the stairways and for the fact that Scorsese, as he did in the second Belmore Cafeteria sequence, has given Travis his personal lighting scheme (the familiar neon pink) that sets him apart from his setting in the shots devoted to him.

As Travis continues his prolonged struggle with the timekeeper, a customer emerges from Iris's apartment and shoots Travis. Scorsese devotes a shot to a gun falling from Travis's hand, another shot to the gun rolling down stairs, a third (an overhead shot) to Travis falling to the floor from the impact of the bullet. The effect of this series of shots is, again, somewhat balletic; and the result is, again, a distancing of the events depicted in this segment of the sequence from the zone of realism where they properly belong.

Travis recovers enough to shoot Iris's customer, and there is an overhead shot of the customer's body falling through the beaded curtains of Iris's apartment.

There is a cut to a medium shot of Travis's blood-covered face and upper torso; the shot features the drained, washed-out color scheme that has been inconsistently associated with Travis. The camera tilts up as Travis rises and then walks toward the stationary camera to create an extreme close-up of his bloody face. There is a cut, and now the camera is tracking into Iris's apartment with Travis and the timekeeper, both of whom seem near death. They fall to the floor of the apartment, locked in a strange symbiotic embrace. Scorsese then intercuts shots of Travis and the timekeeper struggling with shots of Iris screaming.

Scorsese concludes the sequence in a burst of unabashed virtuosity. There is first a sustained shot of Iris that features as a light source a number of small votive candles and in which all sound has been eliminated from the soundtrack save that of blood dripping from Travis's body (Travis is now off-camera; the timekeeper has finally expired). This is followed by a cut to a sustained medium shot of Travis kneeling beside the couch in Iris's apartment. He rises and sits down on the couch; and Scorsese, without a cut, composes another medium shot that is sustained for a considerable time. In this composition, Travis is at the center of the frame, staring at the ceiling; Iris is at the right, her head resting on an arm of the couch, crying. There is then a cut to a shot of pistols extending from the left of the frame. This is followed by a shot in which the back of a policeman is seen in the foreground of the frame, Travis and Iris in the background. A medium shot dominated by Travis's bloody hand follows. The camera tilts up with Travis's hand to a close-up of him as he mockingly shoots himself in the temple with his hand, which is cocked like a pistol. There is then a sustained shot of Travis looking up at the ceiling. Then, in what is perhaps the single most outrageous example of inorganic virtuosity in *Taxi Driver*, Scorsese cuts to an overhead shot in which the camera cranes over the whole bloody tableau in Iris's apartment; this shot, with its unmistakable sense of geometric abstraction, completes the undermining of a sense of this sequence as a realistic rendering of Travis's crazed response to the unrelieved sordidness in which he functions.

Scorsese, as if recognizing that having gone this far into mere virtuosity, he may as well go all the way, concludes the sequence with a series of seven dissolves, the first six of which create a series of perversely beautiful still lifes as the camera observes the blood stains, abandoned pistols, and corpses that are the evidence of Travis's perhaps imagined rampage. The last dissolve is to a crane shot, in slow motion, of police and onlookers gathered outside Iris's building.

The excessive directorial style exemplified in the climactic sequence of *Taxi Driver* is frequently described as "operatic," a nebulous term that presumably connotes an expansive demonstration of the expressive power of film that is unrestrained by considerations of the requirements of thematic coherence. The epilogue of *Taxi Driver* could probably be described as "poetic," a designation for the use of the modalities of cinematic communication to create mood rather than meaning. In the epilogue, Scorsese, relying on a voice-over of a letter from Iris's parents to Travis and panning shots of newspaper clippings tacked to a wall, establishes that Travis's bloody rampage, which apparently (though not surely) actually took place, has been interpreted by the media and the public as a heroic act to save a young girl from a life of unspeakable degradation. The film concludes with Travis, now apparently recovered from his wounds (if, that is, he ever had any), giving a ride to Betsy, who is inclined to be more friendly to Travis now that he has attained folk-hero status. Travis, however, perhaps projecting another fantasy, rebuffs Betsy's overtures; and *Taxi Driver* concludes with shots of the neon-lit streets of New York City as seen from the distorting perspective of Travis Bickle's taxi.

Taxi Driver and *Carrie*, considered together, stand as a seminal event of the New Hollywood era. The surprising box office success of the former suggested that "challenging" subject matter could be sold to the public so long as it was subordinated to a display of eye-catching directorial virtuosity, while the surprising critical success of the latter legitimized (for a time, anyway) the idea that pure cinema could be found in films in which a director's virtuosity transformed trash into trash. Thus were the two strains of the Hitchcockian fallacy — Scorsese's high-brow virtuosity, DePalma's low-brow virtuosity — established in the New Hollywood.

The Scorsese strain can be seen in his own *New York, New York* (1977), in Michael Cimino's *The Deer Hunter* (1978), in UCLA Film School graduate Richard Rush's *The Stunt Man* (1979), in Ridley Scott's *Blade Runner* (1982), and in two films from the irrepressible Francis Coppola, *One from the Heart* (1982) and *Rumblefish* (1983). DePalma extended the pulpy virtuosity of *Carrie* into *The Fury* (1978), *Dressed to Kill* (1980), and the absurdly operatic *Scarface* (1983). The DePalma train of the Hitchcockian fallacy also pervaded Philip Kaufman's *Invasion of the Body Snatchers* (1978), Irvin Kershner's *Eyes of Laura Mars* (1978), USC Film School graduate John Carpenter's *Halloween* (1978), and the eclectic Paul Scrader's *Cat People* (1982).

All of these films asked audiences (who, of course, have been the big losers of the New Hollywood era) to sacrifice meaning and intelligent involvement in exchange for self-contained exercises that in the final analysis have no need of audiences; and they asked increasingly resistant critics to defend what were, at bottom, indefensible examples of inorganic filmmaking. The perversion of the legacy of Alfred Hitchcock attained a symmetrical perfection: his New Hollywood successors made films that sacrificed *both* components of the Hitchcockian synthesis, the accessibility of popular entertainment and the artistry of organic direction.

Notes

1. David Kehr, "Hitch's Riddle," *Film Comment*, June 1984, p. 9.
2. Ibid.
3. Wood, *Hitchcock's Films,* pp. 15, 19.
4. Perkins, *Film as Film*, pp. 122–23.

5

The Hawksian Fallacy

M*A*S*H (1970)
Jaws (1975)
Raiders of the Lost Ark (1981)

That no contemporary American film can be said to be in the tradition of Howard Hawks is perhaps the most revealing measure of the distance separating the New Hollywood from the Old; for, along with that of George Cukor, the Hawksian canon is the quintessential expression of the art of the Old Hollywood, an art "that has largely disappeared: to find anything comparable we have to go back to the Elizabethan drama. No other art form has been able to speak to all social and intellectual levels simultaneously and show a comparable achievement."[1]

The precise nature of Hawks's genius has proved remarkably resistant to critical analysis, but a handful of critics have met the challenge admirably. In his seminal essay on Hawks, Jacques Rivette identifies two defining features of the Hawksian genius:

> Hawks's *oeuvre* is equally divided between comedies and dramas—a remarkable ambivalence. More remarkable still is his frequent fusing of the two elements so that each, rather than damaging the other, seems to underscore their reciprocal relation: the one sharpens the other.... Hawks epitomizes the highest qualities of the American cinema: he is the only American director who knows how to draw a *moral*. His marvelous blend of action and morality is probably the secret of his genius.[2]

In his full-length study of Hawks, Gerald Mast locates Hawks's genius in his remarkable success at accomplishing "the task that entertaining stories are supposed to accomplish in our democratic culture: not to exclude all except the specially equipped but to include as many as possible."[3] Mast, echoing Rivette, also emphasizes Hawks's success in conveying on film "such essential human issues as the moral and emotional dynamics of vocational and personal relationships, the existential defiance of mortality when mortality is inevitable and unavoidable, and the expressing of feelings by actions rather than talk."[4]

It is perhaps unreasonable to search for Hawks's achievement of embedding comedy in drama and drama in comedy in the work of other directors. It does not, however, seem unreasonable to expect to find at least traces in other directors' films of the other great Hawksian achievement, the creation of expansive, accessible narratives that are at once entertainments and explorations of human responses to timeless elements of the human condition. That such traces are barely discernible in contemporary American films is one of the most damning facts about the New Hollywood: while a number of New Hollywood directors and writers have repeatedly professed admiration for the work of the Old Hollywood masters, the legacy of one of the quintessential masters, Howard Hawks, has been either ignored or dishonored in the New Hollywood.

It is not quite accurate to speak of the Hawksian fallacy when one considers the comedy films of the New Hollywood, for the Hawksian achievement in film comedy has been more ignored than fallaciously interpreted by the directors of the New Hollywood era. Comedy in the New Hollywood has been largely a matter of television-fallacy products like *Bananas* and the *Animal House* variations, the sometimes labored parodies of Mel Brooks, and the rather claustrophobic literary-fallacy works of Woody Allen's middle period. An occasional gem like Paul Mazursky's *An Unmarried Woman* (1978) has done little to improve the generally dismal state of contemporary film comedy.

Robert Altman's *M*A*S*H* is perhaps the closest the New Hollywood has come to Hawksian comedy. That it is not all that close increases one's respect for Hawks's achievement and underlines Altman's status as perhaps the most critically overrated (at least through the mid-seventies) director of the New Hollywood era.

M*A*S*H lacks the thematic richness of *Bringing Up Baby, Ball of Fire* and *Monkey Business*, with their relatively subtle themes of maturity and infantilism, responsibility and spontaneity; or of *His Girl Friday* and *I Was a Male War Bride*, with their satirical variations on established sex roles and their comic consideration of marriage as a dynamic partnership. *M*A*S*H*, however, while failing to meet such high Hawksian thematic standards, might nevertheless have succeeded as an effective film comedy had it not been for the considerable problem of its director's underlying attitude toward his material.

Robin Wood has provided an indirect insight into the attitudinal problem that undermines *M*A*S*H*. Writing of Hawks, Wood has observed that "there is nothing glib or sentimental about [his] treatment of his characters, but if he can possibly steer them toward salvation, he does. This spirit of generosity, the most creative human characteristic, vivifies all his best films."[5] Altman's attitude toward his characters is notably lacking in a spirit of generosity, and his treatment of them is at once insufferably glib and sentimental in an archly hip way. His film does not convey a sense of his characters moving toward anything, let alone salvation: the favored ones are saved from the beginning, and those out of favor remain so at the end.

Thus, while *M*A*S*H* has a number of apparent affinities with Hawksian comedy — the sense of a group in an absurd situation, screwball responses to realistic events, sharp comic dialogue — it fails as film comedy because of its lack of the deeper comic attributes that have been particularly associated with Hawksian comedy.

M*A*S*H opens with a series of helicopter and zoom shots that depict the M*A*S*H (Mobile Army Surgical Hospital) unit in action as it provides on-the-spot medical treatment to wounded soldiers strewn over a rocky stretch of what we soon learn is a Korean landscape.

From the shots of action in the field there is a cut to a medium shot prominently featuring a sign reading "Officer's Latrine." Captain Hawkeye Pierce (Donald Sutherland) enters the frame and walks toward the camera; in the background of the frame, out-of-focus hats of Korean peasant women can be seen. The camera moves left, eliminating Hawkeye from the frame. Jingoistic quotations from Generals MacArthur and Eisenhower about the Korean War are superimposed on the image. Hawkeye then reenters the frame; as he approaches the foreground, the camera tilts up on him, at the same time bringing the peasant women into focus.

This shot is about as far as one can get from what Jacques Rivette has called the "basic honesty" that characterizes Hawks's mise-en-scène.[6] In particular, Altman's decisions as to what to enclose in and what to exclude from the frame suffer in comparison to Hawks's framing decisions. It is next to impossible to infer anything but rather glib sarcasm from the visual data included in this shot: no clear relationship is established between Hawkeye and the peasant women, and the shot is virtually devoid of inanimate objects that might be a source of meaning. Altman's seeming indifference to what he includes in his compositions becomes a major weakness in *M*A*S*H*; for, as Hawks well understood, one of the primary sources of true film comedy is the establishment and exploitation of the tension between the photographic objects, human and inanimate, that are forced to interact within the boundaries of the frame.

Altman soon reveals his failure to learn another basic lesson of film comedy that Hawks never failed to apply. After an effective crane shot of the military compound Hawkeye has been walking through, Altman devotes a series of shots to Hawkeye preparing his duffel bag while talking to a rather officious soldier whom he encounters standing near a jeep. The problem here is Donald Sutherland seems totally devoid of a comic sensibility, and Altman does not help to compensate for the deficiency. Altman offers little evidence of having absorbed the great Bergsonian insight, demonstrated by the silent comic geniuses as well as by Hawks, that the human form and human gestures, when emphasized and framed to bring out their inherently comic qualities, are a primary source of benign laughter in film. Altman permits or encourages Sutherland to engage in a series of facial expressions that were presumably intended to be funny but that seem only annoying smug. This series of shots featuring Hawkeye is an unfortunately accurate portent of what is to come in *M*A*S*H*, a film in which smugness frequently stands in for true humor. Altman, who apparently lacked Hawks's unerring instinct for casting, also lacked his ability to make human gestures a source of satisfying, expansive comedy.

Gestures reveal attitude, and it is Altman's failure to find and convey an appealing comic attitude in his characters that is one of the deepest failures in *M*A*S*H*. That failure is illustrated in the next shot, which begins as a close-up of Hawkeye's hands as he fastens his duffel bag. There is a reverse zoom to show a truck carrying Captain Duke Forest (Tom Skerritt) pulling into the background of the frame. Hawkeye mistakes Duke for a private assigned to chauffeur him to M*A*S*H headquarters, and Duke plays along with the mistake. In their dialogue exchange beside the jeep, Hawkeye and Duke both assume the languid, disengaged posture that typifies the "laid-back" tone of the film. Their bodies and gestures do not convey the misplaced, obsessive, ultimately hilarious *seriousness* that is one of the bases of brilliant comic characterizations. Neither Duke nor Hawkeye ever conveys the comic obsessiveness of, for example, Susan Vance for her leopard or David Huxley for his intercostal clavicle in *Bringing Up Baby*, or Walter Burns for scooping his rivals in *His Girl Friday*, of Barnaby Fulton for discovering a chemical fountain of youth in *Monkey Business*. Hawks understood that a character's utter seriousness,[7] conveyed through the body language of the actor playing the character, could be a rich source of deeply satisfying laughter; Altman ignores this insight in *M*A*S*H*, directing his actors to convey not maniacal seriousness but glib indifference. The laid-back style might be quite effective in college dormitories; but it makes for slack, overly verbal humor in film, which seems to require the comic tension growing out of single-minded, Keatonesque seriousness.

Duke and Hawkeye drive off in a jeep toward the M*A*S*H headquarters. Altman intercuts helicopter shots of the jeep making its way through the Korean countryside with shots of soldiers and MP's back at the supply base engaging in broad physical comedy as they react with comic ineffectiveness to Hawkeye's unauthorized use of the jeep.

Altman's initially fussy mise-en-scène undermines the effectiveness of the next sequence, in which Hawkeye and Duke (who has revealed his true rank and status) are seen in the officers' mess of the M*A*S*H compound. The camera tracks into the mess with Duke and then tilts down (effectively suggesting the leeringly condescending attitude of both Duke and Hawkeye) on the well-endowed Lieutenant Dish (Jo Ann Pflug). Altman then, for some reason, repositions his camera to a shot of Duke's lower torso, as he passes through the cafeteria line. The camera then tilts up on a medium shot of the unit commander, Colonel Blake (Roger Bowen), who has taken notice of the two strangers in the mess. The camera next tracks left with Hawkeye and Duke as they sit down at a table with Lieutenant Dish. Altman then uses a series of close-ups and medium shots of Hawkeye, Duke, Dish and Colonel Blake; the fragmentation that results means that Altman, who never had Hawkeye and Duke together in the frame and never conveys an overall sense of the mess tent, misses the chance to establish the potentially promising comic interaction between Hawkeye and Duke and the other officers of the unit.

That missed opportunity is partially compensated for in the remainder of the sequence. Altman composes shots in which various members of the unit introduce themselves to Hawkeye and Duke, whose upright positions are contrasted to the outstretched arms, arched backs and disembodied hands of the other officers who are crowded into the frame.

The united apartness of Hawkeye and Duke is emphasized in the next sequence, but Altman exploits their apartness for rather sour humor. Hawkeye and Duke discover that they are to share a tent with Major Burns (Robert Duvall), a humorless, unctuous officer whom they first encounter giving instruction in Christianity to a Korean boy. Altman uses a series of shots to contrast the relaxed, disengaged postures of Hawkeye and Duke with the rigid, pedagogical stance of Burns. Later, when Hawkeye and Duke return to their tent to find Burns at prayer, Altman uses alternating close-ups of the three of them to contrast the contemptuous expressions on the faces of Hawkeye and Duke with the earnestness of Major Burns. When Hawkeye and Duke start to sing a mocking rendition of "Onward, Christian Soldiers," the camera leaves the tent to show that other officers and nurses passing nearby have picked up the song and have joined in the mockery of Burns. Hawkeye and Duke, so recently outsiders, have apparently won over the entire unit to their rather cruel kind of humor. Altman underlines the nasty tone of this sequence by concluding it with a close-up of Burns's eyes, a shot that emphasizes the isolation of the man.

Between the two encounters with Burns, Altman introduces the most problematic strain of the film. Hawkeye and Duke are seen in the unit's surgery tent, operating on wounded soldiers. The camera first tracks left, pausing to observe the operation Duke is performing; it then resumes tracking left and pauses to observe the operation Hawkeye is engaged in. The tracking shot is followed by a series of rather graphic shots of the operations. The problem here is, of course, the introduction into an essentially comic film of such a serious theme as that of saving the lives of grotesquely wounded soldiers. The problem is compounded by the continuing insistence, throughout the film, on the cynically glib attitude of Hawkeye and Duke: Altman wants us to believe that these chronically laid-back, disengaged men are dedicated surgeons; but it is not easy to reconcile the two images, particularly when the hip-cynical patter the two of them indulge in while performing operations is taken into account. Altman, instead of following the Hawksian route of finding humor *in* his characters' seriousness, follows the route of establishing two tracks for the film, with his characters' unrelieved glibness about everything else running alongside their ostensible seriousness about surgery. It is a risky strategy, and Altman does not quite bring it off in *M*A*S*H*.

After a second operating scene that features the ineffectual camp spiritual adviser, Father Mulcahy (Rene Auberjonois), the third principal character of the film is introduced. Trapper John McIntyre (Elliott Gould), a well-known surgeon in civilian life, is first seen in a sequence set in Hawkeye and Duke's tent, to which Trapper John has been assigned. Altman uses a series of medium shots that isolate the three men throughout most of the sequence so a sense of their group solidarity is not conveyed through framing. Altman's compositions, however, emphasize the laid-back posture of each of the men, so Trapper John's posture identifies him as an ally of Hawkeye and Duke. It is an altogether smug little group, lacking the comic internal tension of, say, Susan and David in *Bringing Up Baby*; and there is no significant external tension, since the hapless Major Burns is hardly a serious source of comic opposition, and the rest of the unit has apparently happily adopted the group's too-cool-to-be-bothered style.

M*A*S*H definitely needs a worthy comic foil for its trio of glib protagonists, and in the next sequence she appears. Her name is Major Margaret Houlihan (Sally Kellerman), and her arrival at M*A*S*H headquarters occasions one of the most effective sequences in the film.

The sequences begins with a medium shot of Blake, his indispensable assistant Radar (Gary Burghoff), and others standing in front of a jeep. A helicopter is in the background of the frame, and the camera tracks with it as it lands. The camera zooms in on Major Houlihan as she emerges from the helicopter. Altman immediately establishes her character through her posture: she stands ramrod-straight, in an impeccably crisp uniform, as she salutes Blake and the other officers, who, stooping to avoid the rotating helicopter blades, come forward to greet her. As Houlihan and the others walk away from the helicopter and toward the camera, Altman's composition sets her utter verticality against the spinning blades (whose whirring drowns out the conversation between Houlihan and Blake) of the helicopter.

There follows a scene in which Trapper John becomes furious with Major Burns after the latter has blamed a hapless young soldier for the death of a patient. Trapper John is just about to assault Burns when Blake arrives to introduce Major Houlihan (who is to be in charge of the M*A*S*H unit's nursing staff) to the unit's surgical staff. In one of the film's funniest passages, Houlihan, whose military erectness is contrasted with the horizontals of the operating tables and the stooped postures of the surgeons performing operations, engages in militarily crisp "carry on" exchanges with doctors who are attempting to perform delicate operations in less than ideal conditions and do not have time for pleasantries. The establishment of Houlihan as a force opposed to Duke–Hawkeye–Trapper John is confirmed when she watches in horror as Trapper John physically attacks Major Burns.

There follows a brief scene in which Blake comes to the tent of Hawkeye, Duke and Trapper John to discuss his intention to name the latter Chief Surgeon. The scene is another instance of Altman's rather slack mise-en-scène and overactive montage, featuring a monotonous series of cuts among medium shots of the four men. Altman in this instance creates neither a sense of comic tension (by contrasting Blake to the three protagonists) nor a sense of comic unity (by creating unfragmented compositions in which all four men are united in the confining space of the tent).

M*A*S*H reaches another high point in the sequence that follows.

A hand-held camera and overlapping dialogue convey the easy conviviality of a party in the _M*A*S*H_ unit. Clockwise from the lower left, Tom Skerritt, Elliott Gould, Corey Fischer, Kim Atwood, Carl Gottlieb, _M*A*S*H_ (Twentieth Century–Fox, 1970).

Altman effectively uses a close-in, hand-held camera and his signature overlapping dialogue to convey the easy conviviality of a party celebrating Trapper John's promotion to Chief Surgeon. During the party, Radar and a couple of cohorts rig the tent of Major Houlihan to broadcast throughout the camp the audible portions of a surprisingly passionate tryst between her and Major Burns; as he does elsewhere in the film, Altman makes excellent comic use of the camp's loudspeaker in this sequence.

Then _M*A*S*H_ once again descends into its characteristic glib-cruel humor. Hawkeye cruelly knocks Burns and Houlihan (now known throughout the camp as Hot Lips) the day after their notorious lovemaking session. In one of the nastiest compositions in the film, Altman follows a shot in which the devastated Major Burns is seen being taken away in a straitjacket when a zoom in on Hawkeye and Trapper John enjoying the sight of Burns's humiliation. This composition is about as far removed from the spirit of generosity that animated Hawks's comedies and adventure dramas as one can imagine. Another instance of sour humor follows in a scene in which an announcement over the camp's loudspeaker regarding the dangers of marijuana is a voice-over in shots featuring Hawkeye engaged in a particularly bloody operation.

Another defining quality of Hawksian genius that one misses in Altman's film is Hawks's sense of the appropriate shape for a film, his instinct for what to select or omit, what to emphasize and what to treat lightly. That Altman lacks that instinct is clear from the next sequence of *M*A*S*H*, in which an inordinate thirteen minutes are devoted to a fake suicide and mock resurrection devised by Hawkeye, Trapper John and Duke to restore the self-confidence of Painless (John Schuck), the M*A*S*H unit's dentist. The idea of this passage is sound, and it might have worked had Altman rendered it in a more off-hand manner. As it stands, what Hawks would have treated as an anecdote becomes, in Altman's hands, a belabored, ill-paced sequence that is much funnier on paper than it is on film.

Altman recovers in the next sequence, which again involves Hot Lips.

The sequence begins with an extended emphasis on posture, which has attained the status of a major motif by this point in *M*A*S*H*. After a crane shot that reveals Duke, Hawkeye, Trapper John and other soldiers sunbathing on slabs of rock near a river, Altman devotes a total of ten medium shots to his three protagonists, who are stretched out under the sun and sipping martinis.

The emphasis on horizontality is continued with a variation in the next shot, in which the unit's nurses are seen marching single file toward the camp's shower facility in a composition that emphasizes the horizontal line created by the marching nurses. The camera tracks back from the women, past Trapper John and Hawkeye, who have returned from the river and are observing the march of the nurses, now lost from view as they march behind a tent. The camera cranes up as Hot Lips enters the shower in the background of the frame. This is followed by a zoom in on Hot Lips, now in the shower; only her head and legs are visible behind the shower door.

Horizontally gives way to circularity as the three protagonists and other members of the unit pull up chairs to form a semicircle in front of the shower. There is a series of cuts among shots of Hot Lips taking her shower and the circle of men seated in front of the shower facility. At a prearranged moment, the rigged-up shower walls falls away, exposing Hot Lips to the full view of the men who have gathered to see the show.

The conclusion of this sequence is its most effective section, since it lacks the leering quality of the rest of the sequence. Furious at the trick that has been played on her, Hot Lips wraps herself in a towel and marches off to protest to Colonel Blake. She arrives at the entrance of his quarters, and Altman composes a shot of her standing very tall and erect in the doorway. Then, in the film's best play on the contrast between rigid verticality and laid-back horizontality, Altman cuts to a shot of Blake, who is lying in bed with a voluptuous nurse. Cuts between Hot Lips's vertical rage and Blake's horizontal hedonism bring this sequence to a hilarious close.

The rest of *M*A*S*H* is quite unremarkable. A ten-minute sequence of Hawkeye and Trapper John in Tokyo, where they have been sent to operate on a dignatary's son, is merely a tiresome reiteration of their glib contempt for military rules and military personnel. Altman's imagination and sense of proportion continue to fail him when the action returns to M*A*S*H headquarters in Korea. He devotes an astonishing fifteen minutes to a most unorthodox football game between the M*A*S*H unit and the team from regional headquarters. The game was presumably intended as a celebration of group unity (even Hot Lips has been integrated into the group — she is the enthusiastic head cheerleader at the game); but Altman, continuing to indulge his fondness for zoom shots and jump cuts, does nothing to bring out the latent theme of joyous group solidarity.

The concluding minutes of *M*A*S*H* are curiously limp and ineffective, with Altman's inability or unwillingness to direct actors again weakening the impact of his film.

There is a shot in which the camera tracks with a jeepful of M*A*S*H personnel loudly celebrating their football victory. This is followed by a shot in which the camera tracks around a table at which the three protagonists and Hot Lips are playing poker.

There follows a shot of Hawkeye looking despondent as he sits outside his tent. He has received word that he and Duke are to be reassigned stateside. The camera tracks with Hawkeye into the operating tent. It then tracks back to include Duke in the frame. There is a cut to a medium shot of Duke as he received Hawkeye's news. This is followed by a cut to a shot of the fairytale homecoming Duke imagines he will receive.

After a medium shot of the three protagonists in their tent, the camera tracks in on Trapper John and Duke. This would seem to be a moment for seriocomic poignancy as the two friends say farewell, but Duke exits the frame before any such feeling is generated. Hawkeye then enters the frame for a medium shot with Trapper John; Altman, permitting Sutherland and Gould to engage in more of the meaningless smirking that has characterized their performances, again mishandles the opportunity to create a sense of comic poignancy. There is then a cut to a medium shot of Father Mulcahy blessing the jeep that carries Duke and Hawkeye from the camp. The film concludes with a zoom in on the camp loudspeaker, which proceeds to broadcast the film's cast of characters.

In fairness to Altman, it should be said that he quickly recovered from the (aesthetic) failure of *M*A*S*H*. In the year following, he directed the magnificent *McCabe and Mrs. Miller*. In 1973 he gave us two effective genre meditations, *The Long Goodbye* and *Thieves Like Us*. In 1974 he directed what is, along with *McCabe*, his best film: *California Split*, a seriocomic character study that very nearly justified the cycle of "buddy" films of the early seventies. Then, however, came *Nashville*, whose critical reception probably encouraged Altman's attraction to television-fallacy exercises in elaborate meaninglessness.

Steven Spielberg, until his apparent decision to become the Walt Disney of the computer age, was the New Hollywood director who had seemed most interested in working in the adventure drama tradition of Howard Hawks. Spielberg's exploitation of a genre Hawks raised to an art form is another indicator of the aesthetic decline that has befallen the American film during the New Hollywood era.

Spielberg's *Jaws* is, to a remarkable degree, an emblematic film of the New Hollywood era. It represents as well as any single film that inflation and exaggeration of subject matter and graphic representation that, initially conceived as part of a strategy for distinguishing theatrical films from television fare, have become one of the hallmarks of New Hollywood filmmaking.

In addition to its response-to-television qualities, *Jaws* also exhibits a quality which may at first glance seem merely sub-Hitchcockian but is in fact anti–Hitchcockian, a quality which has surfaced in a number of New Hollywood films and which came into its own the year after the release of *Jaws* with *Carrie*. The shark attacks in *Jaws*, in both the first and (as we shall see) second halves of the film, are excellent examples of what Robin Wood has perceptively identified as an essentially anti–Hitchcockian kind of suspense. Wood used a comparison between *From Russia with Love* and *North by Northwest* to clarify his insight, but *Jaws* might well be substituted for *Russia*:

> The suspense in the [*Russia*] sequence is meaningless: the [helicopter] attack is just an attack, it has no place in any significant development, there is no reason apart from plot — no *thematic* reason — for it to happen

In *Jaws* suspense is used to titillate and manipulate the audience rather than highlight character development and thematic concerns. Crowd scene, *Jaws* (Universal Pictures, 1975).

to Bond then or to happen in the way it does; it has no effect on his character. The suspense consists solely of the question: Will he get killed or not? . . . it has no effect beyond a purely physical titillation. In *North by Northwest* the crop-dusting sequence has essential relevance to the film's development. The complacent, self-confident Cary Grant character is shown here exposed. . . . The man who behaved earlier as if nobody mattered except himself is . . . reminded . . . of his personal insignificance in a vast, potentially inimical universe. The sequence marks a crucial stage in the evolution of the character and his relationships, and through that, of the themes of the whole film.[8]

The anti–Hitchcockian audience manipulation of the first half of *Jaws* need not detain us, beyond a summary of its plot developments. Amity Island, a resort that lives off the summer tourist trade, is suddenly plagued by a series of shark attacks just as the tourist season is about to begin. At first the mayor (Murray Hamilton) dismisses the threat, over-riding the efforts of the police chief, Martin Brody (Roy Scheider), to put Amity on a full-scale shark alert. Eventually, however, the shark attacks become too horrible and too frequent to ignore; and Brody, an ichthyologist, Roy Hooper (Richard Dreyfuss), and a gruff, experienced shark hunter, Quint (Robert Shaw) set off in Quint's boat to locate and destroy the Great White.

It is the shark hunt, which takes up approximately one-half of the total running time of *Jaws*, that is relevant to an examination of the fate suffered by the Hawksian adventure drama in the New Hollywood.

On paper, the shark hunt section of *Jaws* would appear to be comfortably within the Hawksian tradition: a small group of men, set apart in a self-contained world, are engaged in an activity that requires both courage and expertise. In execution (which is, of course, all that really counts), however, Spielberg's adventure shows little affinity with great Hawksian adventures like *The Dawn Patrol, Only Angels Have Wings, Red River, The Thing* and *Hatari!*

The first half of *Jaws* plays as a rather crude manipulation of audiences because Spielberg failed to follow the great Hitchcockian rule of creating an organic relation between suspense on the one hand and character development and thematic concerns on the other. Similarly, the second half of *Jaws* — the shark hunt — fails because Spielberg failed to follow the great Hawksian rule of creating an organic relation between action on the one hand and human relations and universal aspects of the human condition on the other. In the shark hunt section of his film, Spielberg fails to convey the Hawksian sense of men becoming more truly human in the process of engaging in a dangerous, perhaps foolhardy, adventure. As a consequence of that fundamental failure, the second half of *Jaws* plays as merely the rendering of the hunt by three men for a preposterously destructive sea monster.

The shark hunt begins with a prelude in which Brody, Hooper and Quint gather in the latter's house prior to setting off on their mission. Spielberg uses movement within shots and a fragmented montage to create an air of tension among the three men. Quint's status as the dominant figure in the group is given considerable emphasis. Spielberg composes a shot in which Quint is framed between the rungs of a ladder, and then follows with a low-angle shot of Quint standing on the upper level of his house. That suggestion of Quint's superior status is followed by a shot in which the camera, seemingly activated by Quint's movements, cranes down the ladder with him as he descends to the lower level. Later in the sequence, Quint's strength is emphasized in a close-up of his hand, which threatens to crush Hooper's hand and which obscures Brody, who is in the background of the frame. The cumulative effect of Spielberg's choices is to suggest that the tensions in the group will be resolved through

Quint's leadership. Spielberg has thus taken on two Hawksian tasks: to show, through the action of the ensuing shark hunt sequence, the resolution of the tensions; and to demonstrate the basis of Quint's superiority — the morality, to use Rivette's term, of Quint's leadership.

The party sets off in Quint's boat, the *Orca*. Spielberg dissolves from a shot of the boat leaving the harbor to an image of the blood-filled water superimposed on an image of the boat moving in the high seas.

The party makes its first contact with the shark in a five-minute sequence that features forty-five cuts. The rather extreme fragmentation of the sequence prevents the emergence of a sense of men engaged in demanding and complex work: we do not get the Hawksian pleasure of becoming involved in watching people "doing what they do, and love to do, and do well."[9] Moreover, Spielberg's compositions do not convey a sense of a group coming together under Quint's leadership. There are repeated low-angle shots of Quint that emphasize his stature, and Brody and Hooper each get a low-angle shot of their own; but in the entire sequence there is only one, briefly held, Hawksian eye-level shot of the group working together. After this sequence, it appears that Spielberg, if he is to touch on morality at all, will promote the un–Hawksian morality of the individual functioning autonomously, even in situations that require the unity of group effort.

The hunting party's second encounter with its prey is an exciting sequence, with Spielberg's frenetic montage aptly conveying the violence of the shark's attack on the ship and the crew's attempts to subdue the monster by shooting harpoons into it.

The sequence, however, is merely a roller-coaster experience: it is strong on visceral thrills, weak on conveying Hawksian themes of men engaged in work and men coming together in a union with moral implications. Spielberg's rejection of Hawks's relatively uncomplicated, unfragmented, "honest" mise-en-scène assures that the sense of men engaged in involving work will not be achieved. As for Hawks's grand theme of men coming together in a moral union, Spielberg at this point in the film seems to be continuing his movement toward an anti–Hawksian "charismatic man" theme. He begins the sequence with another low-angle shot of Quint. There is then a cut to a crane shot that concludes with a close-up of Quint; without a cut, Spielberg then moves his camera to create an overhead shot of first Hooper and then Brody, both of whom look predictably insignificant. As in the preceding sequence, Spielberg does not balance this emphasis on Quint with attention to the men functioning as a group. Spielberg's insistence on the towering superiority of Quint is beginning to become disturbing, particularly as the moral basis of Quint's superiority has still not been suggested through his actions. Hawks's essentially democratic theme of men forming a values-based, cohesive group is not yet in evidence: Spielberg seems to be insisting on the charismatic, essentially amoral superiority of Quint, the kind of unexamined superiority found in comic book heroes.

There is a lull after the second encounter with the shark. As night settles on the ocean, Quint, Brody and Hooper gather around a table in the ship's cabin for conversation and rounds of drinks. This would appear to be the moment when Spielberg will at last establish the solidarity of men who have formed a moral and vocational unit, something he has been unable to achieve *through* the men's actions, as Hawks typically did, but that he may be able to accomplish in an actionless interlude. Even this more limited achievement, however, eludes Spielberg. His compositions continue to fragment the group, even when the men engage in a quintessentially Hawksian sing-along. Spielberg devotes an inordinate number of shots to Hooper, suggesting that this moment has special significance for Hooper without establishing what the significance is. When Spielberg cuts to an exterior shot of the anchored boat, with the group sing-along continuing as a voice-over, one begins to suspect that this interlude is merely an element in Spielberg's rather manipulative suspense scheme, a lull during which the audience is supposed to be on alert for another shark attack. That suspicion is strengthened when shots of the cabin being jolted by the impact of the shark against the boat are intercut with medium shots of Quint relating to Brody and Hooper his experience on a naval vessel whose crew was subjected to a horrifying series of shark attacks. Quint's monologue initially appears to be the vehicle through which his moral authority will be established, but Spielberg's editing of the monologue eventually reduces it to just another device for the generation of suspense. One can not help but think that Hawks would have provided a respectful closure to Quint's monologue, perhaps fading from it to the commencement of the next attack. Spielberg's very different handling of the monologue indicates, again, that his primary interest in *Jaws* is audience manipulation, not the establishment of a Hawksian ethic of men in action.

The third encounter between men and shark is a ten-minute sequence featuring 120 cuts. Spielberg's montage serves to create a sustained sense of excitement, but his mise-en-scène again fails to convey a Hawksian sense of men coming together through the mediation of a task that requires genuine, deep-seated group solidarity.

Things initially look more promising in the lull that follows the third encounter. The sustained battle with the shark has left the group in a most precarious position: the engine of the ship has exploded, and the great force of the shark's assaults on the ship has left it shattered. Quint, veering toward an Ahab-like madness as a result of the unprecedented tenacity of this shark, is losing his charismatic leadership. From a medium shot of Brody on the upper deck of the ship, Spielberg pans down for a close-up of Hooper on the lower deck and follows with medium shots of an anguished Quint inside the ship's cabin. A cut to a shot of the shattered ship sitting very low in the water forcefully confirms the desperate plight of the group and promises a subsequent emphasis on the restoration of the group's spirit and effectiveness, possibly in a manner that carries the emotional-moral overtones that are a characteristic of Hawks's group adventures.

Unfortunately, that promise is not kept. Hooper insists on attempting to kill the shark by submerging himself in a specially designed, reputedly sharp-proof cage that will allow him to get close enough to the creature to inject it with deadly poisons. While Spielberg's mise-en-scène in the early part of the sequence gives Hawks-like attention to the details of a professional, Hooper, at work with his tools, it does not convey the sense of performing a difficult task. Indeed, Spielberg's compositions only suggest that the supremacy of the technocrat Hooper has been substituted for that of the charismatic Quint, a transfer that might be seen as a (surely unintended) reflection of the New Hollywood ideology, if there is such a thing. In any case, Spielberg's direction of the rest of the cage sequence again exposes his lack of interest in Hawksian issues of leadership and union. In an extended underwater segment, Spielberg emphasizes the kind of anti–Hitchcockian suspense that has prevailed throughout most of *Jaws*. His editing and compositions narrow the interest of the sequence to the single question: Will Hooper's cage withstand the shark's repeated assaults on it? This lowest form of suspense has no thematic implications, and it certainly does not connect with larger issues of group unity and moral courage that deepen the action sequences of Hawks's adventure dramas.

Hooper, his cage having provided only token protection against the shark's unheard-of force, is apparently killed by the indestructible monster. Spielberg then returns to the action on the ship. The shark attacks the already shattered ship; and, in an especially grisly scene, mutilates and then swallows Quint. Brody is now alone on what is left of the *Orca*. Spielberg now suggests that Brody has acquired the stature of Quint by devoting a series of low-angle shots, the angle that has heretofore been almost exclusively reserved for Quint, to Brody in the ship's crow's nest. The emergence and elevation of Brody seem arbitrary, for we have not for we have not seen him growing toward the prominence Spielberg now gives him; the sense, so satisfying in Hawks's adventures, of a man expressing his moral growth through his physical actions is notably absent in Spielberg's treatment of the Brody character.

Brody eventually destroys the shark by setting off an explosive device it has swallowed. Spielberg devotes several shots, both on the surface of the bloody water and underwater, to the explosion of the shark; all of the shots are in slow motion. After this emphatic climax, Hooper reappears; and he and Brody float toward shore on bits of wood from the wreckage of Quint's ship. One might be forgiven for finding symbolism in this conclusion; for *Jaws* can be seen as representing the wreckage of the Hawksian tradition of thoughtful, thematically subtle adventure dramas and the triumph of an adventure genre that seeks only to convey excitement and that achieves its aim through manipulative and thematically empty suspense.

Spielberg's megahit, *Raiders of the Lost Ark*, with its preposterous story line, might at first glance seem to lie outside the framework of a consideration of the Hawksian legacy in the New Hollywood. Yet, with allowances made for the response-to-television inflation of action sequences and the consequences of the availability to New Hollywood directors of technology unknown to Hawks, *Raiders* in essence is no more farfetched than, say, Hawks's *Only Angels Have Wings* or *The Thing*.

Raiders of the Lost Ark can be distinguished from Hawks's adventure dramas not on the basis of its story line but by its director's attitude toward his material, which is revealed in the structure of the film's narrative and in its mise-en-scène.

Robin Wood's observations about Hawks's attitude toward his material (whose apparently frivolous nature was the basis of the dismissal of Hawks that prevailed in the critical community until the dawn of the auteur age) again seem especially relevant to a discussion of the Hawksian fallacy in the New Hollywood: "That Hawks does not feel himself superior to material many may find 'corny,' 'melodramatic' or 'banal' is not a sign of inferior intelligence or sensibility. He responds, directly and spontaneously, to all that is valid in the genre, assimilates it and transforms it into a means of personal expression."[10] While it would be risky to allege that Steven Spielberg felt himself superior to the material of *Raiders of the Lost Ark*, it seems demonstrably true that he did not respond, except in the most detached and calculating way, to what is valid in the adventure genre to which *Raiders* belongs.

His attitude is expressed, in the first place, in his failure to shape his film in such a way as to convey respect for both its material and for the valid pleasure audiences might reasonably expect to derive from it. The shape of *Raiders* does not reflect what Gerald Mast has identified as the organizing principle of Hawks's adventures, the paradox of narrative:

> On the one hand, the events in a narrative must seem to flow spontaneously, naturally, surprisingly; nothing must be expected, nothing foreseen. On the other hand, the events in a narrative must be prepared for, motivated, foreshadowed; nothing is unexpected, everything foreseen.... The narrative that is insufficiently spontaneous and surprising is familiarly condemned as contrived, overplotted, unnatural, and stilted; the narrative that is insufficiently patterned is familiarly condemned as random, wandering, arbitrary, and formless.[11]

Spielberg's *Raiders* falls into the second of Mast's categories, and its insufficiently patterned narrative structure suggests that Spielberg did not take his material seriously enough to structure it and that he presumed audiences, sufficiently entertained by the film's special effects, would not miss the structure that has significantly contributed to the sense of lasting pleasure of adventures as diverse as *Moby Dick, Beau Geste* and *Hatari!*

That same attitude — something very close to contempt for both material and audiences — is reflected in the mise-en-scène Spielberg fashioned for *Raiders of the Lost Ark*. In general, he relies on a mise-en-scène that highlights the superficial pleasures of the genre, rather than on a Hawksian mise-en-scène that brings out, with commendable understatement, its deeper pleasures.

The tone is set in a fourteen-minute prologue that introduces the film's protagonist, Indiana Jones (Harrison Ford), an archaeology professor who roams the globe seeking treasures in exotic places. Beginning the film *in medias res*, Spielberg shows Jones acquiring a precious golden idol hidden in an elaborately booby-trapped cave located in a jungle teeming with hostile natives under the control of Jones's unscrupulous rival, Belloq (Paul Freeman). The mise-en-scène of the entire prologue is an utterly un–Hawksian cheat. Spielberg, by giving visual emphasis to the outlandish special effects of the sequence and by using an editing pattern that emphasizes a series of tongue-in-cheek climaxes undermines the credibility of his hero and fails to establish *how* Jones knows certain things and *how* he is able to accomplish certain feats. If we, the audience, are to derive real pleasure from an adventure, we must be able to follow it intelligently, however farfetched it might be; it is not enough to treat us to a series of technical effects that override coherence.

Spielberg underlines his indifference to the narrative patterning

Mast wrote of by concluding the prologue with a half-hearted introduction of a vaguely supernatural tone as Belloq's voice inexplicably carries and reverberates across a huge expanse of jungle. This occult-supernatural-fantastic element is something Spielberg will pick up and put down through out the film; it is not integrated into the narrative pattern and seems present only to add another superficial kick to the film.

Back at the college where he teaches, Jones and his department head, Marcus (Denholm Elliott), are questioned by two Army Intelligence officers about reports that the Ark of the Covenant, the legendary receptacle containing the tablets on which the ten commandments are inscribed, has been found in Egypt. Army Intelligence is interested because it is feared that if Hitler (the time of the film is the mid-thirties) should obtain the Ark, he might somehow use its powerful religious symbolism to further his nefarious plans. Jones, now in professional suit and tie and exhibiting an almost comical seriousness that recalls David Huxley in *Bringing Up Baby*, engages in a straight-faced recital to the officers of the fantastic lore that has grown up over the years regarding the Ark. Later, in a brief scene set in Jones's house, he and Marcus agree that Jones should find the Ark, both to keep it out of the hands of Hitler and to acquire it for the university's collection.

An indispensable key to locating the Ark is a professor who was Jones's mentor and is the father of his ex-girlfriend, Marion. Since the professor's whereabouts are unknown, Jones must find Marion in order to find her father.

Marion (Karen Allen) is now running a bar in a village in Nepal. She is introduced in a manner that suggests her affinity with a long line of Hawksian heroines: we first see her while she is engaged in a drinking contest (which she wins) with a most formidable-looking Nepalese villager. And Jones, in the course of his first extended exchange with Marion, has a very Hawksian line: "I did what I did. You don't have to be happy about it but maybe we can help each other out now."

Despite these Hawksian elements, the sequence set in Marion's bar is not, in the final analysis, Hawksian because it lacks the pervasive honesty of the Hawksian mise-en-scène and the intelligent structuring of Hawksian narratives. Spielberg's compositions overemphasize Marion's toughness, creating a near-caricature of the Hawksian woman instead of an understated rendering of the real thing. The sequence, moreover, features a dominant smoky-red hue that needlessly emphasizes its unreal, cartoonish quality; Spielberg's choice of color scheme distances us from the events of the sequence, instead of encouraging us to become happily involved in them, despite their essential absurdity. Finally, Spielberg's insistence on emphasizing the superficialities of his material again results in his neglecting to maintain a coherent narrative line. When a troop of Nazis (also interested in Marion's connection, through her father, to the lost Ark) bursts into the bar, the ensuing shoot-out and general mayhem were probably intended by Spielberg as a homage to the Old Hollywood saloon bust-up set-piece. Yet in his eagerness to create an all-out action scene, Spielberg cheats on narrative coherence: it is not clear why a Nepalese villager who has Jones in a death grip first shoots the Nazi who has ordered him to kill Jones and the proceeds to shoot at Jones. Spielberg may have thought he was capturing the marvelously entertaining essence of Old Hollywood adventure films in this scene, but he in fact only exhibits his commitment to the New Hollywood Hawksian fallacy, which uses the adventure drama as a framework for, and an excuse for, an essentially fraudulent mise-en-scène that misses the real values of the genre.

Marion's father is dead; but she does have information about the Ark, information that points to Egypt as the next stop on Jones's quest. Marion, still bearing resentment from her prior association with Jones, reluctantly agrees to accompany him.

In Cairo Jones is reunited with his old friend Salah (John Rhys-Davies), who provides Jones with information about the Ark and about his rival Belloq's efforts to acquire it for the Nazis. Later, Jones is attacked and Marion is apparently killed by a band of Arabs in a market. In what became the film's most famous incident, Jones confronts a sword-wielding Arab in a face-off that recalls the climactic shoot-out of countless westerns. Jones initially confronts the Arab with a whip he has expertly wielded earlier in the film; but then, in what Spielberg probably intended as a direct comment on the heroic conventions of the adventure genre, Jones drops the whip and shoots the Arab point-blank in the head. As Jones makes this anti-genre choice of efficiency over display of skill, Spielberg composes a shot of him in which Jones almost winks at the audience. To me, this incident and Spielberg's handling of it make no sense from any point of view: they seem condescending to the Old Hollywood genre films that Spielberg elsewhere in the film tries to evoke, and they seems contrary to the spirit of the New Hollywood cartoon Spielberg otherwise seems interested in making of the film.

The four-minute sequence that follows, in which Jones again encounters his nemesis Belloq, is one of the better passages in *Raiders*. Spielberg composes an effective medium shot of Jones and Belloq seated at a table in a cafe. Jones, seen in profile, is in the foreground of the frame; Belloq, facing the camera, is in the midground. The composition subtly suggests the possibility that Belloq is merely a more openly unsrupulous version of Jones, that they are on essentially the same moral-ethical plane. While this suggestion is not developed in the film, the shot provides a much-needed hint of dimensionality in Jones, who mostly functions as a cardboard figure in the film.

Later, in another effective shot, Jones is surrounded and eventually engulfed by a swarm of Salah's many children, whose seemingly spontaneous display of affection has the effect of shielding Jones from another attempt on his life. This is another rare moment in *Raiders* in which Spielberg composes a shot that suggests the complexity of the Jones character, who, in quick succession, has been portrayed as a shady character who cuts ethical corners and as a man whose essential goodness attracts the affection of children.

In the next sequence a friend of Salah's interprets the meaning of a key clue to the location of the Ark and Jones is fortuitously saved from a delightfully evil monkey, which has been planted on him by his enemies to administer a lethal poison.

Using the information provided by Salah's friend, Jones discovers an underground room that provides definitive information about the location of the Ark, which the Nazis and Belloq, who have established an excavation site in the Egyptian desert, are also on the verge of discovering. Jones also learns that Marion was not killed in the Cairo market but is being held prisoner in one of the tents in the Nazi compound.

Spielberg's mise-en-scène in the next sequence creates a degree of incoherence that inevitably decreases the audiences' level of involvement in the sequence. Spielberg muddles credibility by failing to establish in his mise-en-scène the spatial relationship between Jones, who is supervising the surreptitious excavation of the indicated location of the Ark, and the Belloq-supervised Nazi excavation activities. The mise-en-scène also makes a mess of chronological coherence, as Spielberg juxtaposes a scene of Jones and his small digging party in silhouette against the blazing desert sun with a scene of the same party set against a preternaturally stormy nighttime sky. Spielberg's inattention to fundamental coherence is unacceptable, even in an unrealistic adventure tale, because it prevents even minimally intelligent involvement by audiences in the events depicted in the film.

The spatial incoherence of the sequence affects the sequence that follows, one of the weakest in the film. Belloq, leaving the tent where Marion is being held, easily spots Jones's excavation activities, which had gone undetected by anyone else in the Nazi camp through at least one (here the chronological incoherence introduces uncertainty) full, sunny day.

Jones has located the Ark in the Well of Souls, an underground chamber whose floor is covered by hundreds of hissing snakes. Spielberg goes to such lengths to emphasize the number and deadliness of the snakes that he undermines the credibility of the rest of the sequence: when Marion and Jones are thrown into the Well of Souls, which is then sealed off at the top, it seems impossible that they could escape those ubiquitous, menacing snakes. Marion and Jones do manage to escape; but Spielberg, again ignoring an important obligation assumed by directors of adventure films, does not clearly convey *how* they manage it. Careful attention to how heroic deeds are performed, always notable in the best adventure films of Hawks and other Old Hollywood genre directors, is regrettably absent in this sequence, as it is in the film's prologue.

After Marion and Jones escape from the Well of Souls, they attempt to escape from the compound by stealing a small plane; but they are thwarted by a huge, seemingly invulnerable Nazi guard. The fight with the guard goes on much too long and is rather clumsily edited. Eventually, in a characteristically New Hollywood display of graphic violence, which is completely at odds with the overall fantasy tone of the film, the guard is ground to death in the blades of the plane's propellor. Spielberg follows this moment of New Hollywood violence with an Old Hollywood cliché: gasoline that has escaped from the plane ignites, and the entire camp is soon rocked by a series of explosions.

Belloq and the Nazis have removed the Ark from its long-concealed chamber and are leaving with it in a truck-and-jeep convoy. After entrusting Marion to the protection of Salah, Jones (who says, in one of the truest lines in the film, "I'm making this up as I go") sets out to recapture the Ark. In the best sequence in the film, Spielberg expertly details Jones's efforts to stop the convoy from carrying away the Ark. His feats against overwhelming odds are, of course, incredible; but Spielberg, who this time does not allow a frantic montage and an interest in special effects to overwhelm his rendering of how his hero accomplishes what he does, gives the sequence the special kind of credibility that audiences have learned to accept in adventure films. This sequence, which runs seven minutes, is satisfyingly exciting but also compelling in its depiction of the specific and difficult tasks a man must perform to qualify as an adventure-genre hero.

Opposite: **New Hollywood graphic violence is displayed when a huge Nazi guard attempting to kill Indiana Jones is himself killed by the blades of the plane under which they fight. Unidentified actor, Harrison Ford, *Raiders of the Lost Ark* (Paramount Pictures, 1981).**

Jones arrives with the convoy at the port where the Ark is to be loaded onto a ship for transportation to a small island. Marion and Salah have somehow also reached the port; and Jones and Marion arrange passage on the ship carrying the Ark.

The sea-voyage segment runs for nine minutes, and it includes a love scene in which Spielberg uses a stationary camera to record the effective portrayal by Karen Allen and Harrison Ford of the comic-erotic relationship between Marion and Jones. This scene, however, is followed by one in which the camera slowly and deliberately tracks in on the Ark in the ship's hold. The ark is burning from within, scorching the crate that contains it. This depiction of the supernatural power of the Ark, an idea that fitfully appears in the film, is overemphatic; and it tilts *Raiders*, which has been quite effective for the ten minutes or so preceding this scene, back toward the kind of blatantly contrived excitement that has been its characteristic feature.

The Nazis learn of the presence of Jones and Marion on the ship. Marion is again taken prisoner, but Jones eludes capture. On the island, Jones has the opportunity to destroy the Ark and thus foil the Nazi plan to use it in their march toward world domination; but the destruction of the Ark would mean the death of Marion, who is being held at gunpoint by Belloq. In a well-composed scene in which the moral questions that pervade Hawksian adventures at last emerge, Spielberg has Jones, rifle in hand, standing on a hill, looking down on Belloq, Marion, Nazi guards, and the Ark. Jones hesitates for an appropriate amount of time, weighing the morality of sacrificing Marion for the sake of keeping the Ark out of Nazi hands. He then throws down his weapon and is taken prisoner.

Jones and Marion are next seen bound to a stake in what appears to be a huge cavern. One feels that the sequence that follows is the one Spielberg considered the expression of the essence of his film; if that feeling is accurate, it is a powerful indicator of how deeply immersed in the Hawksian fallacy Spielberg is. With Jones and Marion looking on helplessly from a distance, the Ark is opened under Belloq's supervision. The opening unleashes a special effects extravaganza, the most notable feature of which is the melting of the bodies and faces of those exposed to the Ark's power, an event that Spielberg captures in a series of straightforward, sustained medium shots and close-ups.

Marion and Jones somehow survive the horrible destruction unleashed by the violation of the Ark; and this, the climactic sequence of *Raiders*, ends with a long shot of Marion and Jones tied to a stake in the foreground of the frame with the Ark, once again quiescent, in the midground. The climax of the film captures the essence of the Hawksian fallacy: in the New Hollywood, the "fun" of Hawks's adventure films has been reduced to a matter of special effects and a frantic montage taking center stage from a hero who is mostly lacking in moral dimensions and who is not required to take decisive action (or, indeed, *any* action: Jones passively sits out the climax of the film) that reveals, just below its surface, a moral dimension.

There is a one-minute epilogue in which Jones and Marion, now apparently happily in love, are frustrated by Washington bureaucrats' confiscation of the Ark. The last scene of the film shows the Ark, crated and labeled as United States government property, being placed in a huge warehouse, apparently to be forgotten until another attempt is made to exploit its extraordinary power.

The phenomenal commercial (and considerable critical) success of *Raiders of the Lost Ark* consolidated the Hawksian fallacy in the New Hollywood and confirmed Steven Spielberg's position as king of the New Hollywood hill.[12] The Hawksian fallacy perverts Hawksian adventures, characterized by a coherent narrative structure, an involving mise-en-scène, and an emphasis on action as an expression of morality and values into spectacles characterized by narrative incoherence; a mise-en-scène that highlights special effects and is fractured by a supercharged editing pattern, and an emphasis on action totally devoid of a moral dimension. Hawks's genre creations convey significant statements about human behavior in and through their rendering of exciting and enjoyable events; as Gerald Mast observed of a quintessential Hawksian adventure, *Only Angels Have Wings*: "One can see the literal action of *Only Angels Have Wings* . . . as a mere pretext for the real metaphoric interests of the narrative. The real story of *Only Angels* is the subtextual evolution of trust between Geoff Carter and Bonnie Lee, played against a background of vocational commitment, existential assertion, and male camaraderie."[13] The Hawksian fallacy films of the New Hollywood, in contrast to Hawks's genre masterpieces, contain nothing beneath their surfaces: if Hawks's adventures tend toward the aesthetic of the morality play, the Hawksian fallacy films tend toward the aesthetic of the comic book, something that is implicitly acknowledged in *Star Wars* and George Lucas's other fantasy variations on the fundamental Hawksian fallacy.

Notes

1. Robin Wood, *Howard Hawks* (Garden City, N.Y.: Doubleday, 1968), p. 8.

2. Jacques Rivette, "The Genius of Howard Hawks," in Joseph McBride, ed., *Focus on Howard Hawks* (Englewood Cliffs, N.J.: Prentice-Hall, 1972), pp. 70, 73.

3. Gerald Mast, *Howard Hawks, Storyteller* (New York: Oxford University Press, 1982), p. 18.

4. Ibid., p. 130.

5. Wood, *Howard Hawks,* p. 48.

6. Rivette, "Genius," p. 73.

7. Gerald Mast relates a revealing anecdote about how Hawks coaxed a brilliant comic performance from Katharine Hepburn in *Bringing Up Baby.* Mast, *Storyteller*, p. 136.

8. Wood, *Hitchcock's Films*, p. 21.

9. Mast, *Storyteller*, p. 109.

10. Wood, *Howard Hawks*, p. 18.

11. Mast, *Storyteller*, p. 30.

12. In an excellent interview that is mostly a rueful look back at the New Hollywood, Jack Nicholson observes, "Then a few years passed, and Steven Spielberg arrived like the final evolution." "The Bird Is on His Own," *Film Comment*, June 1985, p. 56.

13. Mast, *Storyteller*, p. 130.

6

Redeemers of the Lost Art

McCabe and Mrs. Miller (1971)
Annie Hall (1977)
Breaking Away (1979)
Escape from Alcatraz (1979)

Robert Altman's *McCabe and Mrs. Miller* is, like Arthur Penn's *Bonnie and Clyde* (1967), a stylistically striking New Hollywood film that raises anew questions central to an Old Hollywood genre. *McCabe and Mrs. Miller* is an involving meditation on the principal issue at the heart of the western genre: How is the individual to be reconciled to a society dedicated to an anti-individualistic ideal of organization and capitalism? Altman's answer to that question is embedded in a rather oblique, eccentric style; but his film achieves the essential balance between authorial expression and credibility, and therefore does not fall into the modernist fallacy that has undermined most New Hollywood attempts at creating films that are "personal" in the way modernist novels are.

It is instructive as well as pleasurable to watch Altman avoid the mistakes made by such modernist-fallacy directors as Terrence Malick in *Days of Heaven* and Michael Cimino in *Heaven's Gate*. In contrast to those directors, Altman in *McCabe* does not preempt audience involvement in the reality of his film or preclude a diversity of interpretation of it by making his film a series of inorganic, univocal images. Altman makes of *McCabe* a work whose mise-en-scène respects the complexity and ambiguity of a credible reality while conveying an organic authorial vision of the theme that informs the film.

McCabe and Mrs. Miller is organic because its central theme — the dilemma of the individual seeking community while retaining individuality — is present in every sequence, virtually every frame, of the film. Thus, in the opening sequence, while the credits are still rolling, Altman begins with a series of panning shots that create a powerful sense of place — a gray, rainy, muddy stretch of mountainous desolation — and then cuts to a shot of his protagonist, John McCabe (Warren Beatty), who is alone, mounted on a horse, and moving slowly toward the left of the screen. Altman follows with two shots that suggest the individual-community theme but does not obtrusively impose his interpretation of it. In the first shot, a sustained medium shot, McCabe is seen against the background of an unfinished church steeple, an interestingly ambiguous symbol of community. Then, in a composition that will be repeated in the film and that does much to bring us into contact with the individual humanity of McCabe, he is seen mumbling to himself in a medium shot with an indistinct gray-green background. That cameo of individuality is followed by a cut that eliminates McCabe from the screen and launches a series of images of a crude proto-town rising from the mud and desolation of the wilderness. Having established the convincing reality of both his individual and his community, Altman concludes the sequence with a shot that effectively restates the theme of the film: in a long shot, McCabe is seen at one end of a rickety suspension bridge, preparing to cross it and enter the town.

The next sequence, which runs for six minutes, is a brilliant example of mise-en-scène so immersed in the complexity and ambiguity of credible reality that it contains the author's vision without precluding the possibility that other interpretations may emerge from the richness of the mise-en-scène.

The sequence is set in a saloon, and Altman creates an altogether convincing rendering of a saloon in an incipient town in 1901 in the Pacific northwest. The first shot of the sequence reestablishes McCabe's isolation: he is seen, in profile, outside the saloon, barely visible in a shot that is mostly devoted to capturing the effect of pouring rain. There is a cut, and now the camera is placed inside the saloon, observing McCabe through a window as he approaches the entrance to the saloon. A customer, observing McCabe, moves away from the door as McCabe approaches it. Two shots follow, one of the customer looking at the stranger, and one of McCabe, wearing a derby and lighting a cigar, observing the scene in the saloon from the doorway.

Now Altman cuts to a shot of the hands of a group of men playing poker, following with a shot of a group encircling the table and watching the game. These shots of a proto-community of poker players are followed by one that emphasizes McCabe's singularity as the camera zooms in on his mouth and the cigar clenched between his teeth.

The next several shots are devoted to the reality of the saloon and its customers. Altman cuts among various groups of men distributed over the

crowded space of the saloon, and then his camera follows a woman em-
ployed at the saloon as she waits on the Reverend Elliot, an odd-looking
man with a demonic look in his eyes. There is a cut to a low-angle shot
of Smalley (John Shuck) descending the stairs that connect the saloon's
first and second floors. This is followed by a series of shots of Smalley, the
poker players, Reverend Elliot, Sheehan (Rene Auberjonois), who is the
owner of the saloon, and the bartender. When the camera tracks with
Sheehan as he moves toward the poker table, Altman creates a vivid sense
of the crude, crowded, smoky, low-ceilinged saloon. In this series of shots
and throughout this sequence, Altman uses his signature overlapping
dialogue to excellent effect, creating a sense of the aural, as well as the
visual, reality of this place. By this point in the sequence, Altman has
established the saloon as an entirely credible community that may or may
not welcome McCabe into its ongoing life.

Sheehan, a busybody and a gossip, is eager to pin down McCabe's
identity. He is convinced that McCabe is a gunfighter who was recently
involved in a notorious shoot-out. In a series of medium shots, Sheehan
questions McCabe and McCabe responds with noncommittal answers.
Then there is a cut to the group of poker players, now including McCabe;
he has apparently been accepted into the group. But the threat to
McCabe's acceptance is again emphasized when the camera tracks in on
Sheehan as he moves around the poker table. A series of close-ups of
Sheehan and McCabe follows; the sense of McCabe as part of a group has
been undermined.

There follows a series of shots of the saloon and its customers as
McCabe, embedded in the milieu of the saloon, moves toward its back
exit. The sense of McCabe assimilated into this milieu is, however, again
undermined in the next series of shots. Following a sustained medium shot
of McCabe (who has left the saloon) and Sheehan (who has followed him),
there is a second seris of close-ups of McCabe and Sheehan as the latter
continues questioning the former about his identity. The ambiguity here
is involving: Sheehan appears to be the one obstacle to McCabe's integration into the saloon community, but he appears to be a less than insur-
mountable obstacle because he is so fussy and so seemingly ineffectual.

There is a cut to a medium shot of Sheehan reentering the saloon.
The camera tracks right with him as he moves through the saloon, telling all who will listen that the stranger in town is a well-known gunfighter. McCabe is also now back inside the saloon, talking at the bar with
Smalley and the bartender. Shots of Sheehan trying to persuade McCabe
to rent a bed in the second-floor dormitory of the saloon are then intercut
with shots of Smalley and the bartender engaged in an earnest conversation

about whether the former should shave off his beard. The sequence concludes with a shot that effectively underlines the ambiguous connection McCabe has established with this saloon community. In a tracking shot, the camera follows McCabe and Sheehan as they descend the stairs from the second floor and walk through the saloon. This reiteration of McCabe as part of the saloon community is, however, somewhat undermined as the tracking shot concludes on a medium shot of McCabe, who is again seated at the poker table but who is isolated from the other players by Altman's camera placement and composition. One might thus conclude from this shot and the sequence as a whole that this casual, seemingly unstructured saloon community, so vividly depicted in Altman's mise-en-scène, will surely welcome McCabe. Or one might conclude that even this simple proto-community will reject a man whose unique individuality has been highlighted by Altman's visual treatment of him.

McCabe is next seen in tracking shots as he moves on horseback through mud, rain and snow across bleak terrain. This segment is followed by a series of tracking shots that introduce Bear Paw, a much more prosperous-looking, established town than the one McCabe arrived at in the opening sequence. McCabe, it soon develops, has decided that what the incipient town of Presbyterian Church (so named for the still abuilding structure whose unfinished steeple was featured in the opening sequence) needs is a whorehouse. He has come to Bear Paw to purchase "chippies" for his planned brothel. The chippies move in and out of the corners of the frame as McCabe dickers over their purchase price with their owner. In this series of shots we catch our first fleeting, almost subliminal glimpse of Mrs. Miller (Julie Christie), who is seen in the background of the frame, inside the crude building where the chippies are housed.

Back in Presbyterian Church, McCabe is seen in conversation with Sheehan, who now wants to establish a business partnership with McCabe (several weeks have apparently passed since McCabe's arrival in town). McCabe and Sheehan are interrupted by shouts and screams from the tent compound that is serving as McCabe's whorehouse until his saloon and whorehouse are ready for occupancy. There is a cut to a shot of an apparently crazed woman attacking one of her customers outside her tent. There is then a cut to the squalid, mud-filled tent compound where the whores are lodged. The sequence concludes with a series of shots in which McCabe, with considerable difficulty, manages to subdue the crazed woman. Obviously, all is not running smoothly in the semi-outlaw community McCabe is attempting to establish within the larger community of Presbyterian Church.

Altman extends and complicates the theme of the individual-in-the-community in the next sequence, in which two more strangers arrive in Presbyterian Church.

The sequence begins with the camera craning down on a very odd-looking vehicle—it seems to be a combination of a locomotive and a tractor—pulling into view. A medium shot of three citizens of Presbyterian Church observing the arrival of the vehicle features one of them, a woman, shaking her head and muttering, "More whores."

Mrs. Miller is one of the passengers on the vehicle ("train" does not seem quite the right designation for it), and Altman cuts to a medium shot of her. This is followed by a zoom in on Bart (Bert Remsen), who is expecting his mail-order bride, Ida, to be among the passengers. After another medium shot of Mrs. Miller, there is a cut to a close-up of Bart; Altman's use of the close-up, which he has used sparingly up to this point in the film, in this instance may have been motivated by a desire to highlight Bart as a representative of the "solid citizens" of Presbyterian Church. There is then a low-angle shot of the vehicle passing in front of the unfinished church steeple, another representative of the community and of the respectable town it aspires to become.

Shots of Mrs. Miller, Ida (Shelley Duvall), and Bart are now intercut. Then there is a cut to a shot of McCabe walking left, followed by one of Bart and Ida walking right. In another moment of apparent integration, McCabe is then united in the frame with this solid-looking citizen and his bride-to-be. Altman, however, then, as he has before, undermines the suggestion of McCabe's assimilation into the community by suggesting (and it is important to stress that this is only a suggestion: Altman, here and elsewhere in the film, refrains from imposing interpretation, as a literary-fallacy director would) the continuing problem of McCabe's genuine integration into this community. He follows a close-up of McCabe, which inevitably emphasizes his individuality and isolation, with a shot in which the camera tracks right with Ida and Bart as they exit the frame. Then the camera tracks in on McCabe, who is alone in the frame, his back to the camera.

There is a cut to a shot of Mrs. Miller walking—striding—toward the camera. She walks into a two-shot with McCabe but almost immediately exits the frame, leaving McCabe once again alone in the shot. This is followed by a medium shot of McCabe and Mrs. Miller standing at the entrance to his establishment (the unfinished church is seen in the background). The camera tracks left with Mrs. Miller as she walks into McCabe's place; he follows her.

A medium shot of McCabe talking to Mrs. Miller, who is off-camera, follows; she has said she wants to talk to McCabe, but he has yet to find out about what. There is a cut to a shot of Mrs. Miller, in profile, staring out of a window, followed by a shot of what she sees: the muddy, squalid tent compound McCabe has established for his whores. The profile shot of Mrs. Miller staring out of the window is reprised twice, interrupted by a shot of McCabe walking toward her. Altman's emphasis on Mrs. Miller's perception of the town she has arrived at creates an effective contrast between Mrs. Miller's and McCabe's initial experiences of the town: a dreary, muddy collection of tents versus the (relative) warmth and conviviality of Sheehan's saloon. With Mrs. Miller's perception controlling, one begins to question whether it is even desirable to be accepted into this community.

Mrs. Miller finally turns from the window to face the camera and McCabe. The sequence concludes with a series of alternating close-ups of McCabe and Mrs. Miller, two highly individualistic individuals whose singularity is here emphasized by Altman. During the series, Mrs. Miller, still not revealing what she wants to discuss with McCabe, makes a few sarcastic observations about both the town and McCabe himself, and announcces that she is hungry enough to eat a horse.

McCabe decides to take Mrs. Miller to Sheehan's place for supper (his own kitchen, he sheepishly explains, is not yet in operation). Altman, continuing to devote admirable attention to the specific reality of the community McCabe and Mrs. Miller are attempting to enter, cuts to a medium shot of a man playing a fiddle inside Sheehan's saloon. The camera then tracks back to reveal Sheehan and various customers distributed on various planes of the frame. The camera tracks left with Sheehan as he moves through the saloon; when he exits the frame, the camera stays on the bartender and Smalley, who are still discussing the latter's beard.

In an excellent choice, Altman now cuts to a tracking shot of McCabe and Mrs. Miller walking through town. They seem to be in the town but not part of it. They proceed to walk away from the camera, leaving the screen space to be filled by the crude buildings, puddles and mud of Presbyterian Church.

A remarkable segment ensues. With only three interruptions for shots of others in the saloon, Altman uses a series of more than thirty alternating medium shots and close-ups of McCabe and Mrs. Miller to render their conversation as she eats with remarkable gusto and he sips his drink and observes (with some disdain) her rather unrefined eating habits. The segment furthers the plot: during their conversation Mrs. Miller proposes to McCabe that they form a partnership to build and operate a "proper" whorehouse in Presbyterian Church. Plot development, however, is the least of the achievements of this segment. By withholding the attention to the reality and richness of milieu we have come to expect and instead concentrating singlemindedly on his protagonists, Altman suggests, without preempting alternative interpretations, that McCabe and Mrs. Miller may be just too individualistic to ever be integrated into a community. Moreover, Altman subtly suggests the nature of the McCabe–Mrs. Miller relationship that is evolving: he always initiates the changes in camera placement in the long series of shots with shots of Mrs. Miller, thereby suggesting the control and dominance she will assume in the relationship with McCabe. Altman also uses this segment to initiate his most audacious assault on the conventions of the western. His compositions and his direction of the actors clearly establish the idea that McCabe is a rather "feminine" hero, while Mrs. Miller emerges as a rather "masculine" figure. This in turn relates back to the overarching individual-community theme: Mrs. Miller may well be too aggressive, too masculine, and McCabe too gentle, too feminine, to be accepted in a society predicated on the stereotyped simplicities of sex roles. For all of these reasons, this segment is, if I may repeat myself, remarkable.

In the next sequence Altman uses long shots, reverse zoom shots, and tracking shots to render the arrival (on foot, in pouring rain, through mud) of the whores Mrs. Miller has imported to staff her "proper" house. Altman then cuts between shots of the rain-bedraggled, mud-splattered whores settling into their still-unfinished house and shots of men at a poker game discussing the arrival of the new whores.

The next sequence is set inside the whorehouse, which, if unfinished, is looking considerably better. Shots of the girls in casual conversation with one another and with their customers feature a good deal of overlapping, off-camera dialogue. When one customer requests Mrs. Miller herself and she proceeds to lead him upstairs, Altman, demonstrating his interest in making *McCabe and Mrs. Miller*, among other things, a love story, cuts to a shot of McCabe, who observes Mrs. Miller with her customer and then abruptly leaves the whorehouse, moving right in contrast to the leftward movement of Mrs. Miller.

The theme of the individual and the community is subtly present in Altman's mise-en-scène for the next sequence, which begins with a medium shot of McCabe seated at a table, struggling to make sense of the figures in an accounts ledger. There is then a cut to a long shot of Mrs. Miller walking purposefully through a snowy landscape that includes a few scattered buildings. This is followed by another shot of McCabe working with the ledger; Mrs. Miller becomes visible in the background of the frame, seen through a window near the table where McCabe is seated.

In a remarkable segment of more than thirty alternative medium shots and close-ups, Mrs. Miller eats with gusto and proposes to McCabe that they form a partnership. Julie Christie, Warren Beatty, *McCabe and Mrs. Miller* (Warner Brothers, 1971).

Once Mrs. Miller enters McCabe's saloon-gaming house (this is where he is doing the accounts), Altman uses a series of twenty-three shots in which McCabe and Mrs. Miller react to each other but are never together in the frame. They approach each other repeatedly, but Altman's montage keeps them apart. He also uses the space of McCabe's saloon, which, in contrast to Sheehan's in the earlier sequence, is conspicuously empty, to suggest the distance separating McCabe and Mrs. Miller.

Altman at last brings his two protagonists together (they are arguing about McCabe's conservative business policy, about what Mrs. Miller regards as his lack of vision) in the frame. Even now, however, Altman's compositions and camera movements suggest the distance between McCabe and Mrs. Miller. When she walks into a medium shot with him, he immediately walks right, the camera tracking with him until she is eliminated from the frame. After a shot of Mrs. Miller speaking to McCabe off-camera, there are alternating medium shots of each of them in which each has his or her back to the camera. Then McCabe, with the camera tracking with him, walks past Mrs. Miller, who is now working with the accounts ledger that has befuddled McCabe. There is a cut to a medium shot of Mrs. Miller. She gets up and walks toward the camera. The camera then tracks right with her until she is in the background-center of a medium shot. She is now facing the camera and McCabe, who is separated from her by an expanse of the empty saloon. There is then a cut to a medium shot of McCabe walking out of the saloon door, followed by a shot in which the camera tracks back from Mrs. Miller, emphasizing her solitude in the middle of the empty saloon. The effect of Altman's direction of this sequence is to cast doubt on the romantic notion that McCabe and Mrs. Miller, though they may be isolated from the mainstream community of Presbyterian Church, may be able to form together a community apart, a world of their own. Altman has thus worked another interesting, deepening variation on the film's central theme without resorting to modernist-fallacy images that violate the film's credibility and assert meaning in a way that works against audience involvement in the film's totality.

In a touching interlude that continues both the individualization and feminization of McCabe, he is seen walking aimlessly in the snow and talking to himself; such is the effect encounters with Mrs. Miller have on him. Then, in an incident that reiterates the mores of Presbyterian Church and contrasts the visual solidarity of the community with the visual isolation of McCabe in the preceding scene, Bart is killed in a fight with a group of men who have insulted his wife Ida by mistaking her for one of Mrs. Miller's whores. Among the townspeople who witness the fight is the mysterious Reverend Elliot. In an astute choice, Altman concludes the scene with an overhead shot of the community — or a good portion of it — gathering around Bart's body and carrying it away. This image takes on added importance when it is considered in conjunction with the film's climactic sequence, in which the community fails to rally around one of its threatened members.

The scene depicting the death of Bart also includes brief glimpses (it is characteristic of Altman's direction of the film, with its frequent and thematically significant use of very crowded frames, to introduce important characters in this off-hand fashion) of two more strangers in town, Sears and Hollander. After Bart is carried away, Altman cuts to a shot in which the camera tracks right with McCabe, who, apparently having turned to drink to lessen the bafflement and anger caused by Mrs. Miller, is lurching across the town's version of Main Street. There is a cut to a medium shot of Sears (Michael Murphy), Hollander and Sheehan, who are having a whispered conversation in the dark, left corner of the frame. The camera first tracks right with them, then resumes tracking right with McCabe; Sears calling McCabe's name is a voice-over in the tracking shot of McCabe. After Sears has walked into a medium shot with McCabe, there is a cut to a sustained tracking shot of McCabe, followed closely by Sears and Hollander, walking into his saloon.

Sears and Hollander are agents of a corporation that wants to buy McCabe's holdings; they have already struck a deal with Sheehan to purchase his saloon. At this point, Altman makes what I think is his first false move in *McCabe and Mrs. Miller*. As Sears, Hollander and McCabe, standing at the bar of the latter's saloon, begin sparring about the offer to buy McCabe out, Altman uses an extended series of alternating, stationary-camera close-ups to render their conversation. The decision to devote a number of close-ups to Sears and Hollander seems wrong, an undermining of the individual-community theme that Altman has been organically and suggestively developing in the film. While Altman has included isolated close-ups of Sheehan and Bart prior to this scene, he has for the most part reserved the close-up for McCabe and Mrs. Miller, a stylistic pattern that has artfully suggested their extreme individuality and their alienated status in the community. Altman confuses his theme by now using the same camera placement, for a prolonged period, for shots of Sears and Hollander, who should be rendered as relatively faceless representatives of the corporatism that motivates even a rough-hewn, incipient community like Presbyterian Church.

McCabe, a good poker player, conveys complete indifference to Sears and Hollander's offer, and he leaves them standing at the bar. After an interlude in which Altman effectively evokes an alternative, unconventional community by rendering the familial celebration in Mrs. Miller's whorehouse of the birthday of one of her girls, Altman creates a complex sequence in which he again undermines the possibility of McCabe and Mrs. Miller's creating a community of two, a world apart.

The sequence begins with a low-angle shot of McCabe climbing the back stairs that lead to Mrs. Miller's room. There is a cut to a close-up of Mrs. Miller, inside her room, looking up, startled by the knock on the door. Altman then pans around the room, ending with a medium shot of Mrs. Miller; the effect is to make her appear isolated and misplaced, even in her own room. After alternating medium shots of McCabe knocking at the door and Mrs. Miller staring at the door, there is a cut to a shot in which the camera tracks with Mrs. Miller as she hurriedly hides the paraphernalia she has been using to smoke opium.

Once Mrs. Miller admits McCabe, Altman composes a series of shots that, like those of the account-ledger sequence, emphasize the difficulty McCabe and Mrs. Miller have in coming together. The camera first tracks right with both of them as they move away from the door; but then Mrs. Miller, again assuming the more aggressive role, leads the camera away from McCabe as it tracks left with her. There is a cut to a close-up of Mrs. Miller, followed by a medium shot of McCabe; the asymmetry in this pair of shots is subtly suggestive. In his medium shot, McCabe is seen moving left toward Mrs. Miller; and Altman brings them together in a shot whose composition hardly suggests unity: Mrs. Miller is in the foreground-center, while McCabe is in the background-center. Even this tentative coming together is short-lived, as the tracking camera again follows Mrs. Miller's movement, eliminating McCabe from the frame.

A shot of McCabe talking to Mrs. Miller off-camera (he's bragging to her about how he dealt with Sears and Hollander) is followed by a shot of Mrs. Miller, her back to McCabe and the camera, sitting in front of a mirror and brushing her hair. A medium shot of McCabe beginning to undress is followed by a series of three shots in which a medium shot of McCabe interrupts two shots of Mrs. Miller's reflection in the mirror; Altman here suggests that McCabe is not aware, as we are, that Mrs. Miller is not really "there" for him. When Mrs. Miller at last turns from the mirror and faces McCabe and the camera, the ensuing series of alternating medium shots of them, during the course of which she criticizes his handling of Sears and Hollander, is interrupted by a knock at the door informing McCabe that Sears and Hollander want to see him.

This pointed intrusion of the "real" world underlines the vulnerability of the McCabe–Mrs. Miller relationship. Altman maintains the double focus of this sequence by cutting from McCabe downstairs at the bar with Sears and Hollander to a shot of Mrs. Miller smoking opium in her room upstairs. If McCabe is rather ineffectual in his dealings with the larger community represented by Sears and Hollander (who, in both senses of the phrase, mean business), Mrs. Miller seems to be opting for withdrawing from it altogether.

McCabe again puts off Sears and Hollander and then returns to Mrs. Miller. This concluding segment of the sequence is a series of alternating (once again, Altman's montage assures that his protagonists are not together in the frame) medium shots and close-ups of McCabe and Mrs. Miller as he, chattering happily about his encounter with Sears and Hollander, undresses and she, feeling the effects of the opium, smiles vacantly at him, saying nothing. The capitalist spirit, if not the physical presences, of Sears and Hollander, however, once again intrudes on McCabe and Mrs. Miller. Just as he is about to get into bed with her, she uses hand gestures and nods to indicate he has not yet paid for her. The sequence ends with the camera tracking in on the box where McCabe has deposited Mrs. Miller's fee.

A brief scene of Sears and Hollander discussing how to proceed with McCabe follows. The scene is set in Sheehan's saloon, and this time Altman links Sears and Hollander's single-minded capitalism to the larger community of Presbyterian Church by embedding the two men in a setting and among people that represent the community. Sears favors further negotiation with McCabe; but Hollander, apparently the senior member of this duo, declares that it is time to suggest that their superiors turn to more forceful means of dealing with McCabe.

The next sequence contains the film's most explicit comments on the western genre. It depicts the burial ceremony for Bart, and Altman begins the sequence in a manner that recalls the burial sequences of so many Ford westerns: beginning on a shot of a gravestone, the camera tracks back and then cranes up to show the mourners at the grave site, the town, and the surrounding mountains.

This image of the Fordian community solemnly gathered to bury one of its own is undercut by Altman's handling of the rest of the burial sequence. While he does not insist on this interpretation, Altman's allocation of screen space during the sequence suggests that this is not quite the community celebrated by Ford. Altman devotes most of the early shots of the sequence to Mrs. Miller's whores earnestly singing a funeral hymn, thereby suggesting, as he has before and will again, that the only genuine community in Presbyterian Church is the semi-outlaw community of the whorehouse.

The burial sequence contains a richly suggestive shot. When McCabe, one of the mourners at the grave site, is alerted to the approach of a possibly hostile stranger on horseback, he withdraws from the group of mourners, moving right, toward the stranger. The camera tracks with him, but he is eventually lost from view among the other mourners. Altman continues the shot without a cut, moving his camera rightward until it comes to rest on a close-up of Mrs. Miller. She then moves left, the camera tracking with her. Thus, for the second time in the film, Altman uses camera movement and movement within the shot to create an image of McCabe and Mrs. Miller moving simultaneously but in opposite directions. This ambiguous movement certainly has romantic connotations of an unspoken affinity between the two protagonists, but it also can be read as a continuation of the suggestion that Mrs. Miller is inclined to withdraw in the face of difficulty. Altman, again avoiding the univocal images of the modernist fallacy, insists on neither interpretation, both of which are embedded in a mise-en-scène that respects the complexity of reality.

McCabe's encounter with the mounted stranger is the sequence's second explicit comment on the conventions of the western. In a long shot that includes the town and the surrounding terrain, McCabe is seen slowly approaching the stranger, who is in the foreground of the frame, his back to the camera. After a cut to a shot of Mrs. Miller running through the town, Altman uses a series of alternating medium shots McCabe and the stranger to build to their encounter. This buildup to the classic shoot-out takes on an ironic tone when the stranger (Keith Carradine) a young, gangling, ingenuous cowboy, tells McCabe he wants no trouble, he has come to town because he has heard it has the best whorehouse in the territory. Altman, besides playing with the stylistic conventions of the shoot-out, has exposed the western-bred paranoia (and fundamentally anti-individualistic bias) of audiences, who have been trained to assume that every stranger is a threat.

McCabe and Mrs. Miller now reaches one of its high points in a sequence in which Altman opposes images of an ominous external threat to images of two communities, one unconventional and disreputable, one mainstream and respectable. The question he raises in the sequence — the question to which he will return in the film's magnificent climax, the question that makes *McCabe and Mrs. Miller*, particularly when considered in the context of the western genre, such a thought-provoking film — is whether the threat is really external or whether it is indigenous to the mainstream community the sequence evokes.

The sequence begins with the camera tilting up from horses' hooves to three mounted men, who are partially obscured by the glare of the sun. There is then a cut to a shot of the lower torso of a man wearing long underwear descending the interior staircase of Mrs. Miller's whorehouse. The camera tracks back, revealing that the man is the young cowboy who arrived in town the day of Bart's funeral. The camera tracks with him through the whorehouse; and Altman, suggesting the familial-communal nature of the brothel, pauses for a sustained medium shot of the cowboy and whore who is using a primitive vacuum cleaner on the brothel's carpet. A shot of the cowboy sharing a sofa in the parlour with two whores is followed by a cut to a shot in which McCabe enters the whorehouse and then moves left for a sustained shot of him and two whores at the foot of the staircase (the cowboy, following another whore, enters and then exits the frame as he ascends the stairs). A cut to a medium shot of McCabe starting to climb the stairs to go to Mrs. Miller's room is followed by a medium shot of a whore shaking her head and telling him, "She's got company." A sustained shot of McCabe reacting with his characteristic mixture of hurt and confusion to her statement is followed by a shot of McCabe moving right, past the whore and toward the front door of the brothel. The whorehouse-as-community has been evoked, but McCabe and Mrs. Miller as a couple has again been undermined.

From the shot of McCabe there is a cut to a shot of feet dancing on a slick veneer of mud, followed by a shot of a fiddler playing. There is then a cut to a shot in which the camera tracks back to reveal a man dancing on a kind of mud rink, which is encircled by a group of townspeople observing the dance. Thus a second community, engaged in innocent and imaginative play, has been evoked.

The action then returns to the brothel. A medium shot of Ida, Bart's widow, partially concealed by a frilly undergarment she is holding in front of herself, gives way to a panning movement that catches Mrs. Miller, now holding the undergarment, moving across her room. Mrs. Miller is initiating Ida into the whorehouse community, a process that Altman renders in a series of medium shots in which Ida and Mrs. Miller are mostly together in the frame.

Now back to the larger community. A series of shots of the mud dancer and of men clapping time to the music ends with a shot of Sheehan, a figure who seems to link the innocent proto-community with the incipient and far from innocent capitalist society that seems to both threaten and fulfill that community, suddenly looking as if he intuitively senses that something of importance is about to happen. There is a cut to a white horse, which was seen in the initial shot of the sequence, emerging from the darkness (the white-black element is another link between this sequence and the film's climax). A series of shots intercutting images of the stranger mounted on the white horse and the activities at the mud rink follows. There's then a cut to a medium shot in which Sheehan's saloon is in the background, and the mud dancer and the spectators are in the mid- and foreground of the frame. The shot is held as the music stops and everyone but the mud dancer exits the frame. There is then a cut to a long shot, reflecting the mounted stranger's point of view, of the dancer. A cut to a medium shot of the dancer shows him looking about in confusion. After this powerful — but not unambiguous — image of the stranger's disruption of the community event, the sequence ends with a medium shot of the stranger mounted on the white horse riding left, out of the frame. We later learn his name is Butler, and his companions (seen briefly at the beginning of the sequence) are Breed and an unnamed teenage boy with an incongruous baby face and a Dutch boy haircut.

Apparently, through the operation of a small-town grapevine, it soon becomes known that the three armed strangers are agents of the corporation that wants to buy out McCabe. Before the inevitable meeting between McCabe and the men who have come looking for him, there is a sequence in which Mrs. Miller warns McCabe about the implacable danger facing him.

The sequence is again set in McCabe's empty saloon, a setting with connotations that further the idea of McCabe and Mrs. Miller's isolation from the mainstream community of Presbyterian Church. In this sequence, however, Altman's mise-en-scène at first glance suggests a possible alteration in another of the film's established ideas, the idea that McCabe and Mrs. Miller are unable to come together in their shared isolation. Altman intersperses among a series of alternating medium shots of McCabe and Mrs. Miller five shots in which they are together in the frame. The mise-en-scène of these shots, however, emphasizes the tentativeness, ambiguity and vulnerability of McCabe and Mrs. Miller's union. In two of the shots, she is facing the camera while he is seen in profile; and in two others — one an overhead shot, the other a rather distant medium shot — their isolation and smallness receive more visual emphasis than their union. In any case, Altman ends the sequence in a way that seems to renew the idea of his protagonists' disunity: a medium shot of McCabe (who has refused to accept Mrs. Miller's advice to settle with the corporation before its hired guns kill him) walking out of the saloon door is followed by a startlingly lovely close-up of Mrs. Miller, who is seen gazing at something off-camera, lost in thought, sadness and solitude.

McCabe's encounter with Butler, the leader of the hired gunmen, begins in a way that reiterates the idea of McCabe's isolation and asserts the idea that men like Butler are products of, rather than aberrations from, communities like Presbyterian Church. The sequence begins with a long shot of McCabe walking through a gray, snowy landscape and crossing the suspension bridge that leads to Sheehan's saloon. This image of McCabe's isolation is immediately followed by an image of Butler's assimilation: in a medium shot set inside Sheehan's saloon, Butler is in the foreground of the frame, partly encircled by a group of town citizens who are listening to him. As if to emphasize that McCabe, not Butler, is the intruder, Altman pans left to McCabe as he enters the saloon and then immediately cuts to a shot that reprises the composition of Butler in the midst of the saloon customers.

Butler at last turns his attention from the group of townspeople to the solitary McCabe. Altman shoots their conversation — in which McCabe rather pathetically agrees to accept the offer of Sears and Hollander, and Butler simply states that it is too late to make a deal — as

a series of medium shots and close-ups of McCabe and Butler, with interruptions for shots of Breed, the baby-faced gunfighter, and, significantly,
Sheehan. The sequence concludes with McCabe, muttering something
about contacting Sears, exiting the saloon. Butler, in a close-up, says to
Sheehan (who has apparently related to Butler his ill-founded belief that
McCabe is a notorious gunfighter), "That man? That man never killed
anyone in his life."

The scene now abruptly changes (the film's lack of narrative transitions is sometimes annoying in its self-conscious modernism but more
often — the climactic sequence is the leading example — the effect is to lend
the film the rhythm of real life, which seldom proffers elegant transitions)
to Bear Paw, where McCabe has gone to consult a lawyer (William
Devane) about his problems with the corporation that has apparently
marked him for death. The lawyer, a former senator, assures McCabe
that the courts and the threat of negative publicity will protect him from
the corporation. McCabe seems reassured, but the bombastic tone of the
lawyer's monologue sows substantial doubt about the efficacy of the
course of action he proposes.

McCabe returns to Presbyterian Church for an encounter with Mrs.
Miller that is another of the film's high points. Altman's mise-en-scène —
particularly his use of space, decor and movement within the shot — speaks
eloquently about the relationship between McCabe and Mrs. Miller and
about their growing awareness of their alienation from the community.

The encounter begins with a shot of food frying on a stove. The
camera tilts up with the frying pan as it is lifted from the stove, the camera
movement concluding on a profile close-up of Mrs. Miller; McCabe enthusiastically relating what the lawyer told him is a voice-over in the shot.
After a cut to a close-up of McCabe, there is a cut to a shot that is a visual
rendering of the division separating McCabe and Mrs. Miller, who puts
no faith in the law's power to stop Butler and his friends (in her distrust
of the law, as well as in her greater aggressiveness, Mrs. Miller is much
more a traditional western "hero" than McCabe is). The shot is a medium
shot, with Mrs. Miller in the foreground of the frame, her back to the
camera, and McCabe in the midground, facing the camera. The camera,
reflecting McCabe's passivity, remains stationary as he passes in front of
it; then, as it has before, it follows Mrs. Miller's movement within the
shot, eliminating McCabe from the frame. A medium shot of McCabe
talking to Mrs. Miller off-camera is followed by one of her shouting at him
off-camera. The camera tracks slightly right with her and then holds as
she moves to the rear of the frame, where she is partially concealed by
white drapes that make a kind of alcove in the room.

A shot of McCabe walking toward Mrs. Miller is followed by a medium shot of her, her back to the camera, framed by the drapes. A second shot of McCabe walking toward her and the camera becomes a profile close-up of him speaking to Mrs. Miller off-camera.

There is a cut to a medium shot in which Mrs. Miller, still partially concealed by the drapes, is in the background of the frame; McCabe, his back to the camera, is in the foreground. This image of alienation and isolation is altered when Mrs. Miller begins to walk toward McCabe in the foreground of the frame. Then, in an excellent choice that conveys the deep ambiguity at the heart of his film's central relationship, Altman has his camera track right-left with Mrs. Miller as she paces about the room; the effect of the camera's movement is to create a pattern in which McCabe (who remains inert) is irregularly eliminated from, and restored to, the frame. The last shot of the sequence effectively recapitulates both the impasse McCabe and Mrs. Miller have reached and their isolation. In a medium shot, McCabe is at the left of the frame, with the center and right empty. The camera tracks back; and in the new composition McCabe is sitting in the midground-left, while Mrs. Miller is standing, with her head bowed, in the midground-right; the center of the frame is empty. Altman sustains this shot for several seconds after the McCabe–Mrs. Miller conversation has given way to silence.

Altman makes his only serious fall into the modernist fallacy in the next sequence. The young cowboy who arrived the day of Bart's funeral and who has apparently spent several days and nights in Mrs. Miller's whorehouse is at last leaving town. After fond farewells to the whores, he rides off, dismounting to cross the suspension bridge leading to Sheehan's saloon. At the opposite end of the bridge, the baby-faced teenage killer is engaged in target practice. He challenges the young cowboy, a totally likeable innocent who has no expertise with guns, and then kills him in cold blood. A slow-motion shot captures the cowboy's body falling into the partially iced-over river that runs below the bridge. Brief shots of Butler, Breed and Sheehan at the killer's end of the bridge are intercut with shots of the psychotic teenager himself. This passage strikes me as a modernist-fallacy image-sequence, an instance of Altman's asserting an univocal image whose meaning — the stark contrast between, on the one side, Butler and his friends (and, ultimately, the corporation they represent) and, on the other, a strikingly "average" citizen — is an oversimplification of, and possibly a contradiction of, the more subtle rendering of the individual-community theme Altman has been organically and compellingly developing in his film.

McCabe and Mrs. Miller reaches another high point in its penultimate sequence, which begins with a medium shot of Mrs. Miller, in profile, sitting up in her bed at the left of the frame. A soft glow from a nearby light falls on the pillow beside her; most of her face is in darkness. There is a cut to a medium shot of McCabe, wearing a nightshirt, moving left across Mrs. Miller's room, toward the bed. He sits down at the edge of the bed; Altman composes the shot so that McCabe's profile is a symmetrical match of Mrs. Miller's in the preceding shot.

An extraordinary series — interrupted by only one medium shot of McCabe with his back to the camera — of nineteen alternating close-ups of McCabe and Mrs. Miller follows. Altman's montage and his commitment to the close-up in this instance seem right, for they contribute to the development of three of the film's thematic preoccupations. First and most obviously, the close-ups emphasize the individuality of Mrs. Miller and McCabe. Second, they emphasize their confinement, their isolation. Third and paradoxically, Altman's emphasis on the individual beauty of his two protagonists, which gives the sequence a strongly romantic tone, necessitates a montage that keeps them apart, that emphasizes their separation from each other. Thus Altman's series of close-ups ends up again undermining the romantic notion that McCabe and Mrs. Miller can somehow form a union that might be able to exist apart from the larger community.

Throughout the series of close-ups, McCabe has been rather incoherently telling Mrs. Miller about his hopes and fears; she has said nothing, has simply listened, an enigmatic smile on her face. In the beautiful concluding shot of the sequence, McCabe is seen in another medium shot in which his back is to the camera; Mrs. Miller has been eliminated from the frame. The camera holds as McCabe gets into bed beside Mrs. Miller (this time, she has not insisted that he pay). Then the camera tracks in for a sustained, totally silent medium shot of McCabe resting his head on Mrs. Miller's breast as she gently strokes his hair. The shot suggests that, perhaps, McCabe and Mrs. Miller have at last found each other but that their coming together has, perhaps, come too late.

The great, overarching theme of the western genre has been the reconciliation of the individual and the community. The classic westerns of the Old Hollywood had worked out a successful formula that affirmed the possibility of such a reconciliation. In *McCabe and Mrs. Miller* Altman reopens the individual-community question; and, in the film's climax, he concludes his revisionist examination of the Great Reconciliation that has been the consoling message of the Old Hollywood western.

The final sequence, which runs for some twenty minutes, is altogether extraordinary. It contains remarkable images, among the most memorable of the New Hollywood era; but they are not imposed, preemptory, modernist-fallacy images — they are images that are embedded in a credible, compelling mise-en-scène that invites audiences to discover its meaning. The sequence is certainly a culminating statement on the film's central subject — i.e., what kind of society characterized the United States at the beginning of its modern era, and how did that society accommodate individualism? But this culminating thematic statement, precisely because it *is* contained in an utterly cinematic (because it achieves a balance of credibility and expression) mise-en-scène, has none of the didacticism of traditional literary-fallacy films.

The sense of a fated encounter — the result of Altman's avoidance of narrative transitions — informs the final sequence: McCabe seems somehow to know, as he descends the exterior stairs from Mrs. Miller's room, that today is the day he must confront Butler and the other two hired guns. The early shots of the climactic sequence, in which McCabe is seen looking for his would-be killers before they can find him, contain impressive black-white images as McCabe, dressed in black suit, black coat, and black derby, hunts for the three gunmen in a town and surrounding environs blanketed with snow.

Altman uses classic cross-cutting to establish the simultaneous hunts of McCabe for his would-be assassins and the killers for their intended victim. The unearthly silence that follows a heavy snowfall is a powerful element of the mise-en-scène.

Altman, who has used images of the town's unfinished church and its mysterious pastor, Reverend Elliot, throughout the film, now brings them to the center of the action. McCabe, seeking a bird's-eye view to locate Butler and the other gunmen, climbs to the top of the unfinished steeple. As he descends the ladder connecting the steeple with the church proper, he confronts Reverend Elliott, who has seized McCabe's rifle. Reverend Elliot, who presumably disapproves of McCabe's introduction of prostitution into the town, refuses to surrender the rifle and even threatens McCabe with it. McCabe gives up trying to convince the crazed pastor that he is in mortal need of the rifle, and he leaves the church. The last shot of this segment, a long shot that reasserts the black-white contrast and forcefully establishes McCabe's isolation, shows McCabe outside the church in a composition that sets him against the overwhelming whiteness of the landscape.

Later, Butler, in search of McCabe, enters the church and shoots Reverend Elliot in cold blood. The reverend drops a lantern he has been holding as he falls.

In an extended, totally silent segment, McCabe is seen getting a gun from his saloon and then tracking down the psychotic teenager, the first of his foes McCabe has been able to locate. Altman, using tracking, medium, and long shots, in this segment reiterates the utter isolation of McCabe by again setting his black-clad figure against snow, bare trees, and the church steeple. McCabe eventually kills the baby-faced killer, sustaining a wound in the process.

Altman then significantly complicates the sequence, adding a third center of action and two more sets of contrasting images. The lantern Reverend Elliott dropped when he was struck by Butler's bullet has started a fire in the church, and the flames are noticed just after McCabe shoots the teenage gunfighter. For the remainder of the sequence, Altman intercuts shots of McCabe stalking Breed and Butler, Breed and Butler stalking McCabe, and the community coming together to save the church.

Fire-snow images are added to the black-white images; and, more important, Altman's mise-en-scène creates contrasting community-individual images as he juxtaposes medium shots featuring crowded frames to show the community battling the fire, and long shots featuring empty, snow-covered landscape to show McCabe pursuing or fleeing Breed and Butler. Altman has thus found a convincing, organic way to restate the film's central concern with the theme of individual-community: while the community has come together to save the church, it is far removed from McCabe's life-and-death struggle. This, at any rate, is the meaning Altman's direction of the climactic sequence suggests; he does not preempt the emergence of other meanings from his mise-en-scène.

McCabe, suffering considerably from his wound, evetually tracks down and kills Breed. Now, in the best tradition of the western, it has come down to a confrontation between two men. Altman, however, has effectively undermined the Manichean nature of the traditional western shoot-out; McCabe, the individual who is alienated from the community he wants to enter, is passive, ineffectual, confused, and rather feminine in his sensitivity; Butler, the ruthless hired gun, is an ambiguous figure who may (Altman's direction justifies, but does not insist upon, this interpretation) be an extreme example of the aggression and unsentimental capitalism the community at large esteems. A confrontation between such a hero and such a villain is far more ambiguous — and far more interesting — than the typical confrontation in the conventional western.

In a medium shot, Butler emerges from behind a snowbank. The camera then tracks slowly left with him. There is a cut to a medium shot of McCabe struggling up a hill. A shot of Butler taking aim and firing follows. Without a cut, Altman cranes up and then down on McCabe's body rolling down the hill, filling the screen with snow flurries as it does. After a medium shot of Butler, there is a cut to an overhead shot of McCabe's body, a slash of black in the unrelieved whiteness. Then the camera tracks left with Butler through the snow toward McCabe's body. The camera cranes up, and then McCabe fires at Butler. There is a cut to a shot of a bullet hole in Butler's forehead, followed by a slightly overhead shot of McCabe's body. McCabe, grievously wounded by Butler's bullet, painfully rises and looks at Butler's lifeless body laid out in the snow.

Several shots, all of them featuring a close-in camera and crowded frames, of the community celebrating the containment of the fire follow. A masterful, recapitulatory shot follows that series: McCabe is seen dragging himself through the snow; Butler's body is in the background of the frame, and the shouts of the celebrating firefighters are a voice-over. The camera remains stationary as McCabe collapses in the snow.

Altman now alternates shots of McCabe's inert body with shots of the firefighters and the still-intact church. There is then a cut to a slightly overhead shot of McCabe's body slumped against the window of a nondescript building. The camera remains stationary as McCabe dies. Altman holds the shot as snow flurries fill the screen and the sound of howling wind fills the soundtrack.

There is a cut to a medium shot of several Chinese in their shanty compound. The camera tracks left to the open door of one of the shanties. It tracks through the door, coming to rest on Mrs. Miller, who is lying on her side, her eyes wide open, in an opium-induced stupor. The camera resumes tracking in for an extreme close-up of her. That close-up is paralleled in the next shot, in which the camera tracks in on McCabe's lifeless face, now obscured by snow flurries and caked with frozen snow. This striking death mask is followed by another parallel image, a close-up of Mrs. Miller in a state of total, death-like withdrawal. She reaches out for a small onyx vase lying near her. A shot of the vase is followed by one in which the camera tracks in for an extreme close-up of Mrs. Miller's left eye. This image of extreme alienation, which has been paralleled by the equally powerful image of McCabe's definitive separation from both the community and Mrs. Miller, is followed by a shot of the pattern on the onyx vase, which turns into a process shot of an abstract play of color.

With that image, *McCabe and Mrs. Miller*, a nuanced, compelling, iconoclastic meditation on the great western theme of the reconciliation of the individual and the community, comes to an end.

Somehow, while traversing the distance between the television-fallacy aesthetics of *Bananas* and the literary-fallacy aesthetics of *Manhattan* and *Stardust Memories*, Woody Allen, perhaps inspired by the putatively auto-biographical nature of his material or by the ineffable charm of his leading lady, created in *Annie Hall* an altogether cinematic and richly satisfying film, one of the very few romantic comedy-dramas of the New Hollywood era and one that has rightly taken its place among the classics of that revered genre. Allen's mise-en-scène and his witty, justly famous screenplay (cowritten with Marshall Brickman) make of *Annie Hall* a seriocomic meditation on the couple relationship that bears comparison with the best film on that subject, George Cukor's *Adam's Rib*.

Annie Hall opens with Alvy Singer (Woody Allen) facing the camera and directly addressing the audience. The direct-address device, a favorite of literary-fallacy directors, normally works as a preemptive intrusion on audience involvement in a film; in this instance, however, it is not a negative factor, for reasons of both substance and style. With regard to the former, Allen through this monologue is not telling us what to think, in the manner of the literary fallacy; he is merely introducing the film, in the manner of Old Hollywood voice-over introductions. As for style, Allen's stationary camera concentrates attention on Alvy's naturalistic gestures and movements within the shot, with the result that Alvy really seems to be having a one-sided conversation (rendered, it is worth noting, without the technical intrusions a television-fallacy director might turn to to make the shot "visual") with the audience.

Alvy's monologue introduces the subject of his childhood, and the fractured chronology of *Annie Hall* begins with a three-minute sequence of Alvy as a child. With the adult Alvy's commentary as a voice-over, we see young Alvy and his mother consulting the family doctor about Alvy's obsessive conviction that the inexorable expansion and ultimate demise of the universe make such things as eating and doing homework surpassingly insignificant. In this segment and in the segment set in young Alvy's classroom that concludes the sequence, Allen introduces the thematic use of screen space that is to become increasingly prominent and significant in the mise-en-scène of *Annie Hall*. In both segments, while the adult Alvy's voice-over is a prominent feature, young Alvy is frequently off-camera, as authority figures like the family doctor and Alvy's teacher address their remarks to the unseen boy. This play on screen space will assume an important role in Allen's elaboration of the Alvy-Annie relationship that is at the heart of the film. Allen will use screen space to develop his treatment of the problem, inherent in the couple relationship, of the individual's acquiring and maintaining within the relationship his or her fair share of "space," in the psychological sense that word acquired in the "me decade" seventies, a decade whose zeitgeist *Annie Hall* both reflects and satirizes.

In between the doctor's office and classroom segments of the sequence, Allen creates a segment that, in the best sense of the word, is cinematic poetry. Adult Alvy's narration has informed us that he grew up literally under the roller coaster at Coney Island. Following an a-b-b-a pattern for the segment, Allen begins with a shot of the roller coaster. He then cuts to a deep-focus shot that, as is the nature of such shots, brings audiences into contact with the unmediated complexity and ambiguity of reality, in this instance a richly amusing reality. In the extreme foreground of the frame, a bowl of soup set on a table is seen quivering as young Alvy, in the foreground, attempts to eat it. The midground and much of the background of the frame are given over the living room of young Alvy's house, where his father, apparently unperturbed, is reading the quivering newspaper he holds in his hands. Through a window in the extreme background of the frame, the roller coaster, the cause of the pervasive quivering, can be seen.

There is then a cut that initiates a second snapshot of Alvy's childhood. First there is an establishing shot of the Coney Island pier. Young Alvy, three men in military uniform, and a blonde wearing bright red lipstick enter the establishing shot, running toward and then past the stationary camera; camera placement plus movement within the shot result in a fleeting close-up of the blonde, emphasizing her breasts.

Completing the a-b-b-a pattern, Allen concludes the segment with another shot of an amusement park ride. This time, we see young Alvy driving one of the bumper cars in the Coney Island ride his father operates. The segment, which has moved from roller coaster to bumper car, with a suggestive rendering of the reality of young Alvy's life and an emphatic rendering of the nature of his fantasy life in between, stands as a commendably economic cinematic treatment of the childhood of Alvy Singer.

After the segment set in young Alvy's classroom that concludes the sequence, there is a transitional shot of Alvy's mother saying to him (he is once again off-camera), "Even when you got famous you still mistrusted the world." There is then a cut to a long shot of a New York City upper-income neighborhood. Allen, continuing the suggestive motif of Alvy's absence from the screen, allows his voice on the soundtrack but denies him a physical presence. Alvy (again an adult) is heard complaining to his old friend Rob (Tony Roberts) about the anti–Semitism Alvy claims is pervasive in New York (an example he cites is the frequent elision of

"Did you" into "jew"). Rob dismisses Alvy's complaints as paranoia and urges him, apparently not for the first time, to consider moving to California. When the two men, who have been walking toward the stationary camera, finally reach the foreground of the frame and become clearly visible, the camera begins to track away from them, thus diminishing their presence. The shot concludes with their walking out of the frame. The total effect of the shot is to suggest a significant continuity in Alvy's life: as both child and adult, his presence is established more through verbalizing about his environment than through an active, physical engagement with it.

Alvy has told Rob that he is to meet Annie in front of the Beekman Theatre. While he is waiting for her, he is accosted by two rough-looking types (Alvy later refers to them as Teamsters) who are vaguely but very vocally sure that he is a celebrity. Alvy at first denies that he is, but the two men will not take no for an answer; Allen, by filming the encounter as an uncut long take, suggests the no-escape situation Alvy is in. Alvy (who by this time is a well-known comedian) finally admits he has been on the Johnny Carson show. The admission produces a strong reaction in the Teamsters, who proceed to alert every passerby to the presence of a celebrity.

There is a cut as Alvy, followed by the Teamsters, walks toward the curb to meet a taxi that is pulling up; the camera tracks with him as he moves left. Annie Hall (Diane Keaton) emerges from the taxi, and the camera tracks right with her and Alvy as they walk away from the curb and into the theatre lobby.

It is in the shot following the introduction of Annie that Allen begins to create his study of the couple relationship. In another sustained, uncut shot, Allen begins with a middle-distance view of Annie and Alvy in the theatre lobby. They both approach the camera for a closer medium shot that is sustained. Alvy then exits the frame, and he once again assumes an off-camera role. The camera tracks with Annie as she follows Alvy, talking to him off-camera as she moves; besides continuing his exploitation of screen (and off-screen) space, Allen here initiates the motif of one-half of his couple following the other half, a motif Cukor used to excellent effect in *Adam's Rib*. In this first sustained Alvy-Annie shot, Allen has effectively used framing and camera movement to initiate his ruefully comic examination of two individuals finding their "space" within the confines of the couple relationship.

Annie and Alvy end up seeing Marcel Ophuls's *The Sorrow and the Pity*, a brief excerpt from which is shown. From the excerpt, Allen cuts to a medium shot of Alvy (who wants to make love) and Annie (who does not) in bed. Something Annie says triggers the scene that follows, which depicts Alvy's meeting his first wife, Allison (Carol Kane), about fifteen years before the film's present time. This is followed by a brilliant shot-sequence in which Allen conveys the essence of the Alvy-Allison marriage. Paralleling the just-seen shot of Annie and Alvy, the shot-sequence begins with Alvy and Allison on a bed. The camera tracks circularly with Alvy as he paces around the bedroom, pausing when Alvy does. Allison invades Alvy's space by walking into the frame. As if to confirm Allison's preemption of Alvy's "space" (or rather, since the camera consistently takes Alvy's point of view, his *perception* that she is preempting his space) the camera tracks with her when she returns to the bed, leaving Alvy out of the frame. Alvy then walks into the frame for a restored medium shot of him and Allison. The restoration of an equal sharing of space, however, is short-lived; for Alvy (whose problem, as he fitfully acknowledges and Allen artfully suggests, is that he wants to be involved in a relationship but is continually stepping out of one, fearful of the loss of individual space that a relationship might entail) almost immediately walks out of the frame, leaving Allison talking to him off-camera. In an emphatic camera movement that suggests Alvy's (perhaps unconscious) preference for a detached, verbal kind of presence, Allen pans left to a medium shot of Alvy again directly addressing the audience as he comments on his marriage with Allison, a superfluous commentary, given that the marriage has just been expertly summarized in the shot-sequence.

The film returns to its present time for a delightful scene in which Alvy and Annie have an encounter with several lobsters they are trying to prepare for dinner. After an establishing shot of a house on Long Island, Allen cuts to another lengthy, uncut shot depicting Annie and Alvy's comic battle with the lobsters. This shot again recalls *Adam's Rib*: as Cukor frequently did in that film with Tracy and Hepburn, Allen here uses a long take and unobtrusive camera movement to capture the marvelous naturalism of the rapport between Allen-the-actor and Diane Keaton. Allen's directorial self-effacement — he seems to know there are times when the director should simply allow unmediated acting to convey meaning — is quite Cukorian and, in this instance and others in the film, quite effective.

We next see Annie and Alvy in a long shot, walking against the background of sand dunes at sunset. The camera tracks left with them; we can not see their faces, but their conversation is heard on the soundtrack. Just as they are about to walk out of the frame, there is a cut to a very brief scene from Annie's past in her hometown, Chippewa Falls, Wisconsin. There is then a cut to a scene from Annie's more recent past in New York. We see Annie at a party with her then-boyfriend, a rather self-important actor. There is then a cut to a shot of Alvy and present-day Annie walking toward past-time Annie and her actor boyfriend; the past-time couple is engaged in a seemingly serious conversation. In another sustained shot in which Allen wisely allows a stationary camera to pick up the delightfully nuanced interaction of Allen-the-actor and Keaton, present-day Annie and Alvy are seen exchanging wry observations about past-time Annie and her former boyfriend.

Allen then brings a satisfying sense of closure to the sequence by returning to present-time Annie and Alvy on the dunes. In what works as an effective tribute to the privacy of the couple relationship, Annie and Alvy are never seen in the shot, which is quite lengthy. Their conversation is a voice-over as the camera tracks slowly across the dunes that conceal them from view. This shot, as much as any single shot in the film, shows Woody Allen's freedom in *Annie Hall* from both the television and literary fallacies. A director committed to the television fallacy would not have created a shot of such duration that did not feature either up-front images of the characters or a "technical event" of one kind or another to prevent the shot's being visually dull; a director committed to the literary fallacy, eager to assert the meaning of the shot, would have replaced its suggestive ambiguity (a tribute to privacy is only one of a number of meanings that can be derived from the shot) with a less nuanced "image-text" that declared the author's interpretation of the shot.

Once again, something Annie has said triggers a return to the past. This time, the subject is Alvy's second marriage, to a woman named Robin (Janet Margolin). Allen covers this relationship in three long takes. First, there is a sustained tracking shot of Alvy (reluctantly, contemptuously) and Robin (enthusiastically) making their way among the guests at a literary cocktail party. Next, there is a sustained stationary-camera shot of Alvy, who has slipped away from the party to watch a basketball game on television, futilely trying to make love to Robin, who is outraged at Alvy's preference for basketball over literary chit-chat. Finally, we see Alvy and Robin at home in bed. The camera remains stationary as Robin, unmoved by the desperate pleas of Alvy, declares that, once again, the ambiance is not quite right for lovemaking and that Alvy's insistence on it has given her a headache. Alvy, announcing that he is going to take "another in a series of cold showers" gets out of bed and begins to move to the right. As he exits the frame, this concise reconstruction of Alvy's second marriage concludes.

The next sequence moves forward to the recent past: the day Annie and Alvy met. They meet on an indoor tennis court on a blind date arranged by Rob and his current girlfriend. The sequence is notable on two counts. First, Allen's placement of the camera during the tennis segment of the sequence assigns Alvy off-camera space, with the shots of Annie playing tennis reflecting Alvy's point of view. The result is the first extended passage in the film in which Alvy is denied a physical *and* a verbal presence (the sequence begins with a voice-over of Alvy speaking to Rob, but the voice-over ends once Annie appears, and the device of Alvy's voice-over is not used again until the last minutes of the film). Allen thus extends his thematic use of screen space to film's aural space by suggesting that, from Alvy's point of view, Annie's preemption of his space is so complete that she has even silenced the super-ego voice that has been up to this point the most prominent manifestation of Alvy's presence.

Second, in the latter part of the sequence, when Alvy and Annie encounter each other after the tennis match, Allen turns to a subtle editing pattern with considerable thematic resonance. In a series of sixteen medium shots that alternate between Annie and Alvy, all of the shots of Alvy are held briefly, while several of Annie's are sustained. Allen, who has already shown his sensivity to the thematic connotations of screen space, here subtly uses screen time to deepen his film's preoccupation with the problem of achieving and maintaining balance within the couple relationship. The editing of this segment adds to the sense that Annie is encroaching on Alvy's individuality, diminishing his presence — or, more accurately, that Alvy, whose point of view is explicitly or implicitly controlling throughout the film, *feels* she is diminishing his presence.

After a very funny scene showing Alvy cringing through Annie's hair-raising drive to her apartment (he has accepted her offer of a lift home), *Annie Hall* reaches one of its high points in a sequence that can be numbered among the best romantic-comedic sequences on film.

The sequence begins with a sustained, stationary-camera medium shot of Annie and Alvy engaged in comically awkward conversation on the sidewalk in front of her apartment building. Alvy finally accepts her invitation to have a drink, and the camera tracks right with them as they move away from the curb.

There is a cut to another of the brilliant long takes of the film. The shot begins as a medium shot of Alvy, now inside Annie's apartment. The camera tracks left with him as he moves into a medium shot with Annie. The camera then tracks left with both of them, pausing for another medium shot of them; balance and equality, the twin ideal of the couple relationship, are thus emphasized. Then, however, the balance is broken as the camera tracks left with Annie, leaving Alvy out of the frame. In a marvelous comic monologue that in itself justifies Diane Keaton's Oscar

Annie and Alvy carry on a comically awkward conversation in front of her apartment building. Diane Keaton, Woody Allen, *Annie Hall* (Metro-Goldwyn-Mayer/United Artists, 1977).

for her performance, Annie relates to Alvy (off-camera) an anecdote about one of her grandmother's friends back in Chippewa Falls. The camera then tracks right with Annie as she walks into a briefly held medium shot with Alvy. Balance has been restored.

The camera follows Annie and Alvy onto the terrace of her apartment. There is a sustained medium shot of them sipping wine and exchanging banalities. Allen then creates a passage that both celebrates the couple relationship that is the heart and soul of the romantic comedy genre and acknowledges the tension that always underlines that relationship. In a series of shots that are equally—in terms of both space and time—divided between Alvy and Annie, Allen shows them engaged in polite conversation, while what each of them is *really* thinking is expressed in subtitles that appear across the middle of the screen (example: Alvy is talking about the "relevant aesthetic criteria" of photography; his subtitle reads, "I wonder what she looks like naked"). This series of shots, at once a celebration and an exposé, is the best rendering I have seen of how the mating game is played in contemporary urban America.

After this series of alternating medium shots, the couple relationship is emphasized in a sustained, stationary-camera shot of Annie and Alvy. They agree to meet again on the night when Annie, who is trying to break into show business, is to make her singing debut.

We next see Annie singing "It Had to Be You" in a noisy nightclub full of rude patrons. Annie and Alvy are then seen walking to a deli after her nightclub appearance. The camera tracks with them as they walk, then pauses as they stop for a gentle, tentative kiss. After a brief, very funny scene in the deli (to Alvy's horror, Annie orders a pastrami on white with mayonnaise, lettuce and tomato), there is a cut to a shot in which the camera cranes down on Annie and Alvy in bed. Allen complements that uncharacteristically dramatic camera movement with emphatically romantic lighting for the film's first close-up: the camera holds on the lovers' faces, which are partially illuminated by what might be a street light but has the effect of moonlight.

There is then a cut to the cover of a book whose title is *The Denial of Death*. The camera tacks back to reveal Annie and Alvy in a bookstore; Alvy, asserting his intellectual presence, is steering Annie toward the selection of books on his favorite subject, death. From the bookstore, there is a cut to a scene in which, in a series of rapid cuts, Annie and Alvy comment on the comical variety of people passing in review before the Central Park bench where they are seated.

This dating segment is brought to a romantic close in the sequence following the Central Park scene. It is just after sunset, and Annie and

Alvy are seen on a river bank, walking left-right past the stationary camera. They pause to embrace in a medium shot in which they are in the foreground-left of the frame, while the river, a bridge, and the lights of the city fill the midground and background of the frame. Allen sustains this lovely shot for a considerable period, bringing *Annie Hall* to its romantic peak. The romantic ideal of the couple has now been effectively established and celebrated; the rest of the film will emphasize the more realistic perspective of the couple that Allen has already subtly introduced.

The idealized image of the couple is immediately shattered in the next sequence, in which Allen's montage and mise-en-scène renew the theme of the problem of maintaining both unity and balance within the couple relationship.

The sequence begins with a medium shot of Alvy carrying a carton filled with books. The camera tracks left with him into a medium shot with Annie. It then tracks right with Annie and Alvy as they move to the far background of the frame. The tracking again reverses direction as it moves left with Alvy toward the midground of the frame.

Annie, despite Alvy's reservations about the idea, has decided to move in with Alvy; and the restless, contradictory camera movements of the early part of the sequence convey the tensions in the relationship caused by Annie's determination to invade Alvy's space, literally. Allen reinforces the idea of fissures in the relationship by adding a fragmented montage to his well-established use of screen and off-screen space: as Annie and Alvy continue to argue about the wisdom of the move, Allen uses a series of ten alternating medium shots in which one-half of the couple speaks to the off-camera other half. The sequence concludes with Alvy walking into a two-shot with Annie. The couple has been restored, but the emphasis given in the sequence to fragmentation and separation suggests the tentative quality of the restoration.

One of the weak sequences of *Annie Hall* follows. Annie and Alvy are again at the Long Island house. Alvy is trying to persuade Annie to stop her practice of smoking marijuana before having sex. She reluctantly agrees to forgo it, but her heart is not in the effort. To convey that idea, Allen shows Annie's spirit — her soul, her emotional self — detaching itself from her body as Annie and Alvy begin the preliminaries of lovemaking. Annie's spirit addresses Annie and Alvy, who are off-camera; Alvy, not surprisingly, complains to Annie about her extreme detachment, but she argues that he should be satisfied that he has her body. The sequence is weak because it is one of those violations of the balance between credibility and expression of which V. F. Perkins has written: Allen has not created a world in his film that can tolerate such a heavy-handed, literal depiction of Annie's apparent problem (it is never again dealt with in the film) with bringing emotional commitment to the act of sex.

For the third time in the film, a remark made by Annie triggers a recollection of Alvy's past (Allen's establishment of this pattern strengthens the theme of Alvy's perception that involvement with Annie means a reduction in his space: she even exercises control over his memory). This time it is a recollection of the days when Alvy was writing material for other comedians. In a brief, funny scene, we see Alvy striving to be polite while a Las Vegas–type comic instructs him on the "classy" comic materials he wants Alvy to write for him.

There is then a jump to the more recent past. In an excellent long shot, Alvy is seen performing his own material before a receptive audience of University of Wisconsin students. Alvy, far from being lost in the vastness of the auditorium, has the audience in the palm of his hand as he delivers what is a typical Woody Allen stand-up monologue.

From the stage there is a cut to a medium shot of Annie waiting for Alvy backstage. Alvy enters the frame, and the camera then tracks with Annie and Alvy as they exit the frame. The couple relationship has been restored in a context that suggests Annie has come over to Alvy.

In fact, however, Alvy and Annie are on the latter's home ground: the University of Wisconsin is not far from Chippewa Falls, and Annie takes advantage of Alvy's presence in her home state to introduce him to her family.

The sequence that follows, perhaps one of the best remembered of the film, is Allen's most sustained treatment of one of the sub-themes of *Annie Hall*: the cultural clash between WASP, Midwest Annie and Jewish, New York Alvy.

There is first a witty establishing shot of the picture-postcard, Norman Rockwell home of Annie's family. Allen then uses a series of sixteen medium shots that isolate Alvy from the members of Annie's family during an excruciatingly polite Easter dinner (in one of the shots, Alvy appears in the guise of an Orthodox rabbi; this reflects Alvy's certainty that Grammie Hall, who has been glaring at him throughout the meal, is a rabid anti-Semite).

During the meal, Alvy directly addresses the audience as he muses on the contrast between this family dinner and a typical dinner in the Singer household. Allen then goes to a split screen: in an interesting variation on the film's screen-space motif, Alvy's family at dinner is given three-fourths of the screen, with the meal at the Hall home taking the remaining one-fourth. Mrs. Hall (Colleen Dewhurst) asks questions that are answered by Alvy's mother from her side of the screen; the questions emphasize the gap separating Protestant self-assurance from Jewish guilt.

The film now returns to the present time. In a four-minute sequence consisting of three shots, Allen creates a mise-en-scène that stands as an amusing, nuanced meditation on the dark side of intimacy and the dynamics of coming together and moving apart.

There is first an establishing shot of a brownstone on a New York City street; Annie and Alvy shouting at each other is a voice-over in the shot. When they enter the frame, an extended shot that recalls the great sustained "following" shots of *Adam's Rib* commences. The camera tracks left as Alvy follows several paces behind Annie; she is angry because he has accused her of being involved with the teacher of one of the classes she has been taking (the classes were Alvy's idea) at NYU. The tracking camera plus the movements of Alvy and Annie within the shot create a compelling rendering of a couple that can not find the center. At one point in the shot, Annie is out of the frame and Alvy is following her, shouting at her; by the end of the shot, it is Alvy who is out of the frame and Annie who is following him.

The second shot of the sequence involves a return to the recent past; Annie's voice from the preceding shot serves as a transition. Allen here creates a composition that emphasizes the sometimes suffocating intimacy of the couple relationship. Alvy, his back to the camera, is seen at the sink in the tiny kitchen of his apartment. Annie enters the frame at the left and then moves right; the camera tracks in on her, eliminating Alvy from the frame. Alvy enters the frame for a cramped, uncomfortable-looking two-shot that suggests stifling intimacy. Annie is telling Alvy about her first, very productive session with an analyst. As she talks and moves about the minuscule kitchen, the camera tracks with her, again denying Alvy screen space. Alvy, however, again breaks into Annie's shot, and there follows a sustained medium shot of the two of them. But this center will not hold: Annie, perhaps asserting the independence her analyst has encouraged, walks out of the frame, leaving Alvy alone in the medium shot. Alvy, though he now has the space he always seems to demand, is not content and again moves toward Annie, forcing himself into another tight medium shot with her. The camera, however, again follows Annie's movement and eliminates Alvy from the frame. For the fourth time in the shot, Alvy follows Annie, and a medium shot of the two of them results. Alvy, in what can probably be interpreted as a response to his perceived failure to maintain his space with Annie, falls back on his commentator role, directly addressing the audience about a remark Annie has made. As he verbalizes, Annie exits the frame.

This excellent long take is followed by another equally effective one that brings the film back to its present time. Annie and Alvy are seen in a medium shot, still arguing as she enters a waiting taxi. Annie exits the frame, leaving Alvy alone in the space they had occupied together. In a passage that is both funny and touching, Allen continues the shot without a cut as the camera tracks with Alvy as he randomly stops strangers on the street to solicit their advice on how to sustain a couple relationship. With that, this great sequence, in which Allen's long takes have created a sense of genuine involvement in the disintegration of a couple, concludes.

There follows a comic interlude, an animated segment in which cartoon figures representing Annie, Alvy, and Rob discuss the breakup of the Annie-Alvy couple and what Alvy should do about it.

What he does, reluctantly and on Rob's advice, is date other women. In a funny scene, Alvy is seen enduring a counter-culture event at Madison Square Garden that his date, a *Rolling Stone* reporter (Shelley Duvall) is rapturously enthusiastic about. Later, Alvy and his date are seen in bed; he reacts with Woody Allen's inimitable mix of amusement and contempt when she describes sex with him as a "Kafkaesque experience."

The phone rings while Alvy is in bed with the *Rolling Stone* reporter. That call is the prelude to what may be the best sequence in *Annie Hall*, the one in which Allen's mise-en-scène most effectively renders the complicated tension-attraction that characterizes the magnetic field of the couple relationship.

The phone call is from Annie, who asks Alvy to come immediately to help with an unspecified emergency. There follows a shot that runs for two minutes without a cut. It begins with a medium shot of Annie, her back to the camera, walking toward the door of her apartment. There follows a sustained medium shot of Annie and Alvy at the door. Alvy begins to walk toward the camera, obscuring Annie from view as he moves; but the camera, as if eager to hasten a reconciliation between Alvy and Annie by keeping them together in the frame, tracks back and restores Annie to the frame. Thoughts of reconciliation, however, are premature: Annie exits the frame almost immediately after being restored to it, leaving Alvy the sole occupant of the screen space as he talks to her off-camera. Annie then moves right to reenter the frame, but she immediately leaves it again: this reconciliation, if it is to come, will not come easily. Annie continues to be the active, if indecisive, half of the couple as she moves back into the frame; this time she pauses for another medium shot with Alvy. Then there is a camera movement that suggests the relationship is returning to its status before the breakup: as Annie moves right, the camera tracks with her, eliminating Alvy from the frame. As he has several times before, Alvy forces his way into Annie's screen space; and there is another sustained medium shot of the two of them. Allen's next series of directorial choices suggests that, contrary to the impression created by his preceding choices, Alvy has attained the dominant position in the relationship that he at least subconsciously wants. Alvy moves left, the camera tracks with him, and Annie follows. After a brief period in which Alvy is off-camera, the "following" motif is repeated: Alvy again moves left, and the camera and Annie again follow. It would appear that, if there is to be a reconciliation, it will be based on Alvy's regaining control of the space he had lost (or thought he had lost) to Annie.

The emergency that prompted Annie's call is a spider in her bathroom. There is a cut to a shot of Alvy, tennis racket in hand, entering the bathroom to do battle with the spider. There is then a cut to a superb shot which Allen composes to capture the ambiguity of the Annie-Alvy reconciliation.

Annie is seen curled up on her bed, her head in her hands. Alvy enters the frame, and there is a sustained, stationary-camera medium shot as they quietly and tenderly agree to reconcile. Allen's composition, however, suggests the tentativeness of this reconciliation: Annie and Alvy are crowded into the right corner of the frame, leaving a good deal of screen space unoccupied. In the context of the significance screen space has acquired in Allen's mise-en-scène, the thought that Annie and Alvy will soon be struggling to apportion that unfilled space is unavoidable.

The reconciliation sequence concludes with a sustained, stationary-camera shot of Annie and Alvy in bed. Their second attempt to make the couple relationship work is under way.

Alvy has agreed to let Annie help him have more fun, and the next sequence shows them on a fun outing with Rob to the old neighborhood in Brooklyn. The sequence involves another return to Alvy's childhood: adult Alvy, Annie and Rob are present at a World War II–era party featuring young Alvy, his comical Aunt Tessie, and an obnoxious family friend named Joey Nichols. The sequence is notable as another instance in which Allen's compositions and stationary camera capture the wonderfully naturalistic interaction of Allen-the-actor and Diane Keaton.

When Annie and Alvy return from Brooklyn, he gives her the presents he has bought for her birthday. In what turns out to be the last shot of the film that unambiguously affirms Alvy and Annie as a couple, Alvy enters a shot that had been a medium shot of Annie opening her gifts to form a medium shot of the two of them, which is sustained. Piano music on the soundtrack, serving as an aural transition, leads to the next sequence.

Annie (who apparently has been progressing in her career off-camera) is seen performing a very stylized, polished rendition of "Seems Like Old Times" at a posh nightclub. After her performance, she and Alvy are at the bar of the club when Tony Lacy (Paul Simon), a West Coast record producer, comes up to introduce himself. He invites Annie and Alvy to his hotel suite for a drink. In a series of cuts that explicitly portrays the new fissures in the recently restored Annie-Alvy relationship, Alvy indicates his desire to decline Lacy's invitation and Annie indicates her inclination to accept it. Alvy wins out, but the battle clearly has been rejoined.

Allen uses a split screen for the second time in the film for the next sequence, in which Annie and Alvy are seen in sessions with their respective analysts. Each, of course, is complaining about the other; and their sometimes overlapping dialogue suggests how hopelessly intertwined the couple relationship can become (at one point, Annie and Alvy respond to the same question posed by their analysts about how often they have sex. Annie: "Constantly, three times a week." Alvy: "Almost never, only three times a week"). The split screen is an obvious indicator of the erosion that has occurred in the Annie-Alvy relationship since the reconciliation. It is perhaps significant that, as was the case in the first split-screen sequence, the screen space is not evenly split: Alvy and his analyst occupy three-fourths of the space, with Annie and her analyst obliged to make do with the one-fourth that remains.

A brief scene in which Alvy and Annie are with friends who urge them to try cocaine (Alvy winds up sneezing away two thousand dollars worth of it) serves as an introduction to Alvy and Annie's trip to Los Angeles, where Alvy, bowing to the pressure of his agent, is to be a presenter at an awards show.

Los Angeles–bashing is a subtheme of *Annie Hall* that is fondly remembered by the film's admirers, and Woody Allen's dead-on put-downs of the city have become part of the popular culture. His only sustained visual treatment of the subtheme occurs when Alvy and Annie first arrive in Los Angeles. As they ride through Beverly Hills in a convertible driven by Rob (he has become a Los Angeles resident and the star of a successful sitcom), shots of palm trees, the glaring sun, and the incredible architectural mish-mash of Beverly Hills are contrasted with "We Wish You a Merry Christmas" and other Christmas carols on the soundtrack (it is Christmas time, and Alvy is especially upset about being away from New York for Christmas). Accompanying the visual rendering of Beverly Hills and Los Angeles and sharing the soundtrack with the carols is a running commentary from Alvy on the horrors of Los Angeles, which is counterpointed by Rob's running defense of the city and Annie's expressions of enthusiasm about its hedonistic contrast to New York.

Alvy comes down with a mysterious illness that is probably a severe case of LA-itis. He experiences an abrupt and inexplicable recovery the moment his agent gets him out of his scheduled appearance on the awards show.

In the next sequence, the only instance I am aware of in the Woody Allen canon of a sustained crowd sequence, Allen merges his verbal and visual assault on Los Angeles into a perfectly realized statement that should stand as the last cinematic word on the glitzy emptiness of the upper-showbiz stratum of Los Angeles society.

Annie, Alvy and Rob have been invited to party at Tony Lacy's mansion. After a shot of the three of them approaching the house in Rob's convertible, there is a cut to two guests at the party engaged in a circular conversation about "taking a meeting." There is then a cut to two other guests solemnly discussing the New Hollywood process in which a "notion" becomes a "concept," which in turn is transformed into something called an "idea."

There is a cut to a medium shot of Alvy and Rob (Annie is, in more than one sense, lost in the crowd) observing the scene at the party; the glare of the sun makes the patio and the guests milling in and out of the glass doors which fill the background of the frame almost invisible.

The shot of Alvy and Rob exchanging sardonic remarks about the party guests with the blindingly cheerful California sun blazing behind them is reprised twice, intercut with a shot of a couple Alvy describes as recent graduates of Masters and Johnson and a shot of Tony Lacy's girlfriend (a quintessential California beauty wearing white on white) approaching Alvy and Rob. Three brief shots follow: one of Alvy, Rob and Lacy's girlfriend, one of Annie and Lacy dancing, and one of two guests discussing a third person who "gives good meeting."

There is then a cut to a lengthy, uncut shot covering Alvy and Annie's tour of the Lacy mansion. The camera first tracks left with Lacy and his girlfriend as they lead Annie and Alvy on the tour. The camera remains stationary while the four of them are in the mansion's screening room; during this interlude, Alvy has a hilarious nonconversation with an unidentified guest who declares that *Grande Illusion* is a "great film to see stoned." Lacy and his girlfriend then resume the tour. They exit the frame, leaving Alvy, who is experiencing culture shock, and Annie, who is bedazzled by this glimpse of High Hollywood at play, alone in the frame.

The camera resumes tracking with Alvy and Annie, who then exit the frame. The shot concludes with a marvelous "full-stop" image: one of the party guests (Jeff Goldblum in an all-too-brief appearance) is seen speaking on a telephone, saying with total earnestness, "I forgot my mantra."

The party sequence concludes with three more shots: an overview of the uniformly and unisexually pretty party guests, Alvy with two female guests in front of a most incongruous Christmas tree, and a second shot of Annie and Lacy dancing.

There is a cut to a shot of an airplane flying east, followed by a shot of Annie and Alvy inside a plane. Allen immediately establishes the disunity in his central couple by showing Annie looking out a window from her seat and Alvy staring blankly ahead from his: screen space is fairly and equally divided, but unity appears to have been sacrificed for equality. Allen uses the aural component of mise-en-scène (this seems a good point to mention Allen's generally excellent, almost Wellesian, use of sound in *Annie Hall*) to strengthen the idea of disunity: he alternates fragments of Annie's and Alvy's unspoken thoughts on the soundtrack, thus emphasizing the noncommunication the shot depicts. When Annie and Alvy finally face each other and speak, they almost simultaneously declare that it is probably time to acknowledge that their relationship is going nowhere.

Allen now creates a sequence whose mise-en-scène, with its emphasis on two people moving in and out of the frame and its exploitation of the connotations of an empty screen, recalls Cukor's renderings of the disintegration of a couple in *Adam's Rib*. Allen's mise-en-scène, however, does not quite attain the intensity of Cukor's, perhaps because Allen was more concerned than Cukor was with assuring that his film remained unmistakably a comedy. Whereas Cukor's sequences relied on long takes, which tend to increase involvement and thus intensity, Allen cuts frequently in his sequence, which makes for a less involving but undoubtedly more amusing sequence.

From Annie and Alvy on the plane there is a cut to a medium shot of Alvy standing near a bookcase and speaking to someone off-camera. There is then a cut to a shot in which the camera tracks left with Annie, who is carrying an armload of books. In the companion to this shot, the camera tracks *right* with Alvy as he loads books into a carton. Two medium shots of Annie follow; in them, she is ostensibly speaking to Alvy off-camera, but she actually seems to be speaking to no one in particular as she looks almost straight-on into the camera. These two shots are matched — or, more accurately, *mis*matched — with two tracking shots of Alvy busily engaged in segregating his and Annie's possessions.

The second tracking shot of Alvy turns into the only long take of the sequence. The long take, up to a point, insists on disintegration: after a brief medium shot of Annie and Alvy, she exits right and he exits left, leaving the screen empty. Then, however, in a problematic conclusion of the shot and the sequence, Annie and Alvy reenter the frame for a sustained shot of them in the foreground center of the frame. This conclusion would seem to be inconsistent with the rest of the sequence, with its pronounced emphasis on separation, disunity and moving apart. The conclusion only makes sense in light of the film as a whole: it prefigures the conclusion of the film itself, with its strong suggestion that Annie and Alvy will manage to retain *some* kind of relationship, even after they have given up on the couple relationship.

The breakup is followed by a segment that conveys Alvy's lonely life without Annie. First he is seen again stopping strangers on the street to express his misery and ask advice about how to deal with it. There is then a touching scene in which Alvy attempts to duplicate with another woman his and Annie's joyous frolic with uncooperative lobsters; the attempt is an utter failure, a demonstration that Alvy's capacity for fun is a function of his connection with Annie. There follows a scene in which Alvy walks alone on the river bank that was the setting for his and Annie's first declaration of mutual love. Finally, there's a shot of Alvy on his bed talking by telephone to Annie, who is living in Los Angeles with Tony Lacy. Alvy, unable to persuade Annie to return to New York, decides to go to Los Angeles to continue his campaign.

After a series of brief shots showing Alvy arriving in Los Angeles and attempting to drive the car he has rented, Allen creates what is, appropriately enough, perhaps the most fragmented sequence in his *oeuvre*. He uses twenty-eight shots, divided equally between Annie and Alvy, to cover Alvy's unsuccessful attempt to talk Annie into returning to New York and resuming their relationship (Annie and Alvy are sharing a table at a health food restaurant, where Alvy, with pronounced distaste, has ordered "alfalfa sprouts and a plate of mashed yeast"). Allen's montage brings to completion the motif he has skillfully elaborated through his mise-en-scène: Alvy and Annie have undeniably attained equality of space, but at the cost of being a couple — in the entire sequence they are never on-screen together.

Allen, perhaps again acting out of a desire to keep his film unmistakably a comedy, follows the failed reconciliation sequence with the weakest segment in the film. Alvy, a nondriver, creates havoc when he tries to get out of the health food restaurant parking lot, and he eventually has a run-in with a scrupulously polite but humorless policeman. Alvy winds up in jail, and Rob comes to bail him out. This segment, while quite funny, detracts from our involvement with the Annie-Alvy relationship (or what is left of it) and probably should have been placed at another point in the film (it is quite detachable and therefore constitutes the only clear-cut manifestation in the film of Allen's *Bananas*-era televison fallacy) or omitted altogether.

There follows Allen's most explicit treatment of Alvy's tendency to detach himself from the reality of his circumstances and adopt a highly intellectualized, very verbal stance toward them. We see Alvy in a rehearsal hall observing two young actors reenact the encounter at the health food restaurant we have just seen. For this artistic rendering of a major event in his life, Alvy contrives a happy ending: his script (this is a scene from Alvy's first play) has the Annie character at the last moment agreeing to a reconciliation with the Alvy character. Alvy then directly addresses the audience, rationalizing his transformation of a failure in life into a success in art. The direct-address motif has subtly evolved in the course of the film to the point where it has come to signify Alvy's taking refuge in a detached narrator's role when he has suffered a setback as an involved participant in life. The motif was almost totally absent during the period of Alvy's involvement with Annie; its reappearance now confirms the end of that involvement.

While Alvy devised a blatantly contrived happy ending for his play, Allen creates a bittersweet ending for his film that is, in the best sense of the words, romantic and sentimental, but not in blatant violation of reasonable standards of credibility.

The concluding sequence begins with the return of another long-absent motif, Alvy's voice-over. Alvy's voice, however, shares the soundtrack with a reprise of Annie's haunting (and to Alvy it is literally haunting) rendition of "Seems Like Old Times." Here is another instance of Allen's making excellent use of the aural component of mise-en-scène: if Alvy has lost his space on the screen and has resumed his role of detached verbalizer, Annie shares, and alters the shape of, even the reduced aural space Alvy is now limited to.

With Alvy's voice-over continuing, there is a cut to a long shot of Alvy and an unidentified woman running into Annie and an unidentified man outside a New York theatre showing *The Sorrow and the Pity*. This is followed by a medium shot in which Annie and Alvy are seen through the glass wall of a restaurant laughing their way through a meal; Alvy's voice-over and Annie's "Old Times" still share (and, to some extent, compete for space on) the soundtrack.

The final segment of the concluding sequence is brilliant, as Allen brings the motif of space he has elaborated throughout the film to completion.

First, he again uses montage to amplify and comment upon the theme of individual "space": as "Old Times" dominates the soundtrack, eighteen shots that, in random chronological order, review the Annie-Alvy relationship are intercut in a stunning montage that comes very close to capturing on film the process of memory. Allen, however, does more here than convey the remembrance of a love lost. By crowding the screen space and fragmenting it into a jigsaw puzzle of remembered events, Allen calls into question the film's fundamental preoccupation (which, of course, is *Alvy's* preoccupation, the film being a reflection of his point of view) with the calibrated divisions of space. It is now evident, even to Alvy, that if Annie encroached on his space, she also brought a fullness to his life that he was too insecure or too self-oriented to appreciate.

The last shot of the film confirms the rather melancholy conclusion about Alvy's self-defeating quest for his own, uncrowded space. With Alvy's voice-over continuing, Annie and Alvy are seen in a long shot standing on a corner near Lincoln Center. Annie exits the frame to the left, and Allen holds on the long shot of Alvy standing alone on the corner; the composition and camera placement emphasize his insignificance in a relatively vast space. Then Alvy exits the frame to the right; and Allen, in perhaps the best single directorial choice in the film, holds on the empty scene. Alvy's struggle for individual space has ended in emptiness. The shot of the empty scene continues as "Old Times" comes to an end and Alvy, his voice-over continuing, relates an old joke that suggests he has learned a lesson about human relationships — especially the couple relationship — that he was not ready to absorb during the time when Annie filled his life.

Peter Yates's *Breaking Away* is one of those works of art that should not have happened. Nothing in Yates's uneven filmography (*Bullit, John and Mary, The Friends of Eddie Coyle, For Pete's Sake, The Deep*) would have predicted his Renoiresque direction of *Breaking Away*; nothing in the trend lines of the New Hollywood, which at least since *American Graffiti* has turned material like that of *Breaking Away* into formulaic television-fallacy exercises, would have indicated the appearance of a film that would redeem such material from the lamentable treatment it had been receiving and remind us of the deep pleasures to be derived from the tribal comedy genre when it receives appropriately cinematic treatment.

The comparison to the work of Jean Renoir is not excessive: *Breaking*

Away is solidly within the glorious Renoir tradition, an extraordinarily effective example of what critic Leo Braudy has called the open film:

> In a closed film the world of the film is the only thing that exists; everything within it has its place in the plot of the film — every object, every character, every gesture, every action. In an open film the world of the film is a momentary frame around an ongoing reality. The objects and the characters in the film existed before the camera focused on them and they will exist after the film is over.... The difference may be the difference between finding a world and creating one.... In closed films the audience is a victim, imposed on by the perfect coherence of the world on the screen. In open films the audience is a guest, invited into the film as an equal whose vision of reality is potentially the same as that of the director.

Braudy quite naturally posits a contrast between the open film and the closed film, but expressing the contrast as one between the open and television-fallacy film is equally valid and perhaps more to the point in this New Hollywood era. The television-fallacy film is closed on two levels: on the level of substance, it closes its characters into stereotypes and its stereotyped characters into a "format" (it is perhaps significant that that word, whose differences with the word it has largely replaced, *structure*, are more significant than its similarities, has come into currency during the television era) that makes little connection with recognizable reality; on the level of style, the television-fallacy film is locked into a mise-en-scène that endows the film with a fragmented pseudoreality of highlighted conflicts and carefully timed resolutions that shut out audiences from genuine involvement with the film expereince. In comparison to the television-fallacy films of the New Hollywood, the closed films of Hitchcock and Lang that Braudy uses to elucidate his important insight seem relatively open to a compelling, if highly stylized, reality.

Openness in film is achieved through a director's success in conveying the sense that a film, in Braudy's felicitous phrase, is a "momentary frame around an ongoing reality." That sense in turn is principally achieved through the rhythm created by a director's choices with regard to shot duration, camera placement, sound, movement within the shot and montage. It is these elements of mise-en-scène, plus montage, that are the locus of Yates's achievement in *Breaking Away*, a film whose openness recalls the work not only of Renoir but also of such Old Hollywood masters as McCarey, early Stevens, and middle-period Cukor.

Breaking Away begins with a sequence that effectively conveys the idea, a tenet of the open-film director's art, that the frame simply cannot contain all the reality the film finds; Yates's direction repeatedly implies the larger reality that has overflowed or eluded his momentary frame.

There is first an establishing shot of a quarry containing a small but apparently deep lake. Using the aural component of mise-en-scène to suggest what lies outside the frame, Yates includes in this initial shot a voice-over of an untrained male voice singing a seemingly improvised country-and-western song. Yates leaves the establishing shot to pan right, not to locate the source of the voice-over but to provide a more complete view of the quarry, the lake and the woods surrounding them. Still in no hurry (as a television-fallacy director would be) to focus the film on specific characters, Yates then cuts to a long shot of the woods; four moving figures can be discerned in the background of the frame. The voice-over of the country-and-western song continues.

There is a cut to a sustained shot in which the camera, as if determined to immerse its guests, the audience, in the specificity of this particular place, tracks back from its position within the woods to give a more expansive view of them. Gradually, unobtrusively, four teenage boys enter this place. Mike (Dennis Quaid) and Moocher (Jackie Earle Haley) appear first, followed by Dave (Dennis Christopher) and, finally, Cyril (Daniel Stern). The momentary frame barely catches the four boys as the camera, tracking away from them, finds and then loses them; even when they are within the frame they are partially obscured by trees.

The idea of characters embedded in a defining milieu is emphasized in the next shot, a long shot of the four boys walking through the woods near the quarry. This is followed by a stationary camera medium shot that again conveys the sense of a momentary frame around an ongoing reality: Mike and Moocheer enter the frame, then walk out of it; Dave and Cyril enter and pause in the midground of the frame. The camera tracks left with them as they catch up with Mike and Moocher. Another stationary-camera shot then captures the four boys on a slab of rock overhanging the quarry lake. The frame around them, however, is again only momentary: all four boys (with Cyril again pulling up the rear) quickly exit the frame as they resume their leftward movement.

The next shot confirms Yates's intention to make ambience, the essence of a well-realized milieu, an active presence in the film. He cuts to a medium shot in which all four boys are partially obscured by sun-dappled foliage. The camera cranes down as first Mike and Moocher, then Dave and Cyril, emerge into full view. There follows a cut to a low-angle shot of the four boys jumping down a low hill. The camera, again subtly picking out Mike as a leader, tracks left with him.

Yates now explicitly exploits off-screen space to open each of three shots to the one that follows it. A shot of Cyril, awkwardly jumping down the low hill, catches him talking to the others, who are off-camera. This leads to a long shot of Mike and Moocher, who are sunning themselves on a slab of rock as they talk to Cyril, now off-camera. This is followed by a return to Cyril, who is nearly lost from view amid the foliage of the woods. The circle remains unbroken as Cyril says something to Mike off-camera, but Yates breaks the circle for an evocative culminating shot. The camera returns to the slab of rock, but the boys have apparently vacated that spot and the frame is momentarily devoid of people; the boys' laughter and shouted conversation, and the sound of splashing in the lake are, however, audible on the soundtrack. The sequence concludes on this image, a long shot of a special place the director has immersed us in, accompanied, by the off-camera sounds of four people who have made this place their own.

An open film typically finds its structure in the varied rhythm of the reality it depicts. The unhurried tempo of the opening sequence of *Breaking Away* is followed by another sequence that affirms Yates's sensitivity to the peculiar rhythm of a found world.

The sequence begins with a low-angle shot of a residential street; opera music is on the soundtrack. Dave emerges from the background of the frame; he is riding a racing bicycle, carrying a rather large trophy, and singing an Italian aria.

There is a cut to a long shot of Dave on his bicycle. Camera placement allows Yates to reveal the middle-class neighborhood Dave is riding through and to suggest, as he did in the opening sequence, that Dave is to be perceived as a part of this milieu. Camera movement — panning shots — reflects the swaying rhythm of Dave's side-to-side movement through the neighborhood streets.

There is now a series of cuts whose rhythm is as irregular and unhurried as the meandering movement of Dave's bicycle. The series pairs shots of Dave riding his bicycle with shots that give considerate attention to the homes and people he passes along his route. The attention Yates gives to this setting is as careful as that devoted to the quarry setting, and it establishes a complementary town-woods environment that extends our sense of the milieu Dave is a part of.

The sequence ends with three shots that reiterate the idea of Dave embedded in his milieu and open the sequence to the one that follows. First, an old lady on a porch, observing Dave singing and shouting greetings in Italian to his neighbors as he weaves down the street, remarks ruefully, "He was as normal as pumpkin pie." There is then a cut to a shot of Dave, his back to the camera, as he stops for traffic; Yates composes the shot to set Dave against a picture postcard church in the background of the frame. Dave rides away from the camera. There is then a cut to a shot that points both backward and forward (something open films characteristically do): the same old lady from the first shot of this series is heard muttering to her husband, "His poor parents!"

Dave's "poor parents" are introduced in the next sequence, which initiates one of the outstanding aspects of *Breaking Away*: its sympathetic, unstereotyped portrayal of middle-class parents. Yates and screenwriter Steve Tesich's rendering of Dave's parents — their individuality, their unity as a couple, their relationship with their son — is a singularly impressive achievement, particularly when it is contrasted to the stereotyped rendering of parents in the typical New Hollywood tribal comedy and the facilely hip put-downs of the middle class in general in such influential New Hollywood films as Altman's television-fallacy *Nashville*.

The sequence begins with a lengthy deep-focus shot, a characteristic feature of the mise-en-scène of open-film directors, with their overriding interest in capturing, however fleetingly, the rich complexity and characteristic rhythm of reality. In this shot Yates is interested in conveying the reality of Dave's parents as two individuals who have created a relationship that binds but does not confine.

Dave's father, Raymond (Paul Dooley), is in the foreground of the frame, sitting at a dining room table; his mother, Evelyn (Barbara Barrie, in the supreme performance of a long career), is in the midground, in the kitchen; the window of the back door of the house — an opening onto what lies outside the frame — can be seen in the background. Evelyn approaches Raymond and the camera, pausing in the midground of the frame for a medium shot with her husband. Evelyn then moves back toward the kitchen; but Yates, in an excellent choice that suggests that Evelyn and Raymond are above all else a couple, zooms in on her to restore the same spatial relationship between her and Raymond that was established at the beginning of the shot.

From the kitchen Evelyn moves back toward Raymond at the dining room table (she is serving him lunch); she then moves back toward the kitchen and exits the frame. Yates keeps the linkage between Raymond and Evelyn intact by having him speak to her off-camera. In any case, she soon reemerges into the frame, and the camera tracks left with her. The movement eliminates Raymond from the shot; but Yates, again emphasizing the unity of Raymond and Evelyn, keeps Raymond in the frame by including his reflection in a mirror hanging near where Evelyn is standing. The camera then tracks right with Evelyn past Raymond. She again exits the frame; the camera stays on Raymond, who has yet to make a move in the shot but whose passive presence has been made to seem the equal of Evelyn's active one.

Yates now moves from a sustained, uncut, deep-focus shot to a series of brief shots. His choice has thematic significance, for Raymond and Evelyn are now discussing a subject that has created fissures in the solidity of their couple relationship.

The subject is Dave — specifically, his obsession with bicycle racing and his concomitant obsession with all things Italian. As Raymond complains of, and Evelyn defends, Dave's failure to find a job (he has just finished high school) and his "Itie" obsession, Yates cuts between them for a series of eleven shots. The shots of Raymond are all identical, as he remains inert at the dining room table; Evelyn, in contrast, is shown moving about the house in shots that associate her with openness (she is seen standing by a window), light (she is associated with the subdued sunlight in the living room, which is in contrast to the rather dark dining room Raymond occupies), and life (she is twice shown watering house plants). In this segment Yates extends the unhurried rhythm of the first two sequences of the film by avoiding a staccato editing pattern: his alternating shots of Raymond and Evelyn are not of equal duration, and Evelyn's movements within her shots toward and away from Raymond creates a rhythm consistent with the boys' walk through the woods in the first sequence and the swaying motion of Dave's bike in the second.

Dave then enters the house through the kitchen door and, just as his mother did in the first shot of the sequence, he (with his bicycle and trophy) approaches the camera while moving toward his father, who is still rooted at the dining room table in the foreground of the frame.

The ensuing scene involving Dave and his parents is saved from sitcom silliness by the spatial nuances of Yates's compositions and by the moving apart–coming together rhythm established through movement within the shots.

From the shot of Dave and his bicycle moving toward the camera and his father, there is a cut to a close-up of Raymond addressing exasperated, sarcastic remarks to his son, who is off-camera. This is followed by another lengthy deep-focus shot. It begins with an empty hallway just off the dining room; Dave replying to his father is a voice-over. Then, in another suggestion of the affinity between Dave and his mother, the former enters the frame and moves left (the camera tracks left with him, adding Raymond to the shot), while the latter simultaneously enters from the left. The resulting composition reconstitutes the family: Raymond is just slightly isolated in the foreground of the frame; Evelyn and Dave are together in the midground. Evelyn then exits the frame, leaving Dave in

the midground, Raymond in the foreground. Dave then moves to close
the gap with his father by approaching the foreground; in an excellent
choice, Yates has the camera track with him, so that Dave's move toward
his father also results in Evelyn's being restored to the momentary frame.
The family is now reunited in a triangular arrangement: Raymond is at
the left, Evelyn is at the center, Dave is at the right. In a move that suggests the fundamental unity and equality of their relationship, Evelyn and
Raymond, in the course of their conversation with Dave, exchange places
in the frame. Dave then moves toward his father, kissing him on the
cheeks in the Italian style and presenting him with his latest racing
trophy.

Dave's gesture, however, does not mollify his father: he still thinks
his son should drop this Italian stuff and look for a job, as he did at his
age. There is a cut to a two-shot of Raymond and Evelyn looking right
toward the bedroom Dave has just entered. After a cut to a shot of Dave
putting a Caruso album on his phonograph, there is a cut to a shot of Raymond holding the trophy Dave has given him. He now moves right,
toward the source of the Italian singing that infuriates him. As he exits
the frame, Evelyn moves to occupy the center of the frame, a position
toward which she seems naturally to gravitate.

There is a cut to Raymond, his back to the camera, slamming a door;
cut to a medium shot of Evelyn looking concerned; and a cut to a medium
shot of Raymond entering the dining room from the hallway. Raymond,
looking more shocked than angry, announces to Evelyn that Dave is shaving his legs. The camera holds on Evelyn to capture her expression as it
changes from concern to amused relief. The sequence ends with a cut to
a shot of Dave in the bathroom, shaving his legs (he has read Italian
cyclists do it) and singing "Figaro" at the top of his lungs.

The frame next captures two more moments of the ongoing reality of
the film's found world. First, we see Moocher and his girlfriend Nancy in
the run-down house Moocher lives in by himself (his mother is gone, his
father is in Chicago looking for work). Then we see Raymond at the used
car lot he owns selling a sports car to a college student (Indiana University
is located very near the town where the film's characters live).

The film then returns to the quarry, which is, along with Dave's
home, the spiritual center of *Breaking Away*.

The sequence begins with two shots that again emphasize the idea
of characters embedded in a specific place. The first is a long shot of the
four boys again sunning themselves on the slab of rock seen in the first
sequence. There is then a cut to an only slightly closer view of the same
scene. By sustaining the shot, Yates creates a convincing image of the

carefree hedonism of that brief interlude between childhood's end and adulthood's beginning. The spell is broken only when Mike gets up and moves to the jutting tip of the rock. The camera cranes up with him, eliminating the others from the frame. Mike then dives out of the frame into the lake below.

There follows a segment in which shots of Dave and Moocher, Cyril and Mike (underwater) are intercut. After a time, the other three become concerned about Mike's prolonged absence; they fear he might be trapped in an old refrigerator that lies on the bottom of the lake. There is a cut to Dave, Moocher and Cyril in the lake, swimming and diving near the refrigerator as they search for Mike. There is then a cut to a low-angle shot of Mike, who is back on the rock, looking down on his friends and enjoying the momentary anxiety he has caused them.

Yates, in a choice characteristic of open-film direction, now uses a long shot, the least emphatic of choices available to a director, to introduce one of the major themes of the film: the cultural clash between the Indiana University students and the residents of the town near the Bloomington campus. From the shot of Mike laughing at the trick he played on the others, there is a cut to a long shot of a group of young men and women in bathing suits standing atop the opposite wall of the quarry. There is a cut to a low-angle shot of Mike angrily informing his friends in the water that their special place has been invaded by university students. There is then a cut to Dave, Moocher and Cyril in the water, followed by a low-angle shot of the students that reflects the point of view of the boys in the water. The camera tilts down to follow the beautifully executed dive of one of the students. This is followed by a cut to a medium shot of Mike, who is angrily denouncing the students; and a medium shot of Dave, Cyril and Moocher who are noticeably less upset about the college invasion of the quarry than Mike is. The sequence ends with Dave, Cyril and Moocher getting out of the water and leading a still angry Mike away from the lake. The idyllic moment has been shattered; perhaps more significant, the isolation of Mike from the rest of the group has been established through Yates's compositions and montage. This may yet prove to be a group without a leader: Mike seems to have too much anger to lead what is essentially a group dedicated to carefree living; Dave is preoccupied with bicycles and Italy; Cyril is slow and awkward; and Moocher must worry about hustling to support himself.

Mike is so angry about the invasion of his territory by the Indiana University students that he proposes an immediate drive to Bloomington for a counterinvasion of the campus.

Yates handles the first campus sequence very well, composing a series of tracking shots that quietly but effectively contrast the affluent indolence of the students with the scruffy boys cruising in Mike's beat-up car.

Two shots in this sequence are especially notable. In one, Yates, again revealing his commitment to the open-film style, composes a long-shot view of the university football team at practice. As the players break from a huddle and move right, the four boys sitting on a low hill become visible in the extreme background of the frame. This is the first instance of what is to become a motif in the film: one or more of the main characters "emerging" in a shot initially devoted to a broad setting. It is, of course, a motif that expresses the essence of open-film direction: characters unobtrusively become part of the ongoing reality the frame momentarily captures.

The second shot economically implies two of the film's conflicts, the one between the four boys (who proudly call themselves "cutters," the derogatory name for town residents that refers to the now-waning importance of the quarry to the town's economy) and the university students, and the one within the group of four caused by Mike's bitterness about his lot in life. The shot begins as a rear view of Moocher, Mike and Cyril sitting on the hill and watching the football team at practice below them. The camera tilts up with Mike as he stands up, and then it tracks back from him as he approaches the foreground of the frame. The camera then tracks right with Mike, catching the other three boys in the background of the frame. Mike, a football star in high school, has been bitterly complaining about his bleak present and even bleaker prospects; and Yates's composition and use of movement within the shot have suggested how Mike's bitterness and frustration are removing him from the group. The shot concludes, however, with a suggestion of healing: in a sustained movement, the camera tracks right, away from the playing field, with Dave and Mike, who are closely followed by Cyril; Moocher is out of the frame, but Yates's open style has gathered such strength by this point that we are sure Moocher is just at the edge of the momentary frame.

The next sequence is a light comic interlude, distinguished by Yates's sensitivity to rhythm and his detailed attention to setting.

The sequence begins with a shot of Dave on the Bloomington campus; he is stretched out on a grassy area of the campus, reading an Italian-English dictionary, his bicycle parked behind him. He looks up and spots Katherine (Robyn Douglass), an attractive coed he had seen in the group that invaded the quarry, exiting a campus building. As she gets on her moped, Katherine drops a notebook she had been carrying. Dave gets on his bike, picks up the notebook, and races after Katherine. His pursuit of Katherine is another series of smoothly rhythmical tracking shots; during the course of this series, Yates adds the Indiana University campus to the list of settings he endows with admirable specificity (this attention to specificity and the texture of place is, of course, one of the major characteristics that distinguish *Breaking Away* from television-fallacy films like *American Graffiti*). Dave catches up with Katherine, returns the notebook, and introduces himself as an Italian exchange student (he is, probably unconsciously, afraid to present himself to a college girl as the "cutter" he is). Katherine is sweet and quite friendly; Dave is in love.

The sequence that follows, a triumph of the open style of film direction and one of the high points of *Breaking Away*, would never be found in a television-fallacy film. It allows a character to break away from a linear format, and it trusts audiences to sustain attention through a passage that is not hyped by "technical events."

The sequence is a purely visual expression — among the best of film — of unadulterated joy, and it captures the evanescent quality of that emotion in its pure state. Dave, unable to contain his joy after his encounter with Katherine, is seen riding his bicycle through the cool, calm shade and filtered sunlight of a woods. Yates uses tracking shots, long shots, and overhead shots to convey the joyous passage of a young man through a setting associated with verdancy and life.

Yates stays with the shots of Dave's joyous ride for a considerable time. Then, in a long shot — Yates consistently refuses to distort his open mise-en-scène to give heavy-handed emphasis to conflict elements of the narrative — a carful of college students, Katherine among them, enters the frame, driving alongside the university cycling team. Dave is momentarily out of the frame. As the car and the cyclists move left and then out of the frame, Dave is seen (again, the "emerging" motif) at the side of the road, fixing a flat tire. Yates cuts to a medium shot — not, significantly, a close-up: an open-film director, in contrast to a television-fallacy director, rarely sacrifices the nuances of context for the emphasis of a close-up — of Dave reacting to the cyclists and, especially, to Katherine's presence among them.

Dave is next seen at home, announcing to his parents that he is in love. Evelyn is pleased, Raymond is, characteristically, mildly annoyed.

There follows a particularly good example of Yates's success in conveying a sense of his film as a fragment of an ongoing reality. He begins with a shot in which a bicycle wheel dominates the foreground of the frame; Dave, his back to the camera, is seen working on the wheel; a mailman, moving right-left, is in the midground of the frame. The mailman approaches the foreground and is seen from behind the bicycle wheel as he delivers a magazine to Dave. There is a cut, and now the mailman is in the foreground of the frame, Dave and the wheel are in the midground, and Dave's house is in the background. The mailman exits the frame; and there is a cut to a shot of Dave's hands, seen from behind the spokes of the wheel, turning the pages of the magazine.

The next shot is a quintessential open-film shot. It is a long shot of Dave's house, and Dave shouting "Mamma!" in a voice-over. Dave himself then enters the shot; but he almost immediately runs left, leaving the momentary frame and inviting us to follow him.

There is a cut to a medium shot of Dave standing beside a bush and holding up the magazine to show someone off-camera a particular page. This is followed by a cut to a long shot of Evelyn, who is gardening. She looks toward Dave (who is off-camera) as he shouts the news he has read in the magazine: a team of Italian cyclists, sponsored by Cinzano, is going to appear in Bloomington. There is then a cut to a medium shot of Dave crossing himself and, in Italian, thanking God for his good fortune. This is followed by a reprise of the somewhat more distant shot of Dave standing near the bush; but now the shot includes a wonderful voice-over line from Evelyn: "Oh, Dave, try not to become Catholic on us."

Yates now devotes two scenes to the capturing of a mood rather than to the furthering of a plot. In the first, Dave, full of excitement over the prospect of racing against the Italians, rides away from his home, through his neighborhood, and then completes the long ride to Bloomington in record time. Yates uses a mixture of long shots, medium shots, and close-ups of Dave to capture this intense expression of the young man's excitement. In the second, one of the film's most effective long takes, Dave is seen in his bedroom, talking to and feeling his cat, Fellini. Only an open-film director, committed to exploring the quiet spaces of the world his camera seems to find, would include such an interlude, in which nothing "happens."

The focus of the film then briefly switches from Dave to Moocher, who, over the objections of Mike who thinks the four boys should remain unemployed if they cannot all get jobs together, has taken a job at a car wash. Moocher almost immediately quits the job, however, when his boss makes a disparaging reference to his small stature. Moocher walks away from the car wash and rejoins his friends. The four are reunited, at least for the moment.

One of Yates's great achievements in *Breaking Away* is his success in evoking the spirit of home, the idea of family. How he does it is a formidable challenge to critical analysis; but, as the film's next sequence suggests, his use of lighting, composition, and shot duration constitutes a large part of the explanation.

In a deep-focus shot, Evelyn is in the foreground-left of the frame, standing in the dining room of her home; Raymond is in the midground-right, sitting in the living room; the background is given over to a full view of the living room. The lighting of the shot is notably subdued, creating a feeling of twilight quiet. Raymond approaches the foreground of the frame as he moves toward the dining room table to have dinner.

Evelyn has prepared Italian food for dinner, and this triggers a low-key tirade from Raymond about Italian food (he calls it "Itie" food) and, of course, Dave's Italian obsession. From a shot of Raymond complaining Yates cuts to a shot of Evelyn explaining; the latter shot, repeating a device used in the first Raymond-Evelyn sequence, includes Raymond's reflection in a mirror. After two more medium shots of Raymond and Evelyn, Yates concludes the sequence with a composition that reasserts the unity associated with the ideas of home and family: at the dining room table Evelyn is at the left, Raymond is at the right, and Dave's cat, Fellini, is at the center. Yates, in a choice that recalls the work of Yasuhiro Ozu, another great open-film director, holds this concluding shot for a considerable time, past the conclusion of Raymond and Evelyn's conversation, when they have lapsed into that comfortable silence frequently found in truly close relationships.

The "emerging" motif reappears in the next sequence. It begins with a medium shot of young children playing behind a playground fence. As they run to the left of the frame, Cyril and Dave become visible in the background-right. Cyril is jogging alongside Dave, who is riding his bike. They move to the foreground of the frame, and then Yates turns to a lengthy, uncut tracking shot to cover their movement from right to left. In this characteristically unobtrusive, unemphatic way, Cyril emerges: he is a bright young man whose self-esteem has been weakened by his well-meaning father's apparent belief that his son is programmed for failure. Cyril's monologue at this point is expertly integrated into the film's ongoing reality and is therefore completely devoid of any overtly expository quality.

After a scene set in downtown Bloomington in which the four boys are given a lecture by Mike's older brother, a policeman, Yates creates another of the mood fragments that are a notable feature of *Breaking Away*. In a sustained stationary-camera shot, Evelyn is seen waxing a floor. She is waxing in rhythm with an Italian aria playing on a phonograph. She sings along with the record for a moment, stops her work, sighs; in one of the loveliest moments to come out of the New Hollywood, Yates holds the shot after the sigh, creating another Ozu-like privileged moment in which the essence of Evelyn — romantic yet practical, above all gentle — is captured.

Yates now brings *Breaking Away* to a truly impressive high point in a sequence that conveys the ineffable essence of first love as well as the fundamental identification between first love and mature love.

Dave and Cyril are seen riding on the former's bike past a tennis court on what appears to be the Indiana University campus. There is then a cut to a medium shot of Evelyn and Raymond at the dining room table; candles on the table cast a romantic glow on the setting. As Evelyn asks Raymond, "How about a little music?" there's a cut to a shot of Dave and Cyril emerging from darkness to stop beside a street light. A low-angle shot of a brick building confirms that Dave and Cyril are on the Indiana University campus.

There is a cut to a shot of Evelyn's arms (frilly blouse sleeves) taking a record album out of its jacket. This is followed by a series of four shots: another low-angle shot of the campus building, an overhead shot of Dave shouting "Caterina!" a shot of Katherine appearing in an upper-floor window of the building, and finally a medium shot of Dave looking up at Katherine.

From the medium shot of Dave there is a cut to a shot of Evelyn's hands putting a record on the phonograph. The music, an Italian aria, forms a link to the next shot, in which Dave (accompanied by Cyril on guitar) is seen singing the same aria to Katherine. There is then a cut to a shot in which the camera tilts up from a spinning record to a medium shot of Evelyn, who is now wearing a flower behind her ear.

After a series of shots showing Katherine and her sorority sisters reacting to Dave's serenade, there is a cut to a shot of Evelyn and Raymond at the dining room table. Evelyn gets up and extinguishes the candles on the table; the lighting of the shot changes from a soft glow to a darkness that matches the darkness in which Dave is enveloped as he serenades Katherine.

From Evelyn there is a cut back to the campus and the serenade. Shots of Dave and Cyril are intercut with shots of Katherine and her sorority sisters, one of whom telephones Rod, Katherine's boyfriend (who has been seen diving at the quarry with the other college "invaders" and riding through the woods with one of the university cycling teams), to tell him about the serenade.

There follows a medium shot of Evelyn and Raymond in their bedroom. Evelyn is in the midground of the frame, sitting up in bed and smelling the flower she had been wearing; Raymond, his back to the camera, is in the foreground, walking toward the bed. The glow from a bedside lamp illuminates the scene.

Back to campus for another series of shots of Cyril and Dave serenading, and Katherine and her friends listening from their windows. When the song concludes, the camera tracks right with Dave and Katherine as they ride off into the darkness on the former's bicycle. There is a cut to a shot of Cyril taking bows in response to the continuing applause coming from the sorority house. Suddenly, Rod and some of his friends appear and proceed to chase and, apparently (the darkness obscures the action), assault Cyril. There is then a cut to a shot in which Dave and Katherine are seen walking in the dark. A series of medium shots of them ends with Dave kissing Katherine. From the kiss there is a cut to a sustained medium shot of Dave, followed by a shot in which Katherine, walking away from Dave and the camera, pauses to look back at him. This masterful sequence concludes on the next shot, a medium shot of Dave that is a portrait of unalloyed rapture.

Cyril was rather seriously hurt by Rod and his friends, and Mike declares that revenge must be taken. Mike, Moocher, and Cyril (Dave is, at first unaccountably, absent) drive to campus and end up in a free-for-all fight in the student union. Dave, it turns out, is a witness to the fight: he is in the student union, on a date with Katherine. Before the "cutters" break up the place, there is a moving scene in which Dave, who is still maintaining his Italian exchange student persona, talks to Katherine about the affectionate closeness of Italian families. This scene is an especially notable example of the contribution made to *Breaking Away* by Steve Tesich, who won a well-deserved Oscar for his original screenplay.

The denouement of the donnybrook at the student union is a decision by the university administration to invite the "cutters" to participate for the first time in the university's annual "Little 500" bicycle race. Dave opposes accepting the invitation, while the other three favor acceptance. The divisions in the group are reflected in the next sequence, again set at the quarry, in which Yates's compositions and montage emphasize the separateness of the four boys. Once again, however, a sense of division is followed by a sense of healing, an image of unity: after Mike has injured himself in an impromptu race against Rod across the quarry lake, Yates concludes the sequence on an overhead shot of all four boys, who look small but united in the center of the lake, at the moment when the other three have come to Mike's rescue.

Two brief scenes follow. In the first, a tracking camera follows Dave and Moocher as they walk through the center of town. Dave, troubled by his concealment of his true identity from Katherine, is seeking Moocher's advice about how to resolve his problem. The scene concludes with another demonstration of Yates's commitment to the idea of presenting his characters as embedded in a specific milieu. Dave and Moocher are off-camera; but their reflections, which in turn are superimposed on the reflection of a gothic church, are seen in a store window; their conversation, with a tolling church bell as background accompaniment, is a voice-over.

The second scene is another gem of open-film direction. Moocher and Nancy are going to get married. We first see them in a long shot, set against the background of a convincingly rendered downtown scene. This is followed by a low-angle shot in which the smallness of Moocher and Nancy is set against the looming City Hall. Then Dave rides by on his bike; and the camera, reflecting his point of view, tracks right past Moocher and Nancy as they enter City Hall. There is then a cut to a shot of Dave smiling. Dave then runs a light, causing his father to stall in a car he is demonstrating to a customer. There is a cut to the car being towed away, followed by a shot of Raymond, his head on the steering wheel, moaning, not in pain but in exasperation with his son.

By this point in the film its underlying pattern is clear: moments of expansive unity are interspersed (the effect is not one of schematic juxtaposition, something more likely to be found in a closed film) with moments of contraction, of fragmentation. The serenade sequence has been the supreme expression thus far of an embracing unity: two "cutters" were integrated into the campus milieu; Dave made a major breakthrough with Katherine; and, most significant, the expression of Dave's younger-generation love was integrated with the older-generation, familial love of Raymond and Evelyn. Yet that sequence of cross-cultural, cross-generational unity had not even concluded before fragmentation began. Cyril was attacked by college students; the invitation to participate in the "Little 500" caused dissension among the four; and, in an ambiguous move, Moocher married Nancy, thereby setting himself apart from his three friends.

The fragmentation continues in the next sequence. It begins with a medium shot of Raymond, who is again complaining about Dave's laziness. There is a cut to a medium shot of Evelyn, who is reading in bed and is again associated with the soft glow of subdued lighting. This is followed by another shot of Raymond, who walks to the background of the shot and then exits the frame. There is then a cut to a sustained shot of Dave in his bedroom; he can hear Evelyn and Raymond's conversation in the adjoining room, and the stationary camera captures the gamut of his reactions to the rather cruel attack on him his father is making. Yates's montage now suggests the mediating role of Evelyn: two shots of her looking the essence of serenity as she reads by a soft light are intercut with shots of Raymond attacking Dave and Dave reacting to the overheard attacks. Yates, however, ultimately suggests that, at least on this occasion, Evelyn's mediation fails: the sequence concludes with two shots, one in which Raymond continues his criticism of Dave, and one in which Dave is seen near tears over his father's tirade; the two shots are not interrupted by a shot of Evelyn.

Two more of the film's wonderfully evocative interludes follow (their placement at this point can be taken as evidence of Yates's determination to avoid a schematic unity-fragmentation pattern). First, in a segment that matches the poignancy of the scene in which Evelyn is waxing the floor, Raymond is seen visiting the quarry where, as a young man, he worked as a cutter. He talks with old friends, tries his hand at manipulating the familiar tools, and, in the moving conclusion of the scene, is seen quietly reflecting on, no doubt, the passage of time and the turns a life takes.

The second interlude is a sustained shot in which the camera slowly tracks right as Evelyn and Raymond stroll through a convincingly detailed downtown neighborhood. They are talking about Dave, and Evelyn is again attempting to temper Raymond's anger over his son's alleged laziness. The scene ends on Evelyn's characteristic sigh as she and Raymond walk out of the momentary frame.

It is decided that Dave should go to work for his father, and the next several minutes of the film show Dave working at the car lot by day and training for the upcoming race against the Cinzano team at night. At one point, while Dave is working at the lot, Cyril, Moocher and Mike pass by in the latter's car. They are soon followed by Rod and the other members of his cycling team passing by on their bicycles; in a variation on the "emerging" motif, Dave sees them through the windshield of a car he is cleaning. This is followed by a shot in which Dave is seen, in pouring rain, riding his bicycle on a treadmill set up just outside the car lot office; Raymond occupies the same plane of the frame as Dave, but he is seen through the window of the office.

Dave ends up causing a crisis for his father by suggesting that the latter refund the money a university student paid for an obvious lemon of a car. *Refund* is a forbidden word in the used car business; and Dave's use of it, in the presence of a customer at that, causes a severe reaction in Raymond. He begins to shout, first in anger, then in shock, "Refund! Refund!" There is a cut from the car lot to a shot of Raymond, now in his bed and attended by a doctor, still muttering "Refund! Refund!" Dave has brought on a heart attack in Raymond, whose heart condition was alluded to in the first Evelyn-Raymond sequence.

Dave, who is deeply upset about his father's condition, is next seen sitting on a chair in the living room of his home. There is a cut to a shot of Evelyn standing by a door; she is again associated with openness (she shares the frame with the window on the door) and subdued lighting (in this instance, resulting from the lace curtains on the window).

A series of alternating medium shots of Evelyn and Dave follows. During this series, Barbara Barrie brilliantly responds to the opportunity provided her by Yates and Steve Tesich as Evelyn poignantly confirms her affinity for Dave's joyous romanticism and implicitly urges him not to abandon it prematurely in favor of Raymond's rather joyless practicality. In a lovely shot, Dave bends down to embrace and kiss his mother. Yates sustains this shot for a considerable time; and then, in another directorial choice that recalls the subtlety of Ozu, he concludes the sequence with Evelyn looking right toward the bedroom where Raymond is confined.

The day of the race with the Cinzano team has arrived. Yates covers the race through a series of excellent tracking shots. Also notable is the detailed sense of the decaying Midwest "rust belt" that is conveyed through the scenes the camera captures along the race's route. Dave eventually catches up with and overtakes the Italians; but they, in an action that in the context of this film seems obscenely cruel, cause him to lose the race by jamming the gears of his bike. Yates concludes the race sequence by again moving from fragmentation-isolation to unity-integration: a sustained medium shot of Dave after he's been forced out of the race is followed by a long shot of Dave's bike atop the roof of Mike's car, which is moving away from the scene of Dave's disillusionment and isolation. The long shot reasserts the idea of Dave as part of a milieu, which in this film is to be preferred to the isolation suggested by the preceding medium shot.

The companion to the Dave-Evelyn sequences preceding the race now follows. If anything, it is even more moving than the earlier sequence.

Evelyn and Raymond (who has made a good recovery from his heart attack) are in the foreground-right of a medium shot set in the living room of their home; the shot features the subdued lighting that has become associated with Evelyn. Dave, bruised and dirty from the fall from his bike caused by the treachery of the Italians, enters a door at the midground-left of the frame. Evelyn moves left toward him and then exits the frame, leaving the screen space to Dave and his father.

There is a cut to a medium shot of Raymond sitting in a chair and speaking to Dave off-camera, followed by a cut to a shot in which Dave is in the midground-center and Raymond is in the foreground-right. Yates then cuts to a medium shot of Raymond; in a movement that is the exact reverse of a movement in the earlier Dave-Evelyn sequence, the camera tilts up with Raymond as he rises from the chair and moves toward Dave at the center of the frame.

After an overhead shot of Dave that reflects Raymond's point of view, there is a cut to a shot in which Dave is at the center of the frame, with Evelyn at the left and Raymond at the right. As he begins to tell his parents about what happened at the race, there is a cut to another overhead shot of Dave. The shot is sustained as Dave, sobbing, says, "Everybody cheats. I just did not know."

There is a cut to a medium shot of Raymond as he says, "Well, now you know." Paul Dooley at this moment conveys all the poignancy the moment contains; and Yates, again making a choice that recalls the work of Ozu, holds on Raymond's face to capture the eloquent silence that follows the delivery of the line.

There is a cut to a sustained shot in which Dave and Raymond look at each other. Dave then walks right and throws his arms around his father.

For the shot that follows, Yates has the intelligence to keep his camera still to capture the process of potential stereotypes definitively emerging as people; and he has the courage, rare in the New Hollywood, to be frankly sentimental. The shot is of Dave, his back to the camera, embracing his father. Raymond, facing the camera, initially just pats Dave's back. After several seconds, he raises his arms and returns Dave's embrace.

The sequence concludes, appropriately enough, with a sustained medium shot of Evelyn. She does not say a word, but tears are just beginning to form in her eyes as she observes the now off-camera reconciliation of her husband and her son.

Dave, determined to break away from deception and illusion, is next seen revealing his true identity to Katherine, who is understandably angry about his elaborate deception. Next Dave is seen stripping the posters of Italy from the walls of his bedroom. Raymond enters the bedroom, and there is a sustained shot in which Dave and Raymond are spatially estranged in the frame. Then, in a moment that seems to capture the essence of the open film, Raymond gestures for Dave — and us, the invited guests in this found world — to leave what he is doing and follow him to the next moment of ongoing reality the momentary frame will capture.

We are led to a sequence that is the companion to the serenade sequence, another celebration of healing, of integration.

In a lengthy, uncut shot (Yates's use of the long take is another feature that distinguishes his work from that of television-fallacy directors, who consistently sacrifice the involvement of the long take for the alleged "excitement" of a fragmented montage), the camera tracks back from Dave and Raymond as they walk among campus buildings in the dark. The shot concludes on a medium shot of Raymond, who is sitting on a stone bench, and Dave, who is standing, facing his father.

A trio of shots in which, alternately, Dave and Raymond face the camera follow. Raymond is telling Dave that he and his fellow laborers of an earlier generation cut the stone for the buildings they are walking among now. Yates, in a notably emphatic move, zooms in on Raymond's face as he says how sad it is that people who made the buildings possible began to feel inferior to the institution they helped create. He does not want that feeling of inferiority to pass to the next generation of "cutters."

Yates now returns to a more characteristic camera placement: in a rather distant medium shot, Raymond and Dave are in the midground of the frame, with the glass wall of a college building in the background. The final act of reconciliation of father and son and the integration of both into a milieu that had intimidated them are effectively suggested in this one shot.

The sequence concludes brilliantly. In a medium shot, Raymond is still sitting on the bench, facing the camera; and Dave is still standing, his back to the camera. The camera tilts down with Dave as he sits down beside his father; the camera holds for a medium shot of the two of them sitting side by side. Raymond then rises and moves right; Dave follows. The camera remains stationary as Dave and Raymond slowly recede into the darkness (a reversal of the "emerging" motif); in the enveloping darkness we can just make out that Raymond has put his arm around Dave's shoulder.

Continuing the parallel with the serenade sequence, Yates follows the unity integration of the Raymond-Dave sequence with one that suggests fragmentation.

On a large, cluttered porch, the four boys are seen dispersed in the frame. Dave is working on the bicycle the university has issued for the "Little 500" race. A series of shots of Cyril and Moocher is followed by a shot in which Dave occupies the foreground of the frame and Mike the midground. Mike, who is now opposed to participation in the "Little 500," then moves left. The camera tracks with him, eliminating Dave from the frame. There is then another shot of all four boys together in the frame, but Yates quickly undermines the unity by cutting to a medium shot of Mike and Cyril. Then, in a shot that is repeated after a brief shot of Moocher, Dave confronts Mike. In the two-shot, Mike is seen in profile, while Dave is directly facing the camera; the composition, especially when considered in the context of the preceding sequence, suggests that Dave is squarely facing the no-future represented by Mike's refusal to move toward a closing of the breach between "cutters" and campus. Dave and Mike argue inconclusively about participation in the "Little 500." The sequence ends with Dave walking out of the frame with the bike he had been working on.

There follows a series of shots of Dave working on the university-issued bike (which is inferior to his own but which must be used in the race) and then setting off on it for a practice round at the university race course. In this segment, Yates works in another variation on the "emerging" motif: in a shot that initially shows Dave's house shrouded in predawn darkness, Dave suddenly bursts out of his garage on the bike and rides away through the dark neighborhood streets.

Another scene of integration follows; this time it occurs on the home ground of the "cutters." The camera tracks in on Dave as he exits a fast-food restaurant and sits down against a street sign to eat what he has purchased. This is where Katherine, who has come to say goodbye, finds him. In a series of alternating medium shots, Dave and Katherine heal the breach between them caused by his initial deception of her.

Expansive familial unity — the kind of embracing Italian family unity Dave spoke of in the student union scene with Katherine — is the keynote of the next sequence. In a sustained medium shot, Raymond, Evelyn, Dave and Moocher are seen gathered around the dining room table of Dave's home. Yates keeps the focus of the sequence on Dave and Raymond, interrupting a series of medium shots of them for only one shot each of Evelyn and Moocher. Thus the sense of reconciliation between father and son, so effectively conveyed in the sequence featuring Dave and Raymond on campus, is reiterated. During the course of the meal, Raymond and Evelyn announce that she is to have a baby, the fruit, no doubt, of Raymond and Evelyn's romantic evening alone the night Dave serenaded Katherine.

For all the sequence's emphasis on Dave and Raymond, it concludes with a focus on Evelyn. A medium shot of all four characters at the table — the first group shot since the initial shot of the sequence — initiates the conclusion. In a characteristic movement Evelyn moves to the center of the frame. She presents to Dave and Moocher two of the four T-shirts imprinted with the word "Cutters" she and Raymond have bought for the boys to wear in the following day's "Little 500." The sequence ends with Evelyn's planting a kiss atop Dave's head.

Yates has not structured his film in such a way as to endow the "Little

The idea of community is celebrated throughout *Breaking Away*. Dennis Christopher, Jackie Earle Haley, Daniel Stern, Dennis Quaid, *Breaking Away* (Twentieth Century–Fox, 1979).

500" sequence with the climactic connotations that public events, particularly sporting events, have had in more schematic, television-fallacy films (the "Little 500", in other words, is not a variation on the boxing match that concludes *Rocky*). The race is merely another event in the ongoing reality Yates's camera discovers. The sequence is notable on several counts. Its focus on the two teams of most interest, the "Cutters" and the team that includes Katherine's boyfriend Rod, is not overly emphatic: they simply emerge from time to time in shots that include the other teams and the spectators. Similarly, Raymond and Evelyn are not given heavy-handed attention: they, too, are integrated into the overall reality of the sequence, two spectators of special interest to us who are nevertheless seen as part of the crowd. Finally, the film's remaining conflict, Mike's alienation from his friends and his reality, is resolved in a manner that does not distort the emphasis of the sequence and the film on community, on unity. At one crucial point in the race, Mike must decide if he is going to relieve Dave or not. When he does relieve him — and, as would be expected, he makes his decision in a long shot that does not distract from the sequence's focus on the totality of the race — we know

the "Cutters" will win and that Mike, the film's last unintegrated fragment, will be absorbed into the all-embracing unity (even Rod's team
congratulates the winners with good grace) the film celebrates.

The conclusion of the film is, in a word, masterful. Dave is seen
riding his bike past his father's car lot to the university campus — the
union of town and campus, of "cutter" culture and a broader culture, is
thus unobtrusively and quite cinematically confirmed. On campus,
Dave, who is now a student there, encounters a pretty French exchange
student. There is a cut, and we see Dave, speaking credible French, and
the French girl riding their bicycles. They pass Raymond, and *Breaking
Away*, one of the few genuinely humanist works of recent years, ends with
Dave shouting "Bon jour, Papa" to his father. The final shot of this
eminently open film thus opens to the possibility that the extended family
unity the film celebrates might be extended across political boundaries to
embrace all of our fragmented world.

Alone among directors active in the New Hollywood, Don Siegel,
who served an Old Hollywood apprenticeship as cutter, editor and
second-unit director that seems quaint when contrasted with the accelerated careers of the New Hollywood era, has honored the form and
the spirit of the Hawksian melodrama. In *Escape from Alcatraz* Siegel even
outdoes Hawks by extending the Hawksian narrative into thematic areas
the master did not enter. *Escape* is an admirably terse, compelling entertainment that, in the best Hawksian tradition, expresses a coherent
morality through the actions of its characters and the events of its narrative; beyond that (and *that*, needless to say, is achievement enough),
Escape is an extraordinarily effective treatment of the emotional dimension of confinement and easily one of the most successful cinematic
renderings of the nature and range of human creativity.

The first eight minutes of *Escape from Alcatraz* convey an impressive
amount of information and sustain an emotional tone that is equally impressive in its consistency and intensity.

The film begins with a long shot of the Golden Gate Bridge. The
camera pans left, then right; Alcatraz is now at the center of the frame.
There is a dissolve to a nighttime shot that is blurred by heavy rain. A
reverse zoom locates uniformed guards in the shot. The heavy rain continues.

There is a cut to a shot in which Frank Morris (Clint Eastwood) and
two guards are seen walking left. The camera tracks with them, and then
there is a cut to a shot of the three men standing on a dock. Without a
cut, Siegel cranes up for an overhead shot of the three men walking left

and then descending a small flight of stairs leading to a speedboat. Frank follows the guards onto the boat. There is a cut, and now the camera is tracking left with the boat as it pulls away from the dock. The tracking camera pauses for a brief medium shot of Frank and the guards standing on the deck of the boat, which begins to recede into the rain-filled darkness.

Siegel's maintenance of an objective point of view, one of the most Hawksian aspects of his direction of *Escape from Alcatraz*, continues in the next two shots, in which first Frank and the guards and then Frank alone are seen inside the boat's cabin. Then Siegel makes one of his rare departures (they are as rare as they are in Hawks's films) from a detached, narrator's point of view. He cuts to a shot of Alcatraz as seen from the point of view of Frank, who glimpses the prison from behind the rain-spattered window of the cabin. The rain and the movement of the wipers on the window bring Alcatraz in and out of plain view; in any case, it is barely discernible set against the black sky and the equally black sea. The almost surreal effect of the shot suggests that Frank perceives his movement toward Alcatraz as movement toward an almost illusory void.

After two more shots of Frank and the guards in the cabin, the camera tracks in on them as they descend a flight of stairs to the very dark below-deck area. One of the guards turns on a light to reveal a low-angle shot of Frank, who is partially illuminated by the light. This shot is almost immediately reprised, except that in the second shot precisely half of Frank's face is illuminated. Thus begins Siegel's use of low-angle shots of Frank, a camera placement that will be used to suggest both Frank's superiority to his environment and the oppressive confinement that characterizes that environment.

There is a cut to a shot of Frank, his back to the camera, being shoved by the guards onto a bunk. Frank turns to face the camera, and then the camera tilts down with a guard as he bends over to handcuff Frank's ankles. Siegel then cuts to a shot that is representative of one of his outstanding achievements in the film. It is a medium shot of Frank, who is illuminated by lighting that creates a bar pattern on his face; a guard, his back to the camera, putting handcuffs on Frank's wrists partially obscures his face. This is the first of a number of instances in the film in which Siegel duplicates the Hawksian achievement of integrating images that suggest the psychological state of his protagonist into the ongoing flow of the narrative. Siegel, like Hawks, embeds a suggestive character study into the development of a compelling fast-moving narrative.

The shot of Frank illuminated with a bar-like pattern is reprised after a shot of Alcatraz seen through the boat's window. Siegel then devotes

The psychological state of a man being confined as suggested by images within the ongoing flow of the narrative. Unidentified actors, Clint Eastwood, *Escape from Alcatraz* (Paramount Pictures, 1979).

several shots to Alcatraz looming out of the darkness and the insistent rain.

In an overhead shot that again asks us to consider the psychological state of the man who is experiencing the impersonal, efficient process of confinement the opening sequence depicts, Frank emerges from the speedboat and is immediately caught in the harsh light of one of the prison's searchlights. Siegel cuts to a shot of the searchlight penetrating the darkness and the rain; and the same harsh light is prominent in the next shot: of Frank and the guards walking off the boat onto a dock. There is a cut, and now they are seen climbing steps; the camera has been placed behind a wire fence whose mesh distorts the view of the men. Frank and the guards enter a van, which takes on an eerie blue hue because it is caught in the same light that has been featured in this series of shots. It is a light that blinds rather than illuminates, and Siegel has used it to add to our sense of pervasive confinement.

Siegel cuts from an overhead shot of the van moving right (a searchlight follows its progress) to a shot of Frank and the guards cramped inside the van. After several shots that mix exterior views of the van moving toward the prison with views of Frank and the guards inside the van, Siegel cuts to the shot that concludes the sequence. It is a dramatic, almost expressionistic overhead shot in which the camera looks down the looming walls of Alcatraz onto its central yard, which seems trapped between the walls. Siegel, in this initial five-minute sequence, has created a chillingly unified impression of confinement and has suggested both his protagonist's sense of his confinement and the latent superiority in him that may enable him to overcome his demeaning circumstances. Siegel, in other words, has established the essence of his Hawksian melodrama: a man of stature is pitted against an awesomely confining environment.

In the next sequence Siegel uses camera placement and camera movement to convey a detached, objective, eminently Hawksian view of the process of checking a new prisoner into Alcatraz; his compositions emphasize the narrowness of the prison environment and the constant surveillance and control made possible by an array of monitoring devices. Siegel again manages to focus on the psychological state of his protagonist without interrupting the movement of his narrative: at one point he cuts from a low-angle shot that gives an overall view of one of the prison's cell blocks to a tracking shot that focuses on the face of Frank as he, flanked by guards, walks past a seemingly endless row of cells toward the one that is to be his. Near the end of the sequence, Siegel intensifies the concentration on Frank by composing a medium shot in which Frank's chest (he has been stripped of his clothes and has not yet been issued a prison uniform) is visible behind the bars of his cell. As a guard says, "Welcome to Alcatraz," the lighting suddenly changes and now Frank's face, as well as his chest, is seen behind the bars. Siegel follows this effective moment of heightened concentration on Frank with a return to Hawksian objectivity, concluding the sequence with an exterior shot of Alcatraz at night.

Siegel continues his documentary-like study of life at Alcatraz in the next sequence. After a shot of dawn illuminating Alcatraz, San Francisco Bay, and the Golden Gate Bridge, he uses a mix of long shots and medium shots to show the prisoners of a three-tiered cell block being awakened, counted, released from their cells and marched off to the mess hall for breakfast. Inside the mess hall, Siegel again relies principally on camera placement and camera movement to convey meaning, in this instance the superiority of Frank to his confining environemnt. In a low-angle shot that emphasizes his stature, Frank is seen picking up his tray in the mess hall line. Siegel sustains the shot without a cut as Frank moves toward a table. The effect of the low-angle shot is to pit Frank's stature against the setting, since the camera angle makes it appear that the ceiling of the mess hall is pressing down on Frank.

The coming together of men in a challenging situation, a fundamental theme of Hawks's melodramas, is begun in this first mess hall sequence. At his table Frank meets Litmus (Frank Ronsio), an older, seemingly well-educated inmate who is devoted to a pet mouse he has trained. Siegel interrupts the alternating shots of Frank and Litmus in conversation with a panning shot across the mess hall and a shot of all the prisoners at Frank and Litmus's table; the effect of these interruptions is to place the Frank-Litmus exchange within a larger communal setting. Siegel also interrupts the Frank-Litmus shots with two shots of Wolf, an enormous, remarkably ugly inmate who is eyeing Frank ominously.

Frank is next taken to meet the warden (Patrick McGoohan). The four-minute sequence in the warden's office is notable for Siegel's decision to shoot most of the shots of Frank from a low angle and most of the shots of the warden from overhead; the effect is to continue the intriguing suggestion of Frank's superiority within an oppressive environment, and to suggest the relative insignificance of the warden, a steely-cool, arrogant man. During this sequence we learn that Frank has an exceptionally high IQ, that he was convicted of robbery, and that he was sent to Alcatraz because he attempted to escape from the last prison he was in.

From the warden's office, there is a cut to an excellent long take of Frank in his cell. It begins with a medium shot of Frank's hands as he clips his nails (he has lifted the nail clippers from the desk of the warden, who seems to have an endless supply of them). The shot continues as Frank, shot from the Hawksian, middle-distance camera position, moves about the cell, ending up at its little sink in one corner. The shot has reiterated the terms of the Hawksian melodrama that is the essence of the film: a man of superior intelligence and courage (he had enough of both to steal the clippers), still without sure allies, is confined within a system and an environment that threaten to reduce and ultimately destroy him.

After a scene in the prison shower in which Frank gets the best of Wolf in a violent confrontation, the focus shifts to Frank's second encounter with a potential comrade. He is English (Paul Benjamin), a black man in charge of the prison library, to which Frank has also been assigned. The intial encounter between Frank and English, in the library, continues the consistent emphasis on the ubiquity of a sense of confinement: Siegel's compositions suggest that the tall library bookcases are another kind of cell that limit and reduce Frank and English. Another reiterated idea — the superiority of Frank to his environment — is, however, reversed in the initial shot of the sequence. They are low-angle shots of English and overhead shots of Frank, which suggest that English, an intense, bitter man who has suffered as much outside of prison as within it, may be more in control of his environment than the cool, cerebral Frank. After establishing this initial opposition between Frank and English, Siegel goes on to create images that suggest Hawksian equality and bonding between them: later shots in the sequence, all of them shot with the camera at its somewhat removed, Hawksian distance from the actors, keep Frank and English together in the frame. While creating these images of unity between Frank and English, Siegel does not neglect the equally important idea of the ubiquity of confinement: the last shots of the sequence are brief alternating shots of Frank and English talking across the barriers created by the bookcases.

The sense of men coming together is continued in the next sequence, one of the best in *Escape from Alcatraz.*

Siegel first reiterates the reality of the film's milieu. In a medium shot, Frank, his back to the camera, is seen looking out over the prison exercise yard; what he sees is high, water-stained walls, a few inmates and several guards. The camera begins to track left with Frank across the yard, but this movement is cut short by a cut to a medium shot of Doc (Roberts Blossom), an older prisoner who is standing beside an easel holding the painting (of a flower) he is currently working on. When Frank enters the frame to speak wth Doc, Siegel pulls the camera back for a wider view of the yard. There is then a cut to a shot in which Frank, Doc and the painting of the flower are united in the foreground of the frame; the background is given over to a view of concrete bleachers on which a number of inmates are sitting. There follows a series of shots of Doc and Frank; Doc always shares his shots with the painting, while Frank is seen three times in low-angle shots in which he is set against the inmates sitting on the bleachers.

There is then a cut to a low-angle shot of a number of black prisoners gathered together on the bleachers. The camera cranes up with Frank as he makes his way to the top of the bleachers, boldly invading what is clearly a blacks-only domain. When he reaches English at the top of the bleachers, Siegel sustains a medium shot of the two of them joined in equality on the top row of the bleachers.

Siegel, continuing his strategy of insisting on the reality his characters confront, now cuts to a shot in which Frank and English are in the foreground, while walls, uniformed guards, uniformed inmates and the bay enclosing Alcatraz fill the mid- and background. The camera cranes down with Frank as he starts to descend the bleachers. Then Siegel, continuing his suggestive exploration of Frank's and English's claims to superiority, composes a low-angle shot in which Frank is looking up at English as they resume their conversation. This is followed by a shot in which Frank is seen climbing up the rows of bleachers to rejoin English at the top. The play on climbing and descending, an effective cinematic rendering of the process by which two people form a relationship of equality, ends when Siegel turns to a series of alternating medium shots of Frank and English, who are again sitting together. There follows a medium shot of Frank and English, their backs to the camera, looking out over the yard, its walls, and the bay beyond. As English tells Frank about the tremendous odds against a successful escape from Alcatraz, Siegel covers their conversation in a series of shots that celebrates the now seemingly solid unity the two men have achieved. The shots of Frank in this series all include walls or patrolling guards.

After a scene in which Frank, in his cell, is told he is been assigned to the carpentry shop (a move doubtless motivated by a desire to abort the relationship between Frank and English), the action returns to the exercise yard. The camera first tracks through the yard with Frank and Litmus. Then Wolf, in an unprovoked assault, attacks Frank with a knife. Siegel, again demonstrating his commitment to a Hawksian objectivity, uses a mix of middle-distance, tracking and overhead shots for the fight between Wolf and Frank. Siegel's choices assure that, again, a psychologically intense moment for his protagonist is rendered in a way that embeds the moment in the film's milieu and the events of its narrative. Siegel's camera does not create a strong identification with Frank; as a consequence, we are obliged to continue focusing on *both* terms of this melodrama, the man and the milieu.

Guards eventually manage to separate Wolf and Frank. Both men are sent to solitary confinement in D Block. The passage of the film depicting Frank's time in D Block is an excellent sequence, a textbook example of how credibility, even objectivity, can be balanced with expression in film.

The sequence begins with the camera placed inside a D Block cell as Frank is pushed into the cell, toward the camera. The total darkness of the cell caused by the closing of its door covers a cut to a shot of dawn over San Francisco Bay and Alcatraz.

There is a cut to a momentarily dark screen. Light broken into a bar pattern emerges as a guard opens a cell door. Siegel, again avoiding emphatic concentration on Frank, keeps the camera at middle distance for a shot of Frank in the cell. The shot is sustained as a guard, seen through the barred door, raises a hose nozzle through an opening in the door. A cut to a medium shot of Frank, seen through the bars of the cell, is followed by a cut to a shot of water gushing from the nozzle. In an excellent shot that recapitulates the film's central tension between the reality of confinement and the resilient human spirit, Siegel cuts to a sustained shot, reflecting the guard's point of view, of Frank being assaulted by the powerful pressure of the water. A shot of the guard working the hose is followed by a medium shot of Frank, whose image is blurred by the effect of the water. After a shot devoted to the water gushing from the nozzle, there is a cut to a shot of the guard aiming the water at Frank's writhing body. This is followed by a sustained medium shot of Frank curled up into a ball on the floor of the cell. The guard closes the cell door; the resulting darkness leads to a cut to a shot of twilight on San Francisco Bay and Alcatraz.

There is a dissolve to a shot of a guard initiating the lights-out procedure in the main cell block. This is followed by the screen going totally dark. The opening of a cell door casts a shaft of light on Frank's body on the floor of the cell. A medium shot of a guard is followed by a medium shot of Frank shrinking from the impact of the light. There is then a cut to a shot of Frank, his back to the camera, moving from the rear of the cell toward the light in the background of the frame. When Frank exits the cell, the door closes and the screen returns to complete darkness. This covers an invisible cut to a shot in which the camera tracks left with Frank as he returns to his cell in the main cell block. The camera tracks into the cell with Frank but not all the way in, holding for a stationary shot of Frank, seen through bars, as he curls up on the bunk in his cell.

An excellent long take follows. In a medium shot, Frank is seen in his cell, at the left of the frame; the right side of the frame is devoted to the adjoining cell, occupied by a new inmate named Butts (Larry Hankin). As Frank and Butts, unable, of course, to face each other, engage in whispered conversation, the camera holds on them for a considerable period. The camera then tracks back, left, and finally right as, without a cut, Siegel follows Frank, Butts and the other prisoners on their tier as they fall into line for the march to the mess hall. This is surely one of the best shots in the film: Siegel, in a most economical (and, therefore, most Hawksian) fashion, has again conveyed the process of men coming together wthin an environment designed to prevent genuine communication and devoted to dehumanizing regimentation.

After another scene set in the exercise yard, there is a scene in which the warden, while inspecting cells, discovers that Doc has done a painting of him. He orders that Doc's painting privileges be rescinded. This is followed by a scene in which Doc, Frank, Butts and other inmates are at work in the carpentry shop. Doc, distraught at his loss of painting privileges, seizes a hatchet and mutilates his arm. The scene includes one notable overhead shot of the walkways that crisscross the upper portion of the carpentry shop, allowing patrolling guards to keep an eye on the inmates below. Siegel, even when treating an incident as dramatic as Doc's self-mutilation, insists on maintaining a detached view of the reality of men in confinement.

In the next scene Frank, in his cell, begins to form his escape plan, which hinges on a vent in his cell that might be an opening to escape. English comes by, distributing books from the library. Siegel dissolves from the English-Frank exchange to the mess hall, where Frank is reunited with two brothers he had met in another prison, John and Clarence Anglin (Jack Thibeau, Fred Ward). Frank also has a verbal confrontation in the mess hall with the warden, whom Frank blames for the desperate act of self-mutilation committed by Doc.

The escape plot now begins to take definite shape. Siegel uses a rare series of close-ups to show Frank, using the pilfered nail clippers, digging at the wall around the vent in his cell; the effect of the decision to use close-ups is to suggest an appreciation of the individual intelligence and in-genuity that have created the plan. In the scene immediately following, set in the exercise yard, Siegel uses a sustained, stationary-camera two-shot in an apt and subtle expression of the Hawksian truth that even a superior man needs the cooperation of comrades to reach his goals. After brief scenes in which Butts and English are seen in conversations (under very restrictive, demeaning conditions) with visitors, Siegel cuts to a pair of overhead shots of first Butts and then Frank in their cells. The shots powerfully convey the total confinement of the two men; their effect is powerful enough to constitute sufficient explanation of why Butts, at first reluctant, agrees to join in the escape attempt. Later, in the mess hall, Frank tells the Anglin brothers about the plan. The group has now been formed.

The next several minutes of the film are devoted to the carrying out of the initial stages of the escape plan. In a sustained medium shot that reiterates the key idea of unity, of sharing, Butts and Frank are seen in their cells, waiting for lights out; then, in a series of shots that reiterates the idea of the inherent superiority of Frank, Siegel uses close-ups and low-angle shots to show him, under the cover of darkness, loosening the vent from the wall. Siegel's sustained attention to the accomplishment of the preliminary tasks involved in the escape plan turns this segment of the film into a tribute to creative human intelligence and skill. He uses, for example, sustained medium shots of Frank's hands and sustained medium and low-angle shots of his face to show him fashioning a workable welding tool from the nail clippers, a pilfered spoon, and a pilfered wedge.

In the next sequence Siegel creates a remarkably effective image of the Hawksian group at work. He uses dissolves to link Frank, Butts and the Anglin brothers as they engage in various phases of preparation for the escape. Butts and the Anglins are seen digging around the vents in their cells, while Frank is seen carrying out his ingenious idea for making face masks that each of the escapees will leave in his bunk to fool patrolling guards on the night of the escape attempt.

It is now time for a trial run of the escape plan. There is a dissolve from Frank preparing the mask of his face to an overhead shot of him placing the mask at the head of his bunk.

This is followed by an overhead shot of him in his almost totally dark cell removing the vent from the wall. Three shots of Frank crawling through a very narrow tunnel follow. Once Frank emerges from the tunnel, Siegel makes another judicious departure from the detached narrator's point of view that prevails in the film. He cuts to a low-angle shot that reflects Frank's view of the pipes and scaffolding that loom above the small open space where Frank is now standing.

Siegel also uses variations in point of view in the next two shots: a low-angle shot of Frank as he climbs up a pipe suggests the considerable distance he must climb, while an overhead shot of the same action makes him look small and insignificant in the midst of what are the bowels of Fortress Alcatraz. This sustained departure from the Hawksian head-on, narrator's point of view creates a satisfying sense of the enormity of what this man, who has heretofore been presented as superior to his circumstances, is attempting.

There is a cut from Frank climbing to a shot of a guard patrolling the mostly dark cell block. Then shots of the guard, Butts and the mask standing in for Frank are intercut.

Suspense is now heightened by a cut to another low-angle shot of Frank climbing, which is followed by another overhead shot of him struggling toward the camera. There is then a cut to a medium shot in which Frank's hands (there is considerable emphasis on his hands in the film), then his face, appear through an opening in a floor. This is followed by a classic suspense composition: Frank is seen in the foreground of the frame, a barred door is in the midground, and a patrolling guard is in the background. The camera tracks left with Frank through near-total darkness. The tracking continues in the next shot, and then the camera cranes up to reveal a grate high above Frank's head. Siegel, creating a sustained image of a man of intelligence thwarted by a physical impediment, cuts to an overhead shot, which he holds for a considerable time, of Frank's futile attempts to jump enough to get a handhold on the grate.

The sequence concludes on another note of classic suspense. In a series of brief shots, the patrolling guard is approaching Frank's cell; as he peers in for a close inspection of Frank's bunk, there is a cut to a close-up of Frank asleep in the bunk. He has returned from his trial run just in time.

The four plotters are next seen in the mess hall, where they review the state of the various components of the escape plan. That night, Frank and John Anglin make a trial run of the escape. For this sequence, Siegel uses a mix of low-angle and overhead shots to create a balance between objective and subjective points of view. Removing the grate turns out to be the outstanding obstacle to the success of Frank's escape plan, but Frank believes he can rig up a device to drill through the bars of the grate and thus remove the major impediment to his plan. On the evening following the second trial run, Frank spots a possible component of the drill device he has in mind — a small portable electric fan — in the prison recreation room. In a great tracking crane shot across the recreation room with its innumerable screens and bars, the essence of *Escape from Alcatraz* — the human spirit in conflict with a dehumanizing regime of confinement — is again recapitulated as Frank steals the fan, conceals it in the case of his accordion, and then falls in with the other inmates as they file out of the recreation room.

Siegel now creates another effective, eminently Hawksian passage in which human skill and the human commitment to action are celebrated. In a series of sustained medium shots, Frank and John Anglin, on another trial run of the escape, are seen working, in the dark, on the makeshift drill they hope will remove the one apparent obstacle to the success of their escape plan. After the initial series of shots of Frank and John, Siegel intercuts shots of a patrolling guard into a second series of shots that give meticulous attention to the ingenious creation of the drill.

There is a cut to a low-angle shot of John boosting Frank up to the grate, followed by an overhead shot of Frank hanging from the grate, with John below him; Siegel's decisions regarding camera placement again create a satisfyingly complex perspective, with the low-angle shot suggesting the goal the men aspire to and the overhead shot suggesting the formidable obstacle they face. Siegel continues the pattern in the next series of shots, in which low-angle shots of Frank setting up the drill alternate with overhead shots of John assisting Frank.

The series of shots ends with a cut to a shot in which the camera tracks right with a patrolling guard. There is then a cut to an overhead shot of Frank hanging from the grate; the change to a camera placement that suggests vulnerability for a shot devoted to Frank, who has most often been associated with superiority, subtly strengthens the sense of danger suggested by the shot of the patrolling guard. A medium shot devoted to the drilling device is followed by a shot in which the camera tilts up with the guard as he ascends a stairway that will lead him to proximity to John and Frank. There is then a cut to an overhead shot of John, followed by a shot devoted to the glare of the sparks Frank's drilling device is causing. The sequence concludes with three satisfyingly suspenseful shots: the guard is seen walking left, the direction, we know, that will lead him to Frank and John; in another overhead shot, with its connotations of vulnerability, Frank is seen drilling; finally, the guard is seen walking left, pausing to look up, and then making the crucial turn to the right that means Frank and John will not be discovered.

Suspense gives way to a wonderful scene that is one of the most Hawksian moments in the film. All the prisoners are gathered in a large room watching a war movie. The four conspirators are seated side by side, their faces illuminated by the flickering light emanating from the screen. Siegel sustains a medium shot in which all four are together in the frame as they make whispered progress reports on the various preescape tasks each has been assigned. The scene amounts to a brilliant celebration of group unity in the communal context of watching a film; and it affirms that Frank, the man of superior intelligence and ingenious skill, a natural leader, is well-integrated into a Hawksian group of democratic equality.

The sequence that follows is such a striking departure from the overall directorial style of *Escape from Alcatraz* that one feels Siegel has signaled that he is here treating something that deserves special attention. The sequence recounts an incident in the mess hall: the warden, spotting a flower (which evokes thoughts of Doc) beside Litmus's tray, removes and crushes it; Litmus, driven over an internal line all prisoners must know, rises to assault the warden; he collapses and dies, apparently the victim of a heart attack; Frank intervenes and has another verbal confrontation with the warden. One would expect Siegel to shoot his sequence with the camera at a detached, Hawksian middle-distance from the action, a camera placement that would permit an objective view of both characters and setting. This is how he shot Frank's fight with Wolf in the yard and his first verbal confrontation with the warden in the mess hall. But

Siegel in this instance creates a highly subjective rendering of a confrontation, using low-angle shots of the warden and overhead shots of Frank and Litmus that create a distorted view of both the characters and the setting.

The reason behind this rather marked alteration in style is, I think, that Siegel wanted to suggest that this sequence is the psychological-emotional center of the film. This is the sequence in which he creates his most intense, almost expressionistic, statement about the morality that animates Frank and his comrades. They are escaping *from* oppression (suggested here and elsewhere in the film by overhead shots) and illegitimate authority (suggested by the low-angle shots of the warden that distort his appearance); they are escaping *to* a world in which a man can come to the defense of his friend and in which beauty (the flower) will not be crushed by mindless authority. The moral code espoused in *Escape from Alcatraz* is unconventional and subversive, arising from the assumption that often what is genuinely moral is *conventionally* immoral. The conventionally immoral escape is actually an expression of a deeply felt, authentic morality; and Siegel's change in style in this sequence aptly conveys both the distorted morality Frank and his friends are fleeing from and the true morality their escape represents.

In the next scene Frank bids farewell to English, who has given tacit approval to the escape; they shake hands through the bars of Frank's cell. Then the warden, angered by Frank's defiance of him in the mess hall, inspects Frank's cell and capriciously orders that he be changed to another cell. That, of course, would doom the escape plan, whose success hinges on Frank's escaping from the cell he has prepared. An unlikely and unwitting source, however, saves the plan: when Wolf renews his threat to kill Frank, the latter moves up the escape date to the night before the scheduled change of cell, which, of course, he knows nothing about.

The next sequence, set in the exercise yard, depicts English saving Frank from a surprise attack by Wolf: one superior man, who happens to be black, has again acknowledged his solidarity with another superior man, who happens to be white.

The escape itself is, in sense, anticlimactic: *Escape from Alcatraz* has been preeminently about the morality, human creativity, and group solidarity that have made the escape necessary and possible; it is not surprising, then, that Siegel handles the escape itself rather coolly, mostly avoiding the opportunities for manipulative suspense it contains, refusing to make of the escape the sort of climax found in Hawksian-fallacy films like *Jaws*. Most of the escape sequence is shot from the camera's customary middle-distance, Hawksian position, though Siegel does briefly return to a reiteration of the low-angle–overhead pattern he used earlier in the film. He also uses a series of close-ups, among the few in the film, for the segment in which the escapees, now outside the prison walls, are seen inflating the improvised raft they hope will carry them safely across San Francisco Bay; Siegel's use of close-ups at this point seems an indication of his consistent commitment to rendering the *details* of the ingenious escape plan.

Siegel cuts to an overhead shot as the three escapees (Butts, after much hesitation, finally does not make the escape attempt) as they enter the bay; and then he cuts to a medium shots of each of them before they are lost in the overwhelming darkness of the night and the water. The escape sequence ends with a shot of dawn over Alcatraz.

Escape from Alcatraz concludes with the warden and a search party combing a small island in the bay for evidence of the escapees' presence. The warden claims that the three drowned in the bay, but the others in the party are dubious and seem convinced that the first successful escape from Alcatraz has indeed been accomplished. The warden, while searching among the island's rocks, discovers a chrysanthemum, the flower associated with Doc, Litmus and Frank, placed in a crevice of a rock. He picks up the flower, examines it for a moment, then tosses it into the bay. The last shot of *Escape from Alcatraz* is of the chrysanthemum floating out to sea, toward freedom.

Notes

1. Leo Braudy, *The World in a Frame* (Garden City, N.Y.: Anchor/Double-day, 1977), pp. 46–47, 49.

7

Conclusion

The phenomenon of looking back and lamenting the passing of what seems from the perspective of a disorderly present a golden age has surely colored, to an extent impossible to measure, this examination of the aesthetics of the New Hollywood. However, even with due allowance made for the nostalgia effect, I am convinced that in the passage from the Old to the New Hollywood something real and important has been lost. The nature and the dimensions of the loss are suggested by the following observations on what has come to be regarded as the quintessential New Hollywood film, *Heaven's Gate*:

> I think it likely that audience and critical perception of *Heaven's Gate* as a failure ... came not only from awareness of the scandalously undisciplined method of its manufacture but also from a deeper, more disturbing failure of discipline in the picture itself.... Characters and story were sacrificed to the filmmaker's love of visual effect and production for their own sakes. The "look" of the thing subsumed the sense of the thing and implied a callous or uncaring quality about characters for whom the audience was asked to care more than the film seemed to. Whether those characters were well or ill conceived, they seemed sabotaged by their creator's negligence of them as he pursued, the "larger, richer, deeper" things that surrounded them, obscuring them, making them seem smaller, more shallow.[1]

An appreciation of the loss suffered during the New Hollywood era begins with an understanding of what is meant when one speaks of the Old Hollywood. Robin Wood, writing before there was a recognized need to modify *Hollywood* with *old* or *new*, observed that there are

> two great contradictory truths about Hollywood ... (a) Hollywood is the vast commercial machine where box-office considerations corrupt everyone and everything, where untrammelled artistic expression is impossible; and (b) Hollywood is a great creative workshop, comparable to Elizabethan London or the Vienna of Mozart, where hundreds of talents have come together to evolve a common language.[2]

217

The New Hollywood era has seen the continuation of the Old Holly-wood's reverence for box office success, accompanied by a self-conscious pursuit of artistic expression that was virtually unknown in the Old Holly-wood. The common result of the pursuit of these seemingly antithetical goals (box office success, untainted artistic expression) in the New Holly-wood has been the breakdown of the common language Wood speaks of. The breakdown in turn defines the loss that has been sustained by the American film and the American film audience since the end, in the mid-sixties, of the Big Studio or Old Hollywood era.

The language of the Old Hollywood cinema is as complex as any other sophisticated language, and various theorists and critics have developed a variety of approaches to defining and describing it. A thorough review of these theoretical approaches is beyond the scope of this book; but a brief look at the theories derived from descriptive analyses of the language of the Old Hollywood seems in order, given the present book's underlying premise that the loss of that language appears to be the one notable legacy of the New Hollywood era.

One theoretical perspective, well represented by Robert B. Ray in his recent study of the American cinema, describes the language of the Old Hollywood film in terms of formal and thematic paradigms. The goal and effect of the formal paradigm was to efface any evidence of conscious directorial style, in order "to establish the cinema's illusion of reality and to encourage audience identification with the characters on the screen."[3] The "systematic subordination of every cinematic element [of style] to the interests of a movie's narrative" resulted in what Ray has called an "im-plied contract" between filmmaker and audience: "at any moment in a movie, the audience was to be given the optimum vantage point on what was occurring on the screen."[4]

The formal paradigm, with its aim of disguising the artistic choices that create a film, was complemented by a thematic paradigm which also sought to deny the necessity of choice. The "reconciliatory pattern" that governed the Old Hollywood film denied the necessity for choice among the competing and often contradictory myths embedded in the American culture through the "conversion of all political, sociological, and eco-nomic dilemmas into personal melodramas."[5]

Thus, in this view, the common language of the Old Hollywood was created out of a style that concealed the art in filmmaking in the interests of promoting a sense of realism and encouraging the process of audience-character identification, and out of a deep thematic structure premised on the illusory possibility of the reconciliation of conflicting values held by the majority of the American public.

Another perspective sees the common language as consisting of the plots, themes, stylistic and thematic motifs, and archetypal characters that defined the genres developed during the Old Hollywood era. Leo Braudy's view of the "genre language" is especially relevant to an examination of New Hollywood aesthetics:

> When the genre conventions can no longer evoke and shape either the emotions or the intelligence of the audience, they must be discarded and new ones tried out. Genre films essentially ask the audience, "Do you still want to believe this?" Popularity is the audience answering, "Yes." Change in genres occurs when the audience says, "That's too infantile a form of what we believe. Show us something more complicated."[6]

Braudy would thus argue that the common language of the Old Hollywood has not so much broken down as worn out, and that the wearing out process is inevitable and potentially progressive. The question Braudy does not address and that lies at the heart of the Old Hollywood–New Hollywood issue is: If the Old Hollywood language has worn out, what has taken its place, and does the new language in fact represent the progressive evolution Braudy suggests?

My own perspective on the language of the Old Hollywood cinema is to see it as the result of two sets of interactive relationships, the relationship between form and material, and the relationship between a film (the product of the form-material interaction) and its audience. The guiding principle here has been well stated by V. F. Perkins:

> In the cinema style reflects a way of seeing; it embodies the filmmaker's relationship to objects and actions. But, as a way of *showing*, it also involves his relationship with the spectator. The film's point of view is contained within each of these relationships. Attitudes toward the audience contribute as much to a movie's effect, and therefore its significance, as attitudes towards its more immediate subject-matter.[7]

With regard to the form-material relationship that prevailed in the Old Hollywood, I agree with the paradigm school that the effacement of style was the overriding goal, though I believe the best of the auteurist critics have shown that a number of Old Hollywood directors conveyed a remarkable degree of thematic nuance and displayed a considerable level of personal style within the confines of the commitment to verisimilitude.

I also agree with Andre Bazin that the decade from 1940 to 1950, which saw the refinement of the deep-focus shot and the long take,[8] marked "a decisive step forward in the development of the language of the film" because they (deep-focus and the long take) made possible "a film form that would permit everything to be said without chopping the world up into little fragments, that would reveal the hidden meanings in people and things without disturbing the unity natural to them."[9] With the deep-focus shot and the increasing tendency toward long take, the form-material aspect of the Old Hollywood's language moved ever further from both obtrusive montage and obtrusive expressionism and further toward the thoroughgoing realism Bazin espoused. This formal development in the Old Hollywood langauge thus had clear implications for the film-audience relationship: both the deep-focus shot and the long take, with their tendency to bring out the complexity and ambiguity of a film's subject matter, had the effect of establishing a more involving, complicated film-audience relationship, a relationship that benefited from the audience's relative freedom to interpret what was shown without the dubious "guidance" of a director's analytical montage or interpretive expressionism.

Audience involvement, whether on the rather simplistic level of identification with characters or the more sophisticated level achieved through the deep-focus, long-take aesthetic, was always a more complex feature of the language of the Old Hollywood cinema than the thematic paradigm theory suggests. The Old Hollywood film more often than not fulfilled what Perkins has identified as one of the great potentials of film: "to make us associate with attitudes which are not our own, with thoughts, feelings and reactions which are outside our normal range. . . . [I]n order to work, the movie has to call on the spectator's imagination to complete the necessarily partial presentation of the world."[10]

The New Hollywood era has seen distortions in the form-material relationship that prevailed in the Old Hollywood, with consequent distortions in the film-audience relationship. These distortions can be seen in the context of the rubric suggested by Perkins: "The fiction movie normally discourages awareness that we are interpreting its images and disguises the fact that it is a created object."[11] In the New Hollywood film the vital element of freedom of interpretation, disguised but almost always respected in the Old Hollywood cinema, has either been rendered irrelevant (television-fallacy films, Hawksian-fallacy films) or denied through the imposition of the director's preemptive interpretation (literary-fallacy films); the equally vital element of disguising the fact that a film is the result of a series of creative acts, with its consequent heightening of the sense that audiences are involved with something that at least seems like reality has been abandoned in films that highlight formal elements and the artistry of the director (Hitchcockian-fallacy films).

Some of the New Hollywood directors — whether acting out of a desire for box office bonanzas or simply manifesting the formative influence of the age's dominant medium — have imposed an aesthetics borrowed from television on their films. By doing this these directors have departed from the Old Hollywood language in a formal sense (by rejecting unobtrusive editing and the involving mise-en-scène of deep-focus and the long take, which was becoming prevalent in the American film just before the advent of television) and in a deeper structural sense (by relying on "formats" that, to use Perkins's words, emphatically did *not* "make [audiences] associate with attitudes ... thoughts, feelings and reactions which are outside [their] normal range"). The result has been a film-audience relationship that, not surprisingly, resembles the television-audience relationship, a relationship that severely diminishes the involvement, imaginative participation, and freedom of interpretation audiences enjoyed with Old Hollywood films.

The formal distortion I have called the literary fallacy departs from the language of the Old Hollywood by attempting to make a film work like a novel or an essay; the realism and audience identification that were central to the Old Hollywood cinema are abandoned through the use of such devices as direct address, obvious symbolism, and a mise-en-scène that highlights "ideas" rather than people-in-their-circumstances. What I have called the modernist variation on this distortion constitutes a direct assault on the Old Hollywood film-audience relationship: the director, seeking to make the film form the equivalent of the modernist novel, and perhaps seeking the "untrammelled artistic expression" enjoyed by modernist writers but wisely eschewed by all but a few Old Hollywood directors, diminishes audience involvement in the totality of a well-realized mise-en-scène and preempts the audiences's freedom of interpretation by asserting inorganic, univocal images that declare the director's interpretation of the film experience.

Finally, there are the formal distortions that I have hypothesized derive from New Hollywood misreadings of Old Hollywood legacies. The legacy of Alfred Hitchcock has been misinterpreted to mean that the exploitation of form is the preeminent goal of film direction; the result has been films that require audiences to observe inorganic displays of directorial virtuosity that necessarily intrude on audience involvement in the film experience by highlighting film as a created object. The legacy of Howard Hawks has suffered an equally unfortunate fate. The Hawksian tradition in film comedy has been all but totally ignored; the Hawksian adventure melodrama has been distorted into films that ask audiences to be satisfied with a comic book experience in which elaborate technical effects take precedence over narrative coherence, and manipulative suspense is substituted for Hawks's subtle (and audience-involving) renderings of action as the expression of morality.

The overall result of these formal distortions has been the virtual extinction of the language evolved during the Old Hollywood era and the consequent radical alteration in the film-audience relationship.

To be sure, the language of the Old Hollywood cinema has not been lost in the New Hollywood: on rare occasions, directors have recalled or intuited the Old Hollywood language and have created films that restore the former film-audience relationship. Altman's *McCabe and Mrs. Miller,* Allen's *Annie Hall*, Yates's *Breaking Away* and Siegel's *Escape from Alcatraz* are New Hollywood films that are fully as satisfying as Old Hollywood films. Other good to excellent films of the New Hollywood era are Arthur Penn's *Bonnie and Clyde* (1967) and *Alice's Restaurant* (1969); Bob Rafelson's *Five Easy Pieces* (1970); Irvin Kershner's *Loving* (1970); the musical segments of Bob Fosse's *Cabaret* (1972); Coppola's *The Godfather* (1972); Martin Ritt's *Sounder* (1972); Hal Ashby's *Shampoo* (1975); Michael Ritchie's *The Bad News Bears* (1976); Martin Scorsese's documentary *The Last Waltz* (1978); Paul Mazursky's *An Unmarried Woman* (1978); Blake Edwards's *10* (1979); two by Milos Forman, *Taking Off* (1971) and *Hair* (1979, the most, indeed the *only*, satisfying musical of the New Hollywood era); two by Roman Polanski, *Chinatown* (1974) and *Tess* (1980); two by Jonathan Demme, *Citizens' Band* (1977) and *Melvin and Howard* (1980); two by Walter Hill, *The Long Riders* (1980) and *Southern Comfort* (1981); and two more by Don Siegel, *Madigan* (1968) and *Charley Varrick* (1973).

It is not particularly significant that these films have been far outnumbered by the inferior, weak films of the New Hollywood era: in any art, in any age, the bad have always outnumbered the good. What *is* significant is that so many of the bad films of the New Hollywood era have been not merely utterly routine genre pieces or listlessly undirected star vehicles (descriptions which account for the vast majority of the bad films of the Old Hollywood era) but have been fallacious products that represent fundamental distortions of an art form or experience that once seemed permanently embedded in the American culture and that was once emulated and enjoyed in much of the rest of the world. Some of the most esteemed or popular films of the New Hollywood era readily fall into the aesthetic fallacy categories elaborated in this present book.

The television fallacy has been especially well represented: George Roy Hill's *Butch Cassidy and the Sundance Kid* (1969); John Schlesinger's *Midnight Cowboy* (1969) and his egregious *Marathon Man* (1976); Franklin Schaffner's *Patton* (1970); William Friedkin's *The French Connection* (1971);

and Sidney Pollack's *The Way We Were* (1973), which followed his literary-fallacy film, *They Shoot Horses, Don't They?* (1969). Milos Forman moved from the open-film excellence of *Taking Off* into the television-fallacy category with *One Flew over the Cuckoo's Nest* (1975), then recovered with *Hair* before moving onto the Hitchcockian-fallacy emptiness of *Amadeus* (1984). In 1979 the television fallacy was well represened by Martin Ritt's *Norma Rae* and Robert Benton's *Kramer vs. Kramer*.

The New Hollywood era was in a sense kicked off with a literary-fallacy film, Dennis Hopper's *Easy Rider* (1969). Also in the literary-fallacy category are two by Mike Nichols (who had moved on from his 1967 Hitchcockian-fallacy film, *The Graduate*), *Catch-22* (1970) and *Carnal Knowledge* (1971). (In fairness it should be said that his 1983 film, *Silkwood*, is very good, with Nichols's long takes effectively embedding the film's personal story within its political theme.) Other notable films in the literary-fallacy category are Arthur Penn's *Little Big Man* (1970), a betrayal of the promise of *Bonnie and Clyde* and *Alice's Restaurant*; Sam Peckinpah's *Straw Dogs* (1971), an aberration from the Hawksian-fallacy pattern Peckinpah established with *The Wild Bunch* (1969) and to which he soon drifted back; and the peripatetic Robert Altman's *Three Women* (1977).

As mentioned in chapter four, Martin Scorsese and Brian DePalma have been the leading exemplars of the Hitchcockian fallacy in the New Hollywood; other directors prominent in this category are Stanley Kubrick (*A Clockwork Orange*, 1971, *Barry Lyndon*, 1975); Francis Coppola (*The Conversation* and *The Godfather, Part II*, both 1974); Alan Pakula (*The Parallax View*, 1974); and, of course, Michael Cimino, whose films *The Deer Hunter* (1978) and *Heaven's Gate* (1980) straddle the Hitchcockian- and literary-fallacy categories.

Finally, the Hawksian fallacy has been represented by Peckinpah, by such *Star Wars* spinoffs as Irvin Kershner's *The Empire Strikes Back* (1980), and Steven Spielberg's *1941* (1980), and by his 1984 sequel to *Raiders, Indiana Jones and the Temple of Doom*; and by Hal Needham's *Smokey and the Bandit* (1977) and its various sequels and parodies.[12]

It may be that in the late 1980s small movements and incipient trends are at work that might significantly alter the current state of mainstream American films. Two of the directors prominently featured in this book, Robert Altman and Martin Scorsese, appeared by 1986 or so to be working toward modifications in their filmmaking that could result in their creating more effective, satisfying films,[13] though it would appear from Scorsese's 1985 film, *After Hours*, that he is still trapped in the Hitchcockian fallacy. It may be that a new language is evolving, a language that contemporary film audiences, most of whom are too young[14] to have experienced the Old Hollywood film-audience relationship, will find conducive to a satisfactory relationship with the movies. One can only hope that the creators of this new language will, in the great tradition of innovators in other arts, begin their work with an understanding and appreciation of the enduring values of the Old Hollywood language, the language of a genuine and inestimably precious American art form.

Notes

1. Steven Bach, *Final Cut* (New York: William Morrow, 1985), p. 416.
2. Wood, *Howard Hawks*, pp. 8–9.
3. Robert B. Ray, *A Certain Tendency of the Hollywood Cinema, 1930–1980* (Princeton, N.J.: Princeton University Press, 1985), p. 34.
4. Ray, *Certain Tendency*, pp. 32, 33.
5. Ray, *Certain Tendency*, p. 57.
6. Braudy, *The World*, p. 179.
7. Perkins, *Film as Film*, p. 134.
8. Barry Salt, in his studies of the films of the thirties and forties, makes the interesting point that evidence suggests that both the deep-focus shot and the increased use of the long take were examples of aesthetic considerations leading technological developments, rather than vice versa. See Barry Salt, "Film Style and Technology in the Thirties," *Film Quarterly*, Fall 1976, pp. 19–32; and "Film Style and Technology in the Forties," *Film Quarterly*, Fall 1977, pp. 46–57.
9. Andre Bazin, *What Is Cinema?* 1 (Berkeley: University of California Press, 1967): 38.
10. Perkins, *Film as Film*, pp. 138, 146.
11. Perkins, *Film as Film*, p. 136.
12. The auteur theory should probably be counted among the casualties of the New Hollywood era. The stylistic inconsistencies of Allen, Altman, Coppola, Forman, Kershner, Penn and Pollack and the fallacious consistency of Cimino, DePalma, Kubrick, Peckinpah, Schlesinger and Scorsese would seem to indicate that the age of the auterus has not continued into the New Hollywood era. On the evidence to date, it would seem that only two home-grown New Hollywood directors, Jonathan Demme and Walter Hill, merit consideration in an auteurist context. The other auteur candidates are Old Hollywood survivor Don Siegel; Blake Edwards, a transitional figure in the Old Hollywood–New Hollywood movement; and the foreign-born and (now) foreign-based Roman Polanski.
13. See Stephen Farber, "Five Horseman after the Apocalypse," *Film Comment,* August 1985, pp. 32–35.
14. "A 1977 survey revealed that although only thirteen percent of all movie tickets were bought by patrons more than forty years old (a figure that has scarcely changed since), a whopping fifty-seven percent were purchased by those under twenty-five. (Over the next two years, the youngest part of the audience grew even more dominant — twelve-to-twenty-year-old admissions were up eight percent, mainly at the expense of those twenty-one to thirty-nine.)" J. Hoberman, "Ten Years that Shook the World," *American Film,* June 1985, p. 45.

Film Credits

ALL THAT JAZZ. Columbia. 122 min. Premiere: **December 1979.** *Director:* Bob Fosse. *Screenplay:* Bob Fosse, Robert Alan Arthur. *Director of photography:* Giuseppe Rotunno. *Editor:* Alan Helm. *Musical supervisor:* Stanley Lebowsky. *Choreography:* Bob Fosse. *Producer:* Robert Alan Arthur. **Cast:** Roy Scheider (as Joe Gideon), Jessica Lange (Angelique), Ann Reinking (Kate Jagger), Leland Palmer (Audrey Paris), Cliff Corman (Davis Newman), Ben Vereen (O'Connor Flood), Erzsbet Foldi (Michelle).

AMERICAN GRAFFITI. Universal. 110 min. Premiere: **August 1973.** *Director:* George Lucas. *Screenplay:* George Lucas, Gloria Katz, Willard Huyck. *Director of photography:* Ron Eveslige, Jan D'Alguen. *Editors:* Verna Fields, Marcia Lucas. *Music coordinator:* Karlin Green. *Producer:* Francis Coppola. **Cast:** Richard Dreyfuss (as Curt), Ron Howard (Steve), Paul LeMat (John), Charlie Martin Smith (Terry), Cindy Williams (Laurie), Candy Clark (Debbie), Mackenzie Phillips (Carol), Harrison Ford (Bob).

ANNIE HALL. United Artists. 94 min. Premiere: **April 1977.** *Director:* Woody Allen. *Screenplay:* Woody Allen, Marshall Brickman. *Director of photography:* Gordon Willis. *Editor:* Ralph Rosenblum. *Producer:* Charles H. Jaffe. **Cast:** Woody Allen (as Alvy Singer), Diane Keaton (Annie Hall), Tony Roberts (Rob), Carol Kane (Allison), Janet Margolin (Robin), Colleen Dewhurst (Mrs. Hall).

APOCALYPSE NOW. Zoetrope/United Artists. 154 min. Premiere: **August 1979.** *Director:* Francis Coppola. *Screenplay:* John Milius, Francis Coppola, Michael Herr. *Director of photography:* Vitorio Storaro. *Editor:* Richard Marks. *Music:* Carmine Coppola, Francis Coppola. *Producer:* Francis Coppola. **Cast:** Marlon Brando (as Col. Kurtz), Robert Duvall (Lt. Col. Kilgore), Martin Sheen (Capt. Willard), Frederic Forrest (Chef), Albert Hall (Chief), Sam Bottoms (Lance), Larry Fishburne (Clean), Dennis Hopper (Photo-journalist).

BANANAS. United Artists. 82 min. Premiere: **April 1971.** *Director:* Woody Allen. *Screenplay:* Woody Allen, Mickey Rose. *Director of photography:* Andrew M. Costikyan. *Editor*: Ralph Rosenblum. *Music:* Marvin Hamlisch. *Producer:* Jack Grossberg. **Cast:** Woody Allen (as Fielding Melish), Louise Lasser (Nancy).

BREAKING AWAY. Twentieth Century–Fox. 99 min. Premiere: **July 1979.** *Director:* Peter Yates. *Screenplay:* Steve Tesich. *Director of photography:* Matthew F. Leonetti. *Editor:* Cynthia Scheider. *Musical adaptation:* Patrick Williams. *Producer:* Peter Yates. **Cast:** Dennis Christopher (as Dave), Dennis Quaid (Mike), Daniel Stern (Cyril), Jackie Earle Haley (Moocher), Barbara Barrie (Evelyn), Paul Dooley (Raymond), Robyn Douglass (Katherine).

CARRIE. United Artists. 98 min. Premiere: **November 1976.** *Director:* Brian DePalma. *Screenplay:* Lawrence D. Cohen, from the novel by Stephen King. *Director of photography:* Mario Tosi. *Editor:* Paul Hirsch. *Music:* Pino Donaggio. *Producer:* Paul Monash. **Cast:** Sissy Spacek (as Carrie White), Piper Laurie (Margaret White), William Katt (Tommy Ross), John Travolta (Billy Nolan), Amy Irving (Sue Snell), Nancy Allen (Chris Hargenson), Betty Buckley (Miss Collins).

ESCAPE FROM ALCATRAZ. Paramount. 112 min. Premiere: **June 1979.** *Director:* Don Siegel. *Screenplay:* Richard Tuggle, from a book by J. Campbell Bruce. *Director of photography:* Bruce Surtees. *Editor:* Ferris Webster. *Producer:* Don Siegel. **Cast:** Clint Eastwood (as Frank Morris), Patrick McGoohan (Warden), Roberts Blossom (Doc), Jack Thibeau (Clarence Anglin), Fred Ward (John Anglin), Paul Benjamin (English), Larry Hankin (Charley Butts).

JAWS. Universal. 124 min. Premiere: **June 1975.** *Director:* Steven Spielberg. *Screenplay:* Peter Benchley, Carl Gottlieb, from the novel by Peter Benchley. *Director of photography:* Bill Butler. *Editor:* Verna Fields. *Music:* John Williams. *Producers:* Richard D. Zanuck, David Brown. **Cast:** Roy Scheider (as Brody), Robert Shaw (Quint), Richard Dreyfuss (Hooper), Murray Hamilton (Vaughn).

McCABE AND MRS. MILLER. Warner Brothers. 120 min. Premiere: **June 1971.** *Director:* Robert Altman. *Screenplay:* Robert Altman, Brian McKay, from the novel by Edmund Naughton. *Director of photography:* Vilmos Zsigmond. *Music:* Leonard Cohen. *Producers:* David Foster, Mitchell Brower. **Cast:** Warren Beatty (as John McCabe), Julie Christie (Constance Miller), Rene Auberjonois (Sheehan), Bert Remsen (Bart Coyl), Shelley Duvall (Ida Coyl), William Devane (The Lawyer).

M*A*S*H. Twentieth Century–Fox. 116 min. Premiere: **February 1970.** *Director:* Robert Altman. *Screenplay:* Ring Lardner, Jr., from the novel by Richard Hooker. *Director of photography:* Harold E. Stine. *Editor:* Danford B. Green. *Music:* Johnny Mandel. *Producer:* Ingo Preminger. **Cast:** Donald Sutherland (as Hawkeye), Elliott Gould (Trapper John), Tom Skerrit (Duke), Sally Kellerman (Maj. Hot Lips), Robert Duvall (Maj. Frank Burns), Jo Ann Pflug (Lt. Dish), Rene Auberjonois (Father Mulcahy), Roger Bowen (Col. Blake), Gary Burghoff (Radar).

RAIDERS OF THE LOST ARK. Paramount. 115 min. Premiere: **June 1981.** *Director:* Steven Spielberg. *Screenplay:* Lawrence Kasdan; story by George Lucas and Philip Kaufman. *Director of photography:* Douglas Slocombe. *Editor:* Michael Kahn. *Music:* John Williams. *Producers:* George Lucas, Philip Kaufman. **Cast:** Harrison Ford (as Indiana Jones), Karen Allen (Marion), Paul Freeman (Belloq), John Rhys-Davies (Sallah).

TAXI DRIVER. Columbia. 112 min. Premiere: **February 1976.** *Director:* Martin Scorsese. *Screenplay:* Paul Schrader. *Director of photography:* Michael Chapman. *Editors:* Tom Rolf, Melvin Shapiro. *Music:* Bernard Herrmann. *Producers:* Michael Phillips, Julia Phillips. **Cast:** Robert DeNiro (as Travis Bickle), Cybill Shepherd (Betsy), Jodie Foster (Iris), Harvey Keitel (Sport), Peter Boyle (Wizard).

Bibliography

Alvarez, A. *Beyond All This Fiddle: Essays 1955–1967.* New York: Random House, 1968.

Bach, Steven. *Final Cut.* New York: William Morrow, 1985.

Bazin, Andre. *What Is Cinema?* vol. 1. Berkeley: University of California Press, 1967.

Bluestone, George. *Novels into Film.* Berkeley: University of California Press, 1957.

Braudy, Leo. *The World in a Frame.* Garden City, N.Y.: Anchor/Doubleday, 1977.

Callenbach, Ernest. "Would Someone Care to Say What Is Going on Here?" *Film Quarterly,* Winter 1983–84.

Cook, David. *A History of Narrative Film.* New York: W. W. Norton, 1981.

Corliss, Richard. "We Lost It at the Movies," *Film Comment,* January–February 1980.

Farber, Stephen. "Five Horsemen after the Apocalypse," *Film Comment,* August 1985.

Gelmis, Joseph. *The Film Director as Superstar.* New York: Doubleday, 1970.

Hampshire, Stuart N. *Modern Writers and Other Essays.* New York: Alfred A. Knopf, 1970.

Kael, Pauline. *I Lost It at the Movies.* Boston: Little, Brown, 1965.

Kehr, David. "Hitch's Riddle," *Film Comment,* June 1984.

Madsen, Axel. *American Movies in the '70s.* New York: Thomas Y. Cravell, 1975.

Malone, Michael, "And Gracie Begat Lucy Who Begat Laverne." In *Fast Forward: The New Television and American Society,* edited by Les Brown and Savannah Waring Walker. Kansas City: Andrews and McNeel, 1981.

Mander, Jerry. *Four Arguments for the Elimination of Television.* New York: William Morrow, 1978.

Mast, Gerald. *Howard Hawks, Storyteller.* New York: Oxford University Press, 1982.

Monaco, James. "The TV Plexus." In *Television and American Culture,* edited by Carl Lowe. New York: H. W. Wilson, 1981.

Paul, William. "Hollywood Harakiri," *Film Comment,* March–April 1977.

Perkins, V. F. *Film as Film.* Harmondsworth, England: Penguin Books, 1972.

Ray, Robert B. *A Certain Tendency of the Hollywood Cineam, 1930–1980.* Princeton, N.J.: Princeton University Press, 1985.

Richardson, Robert. *Literature and Film.* Bloomington: Indiana University Press, 1969.

Rivette, Jacques. "The Genius of Howard Hawks." In *Focus on Howard Hawks,* edited by Joseph McBride. Englewood Cliffs, N.J.: Prentice-Hall, 1972.

227

Salt, Barry. "Film Style and Technology in the Forties," *Film Quarterly,* Fall 1977.
_____. "Film Style and Technology in the Thirties," *Film Quarterly,* Fall 1976.
Sarris, Andrew. "After *The Graduate*," *American Film*, July–August 1978.
_____. *The American Cinema.* New York: E. P. Dutton, 1968.
Sontag, Susan. *Against Interpretation.* New York: Delta, 1961.
Vidal, Gore. *The Second American Revolution and Other Essays (1976–1982).* New York: Random House, 1982.
Wollen, Peter. "The *Auteur* Theory." In *Movies and Methods,* edited by Bill Nichols. Berkeley: University of California Press, 1976.
Wood, Robin. *Hitchcock's Films.* New York: Castle Books, 1965.
_____. *Howard Hawks.* Garden City, N.Y.: Doubleday, 1968.

Index

229